Finding the Valuable Person

Finding the Valuable Person

Therapy That Takes Theology Seriously

Chris Steed

Foreword by Steve Motyer

PICKWICK *Publications* • Eugene, Oregon

FINDING THE VALUABLE PERSON
Therapy That Takes Theology Seriously

Pickwick Publications
An Imprint of Wipf and Stock Publishers
199 W. 8th Ave., Suite 3
Eugene, OR 97401

www.wipfandstock.com

PAPERBACK ISBN: 978-1-6667-9086-3
HARDCOVER ISBN: 978-1-6667-9087-0
EBOOK ISBN: 978-1-6667-9088-7

Cataloguing-in-Publication data:

Names: Steed, Chris, author. | Motyer, Steve, 1950–, foreword.

Title: Finding the valuable person : therapy that take theology seriously / by Chris Steed; foreword by Steve Motyer.

Description: Eugene, OR : Pickwick Publications, 2023 | Includes bibliographical references and index.

Identifiers: ISBN 978-1-6667-9086-3 (paperback) | ISBN 978-1-6667-9087-0 (hardcover) | ISBN 978-1-6667-9088-7 (ebook)

Subjects: LCSH: Psychology and religion. | Psychotherapy—Religious aspects—Christianity | Psychology, Religious.

Classification: BF51 S74 2023 (print) | BF51 S74 (ebook)

06/08/23

"And men go abroad to admire the heights of mountains, the mighty waves of the sea, the broad tides of rivers, the compass of the ocean, and the circuits of the stars, yet pass over the mystery of themselves without a thought."

—AUGUSTINE, *CONFESSIONS*

Contents

Foreword by Steve Motyer | ix

Setting the Scene: Oliver Untwisted | xiii

Introduction: History and the "Here and Now" | 1

Part One: Deep-Seated Reasons—Unconscious Influence

1 At 3:00 a.m.: Avoiding the Void | 25

2 Am I OK? Endorsement's Quest | 41

3 Why Am I Hungry? Strivings of the Soul | 49

4 The "I" in the Eye: Identity and Valuable Personhood | 58

5 Models of Mind: Revising the Unconscious | 68

6 Revising the Unconscious: Wired for Belief | 80

7 Revising the Unconscious: The Birth of Worth | 88

8 Widening the Unconscious: Unconscious Bias and the Devalued Self | 97

9 Widening the Unconscious: Violence and Psychopathology and the Roots of Dysfunction | 108

10 A Theory of Emotional Cognition | 116

11 Relational Depth: Dialogue, Defences, and Disguises | 130

Part Two: Domains of Disturbance—REMA Questions

12 Relationality and Object Relations | 145
13 Working in the Second Domain: Embodied Emotions | 163
14 Compulsive Interpreters: Meaning-Making and Human Existence | 177
15 Agency: The Protest, Voice, and Freedom | 189

Part Three: Transformative Repair

16 Sources of Healing | 197
17 Acceptance and Forgiveness (Shame and Guilt) | 216

Part Four: Positions and Foundations

18 Joining the Conversation: Cure of Souls and the Care of Souls | 231
19 Epistemology and Integration: A Proposal | 245
20 Openness to Humanity: The Theology of Personal Experience | 260

Postscript: Spiritual Transformation and the Answering Echo | 272
Finding the Valuable Person: Working with the Model | 277
Endnotes | 283
Index | 305

Foreword

It is a great privilege and joy to contribute a foreword to this masterly exposition of the REMA approach to counseling, put together by Dr. Chris Steed who is currently the program leader for the Theology and Counseling Program at London School of Theology.

I was the program leader at the time when the REMA framework was first developed by the counseling team at LST, in 2014. Until that point the programme had been taught and administered under a "joint venture" with CWR (now Waverley Abbey College), and we used as our core counseling model the "Waverley Framework," which at that time was called "the CWR model." With the end of the joint venture, we needed to develop our own understanding of the core issues at stake, and processes involved, in counseling—building on the experience we had gained since the Theology and Counseling programme began at LST in 1999.

From a powerfully creative team process emerged "the REMA model."[1] Several of the team had trained in "integrative" psychotherapy, and from the start we conceived of REMA as an "integrative" framework—that is, as finding its home not within one of the traditional psychotherapeutic "streams" (psychodynamic, humanistic, behavioral, cognitive), but as working with a view of human being which draws on all of these approaches, as appropriate within an overarching Christian and biblical framework. In this foreword I'd like to pay tribute to the team involved in that initial development, who like me have all now moved on from LST—Irene Davies, Janet Penny, Kirsty Annable, and Lyn Powell. We met all through one summer vacation to hammer it out!

It was a bold venture! We knew from the start that the REMA framework would have to grow and deepen through the experience of ongoing generations of students and their teachers. And so it has been. REMA deepened its psychodynamic roots, and students learned simply to sit alongside people experiencing the "void" at the heart of their sense of self, highlighted by whatever crisis they were going through. Now, under Chris Steed's leadership, the model is widening its social scope, and taking into its heart the cry for value and recognition that moves every human spirit and identifying these as core "drivers" that motivate us. After all, why do people come for counseling anyway? Is it not because something stirs within them, even if not clearly recognized or articulated—a longing for something better, a yearning truly to be seen and valued, not overlooked or (even worse) abused and cast aside?

I'm so glad that the REMA framework is at last receiving a book-length exposition which will help anyone to hear it, and future generations of students to learn it. We knew from the start that a book was necessary, but it has never hitherto been possible. Now, thanks to Chris' persistence and energy, you are reading this and holding this book in your hands.

The REMA framework will stand the test of time, because (I believe) it truly captures the essence of human being and allows for the complexity and messiness that being human always entails. We are born through and into Relationship, which then shapes the entire field of our lives—not least because we internalize the most significant relationships, and we never escape the challenge of relating positively (if possible) to ourselves. And God seems to want to muscle into our relational world. But we can only relate—even to God—because we are Embodied. Our bodies present us with our fundamental "givenness" and with constant challenges to accept ourselves and to manage our process through the world, from birth through all our life stages towards inevitable death. How to find Meaning in that process?—a Meaning which will enable us to *feel* that our lives make sense, have value we can celebrate, and bring us happiness which is deep-rooted and not just an escape from dark realities? That drive towards Meaning and value is the crucial factor at play when we exercise our Agency—that is, when we take decisions and act in the world. The challenge to *act* is an inescapable daily struggle—an unbearable struggle for some—so this is where we often lock ourselves into just fulfilling social expectations, or undertaking repetitive routines or habitual behaviors (even addictive ones) that give a feeling of purpose, even though deep down we might be thinking "there must be more to life than this!—but what?"

Relationship, Embodiment, Meaning, Agency—these are the four poles of the REMA model, capturing the focuses of our longing for authenticity. From a Christian perspective, we are never complete, this side of the new creation. We journey, holding our incompletion and our hope. Each person is unique, and REMA therapists seek to sit alongside each client in their unique journey, seeking to understand the unique ways in which their relational and embodied reality is impacting their hopes and fears and their inner drive for a sense of value.

The REMA framework is not "Christian" in the sense that it is derived from the Bible and is therefore only valid within a Christian setting. Far from it. It is rooted in a philosophy of human being which can be owned by anyone, Christian or not. It has some fairly close parallels "out there" in the counseling world.[2] But for those who want to learn and practice their psychotherapy in a Christian way—in coherence with Christian faith, a Christian anthropology and a Christian spirituality—REMA is exactly the thing. It doesn't fit with all forms of Christian theology, and that is why the Theology half of the LST Theology and Counseling programme is so vital, enabling students to work out how their counseling and their theology cohere and "dialogue" with each other.

Speaking for myself, this partnership between REMA and theology is truly made in heaven. Seeing and experiencing my life through the lens of the REMA framework has immeasurably deepened my sense of myself as a child of God in Christ, and has given me tools to navigate my life with a much clearer sense of belonging and of purpose.

So I am deeply happy to commend this book and can't wait to see where REMA goes next as it continues its journey.

Steve Motyer
June 2022

Setting the Scene

Oliver Untwisted

"Counselling and psychotherapy are umbrella terms that cover a range of talking therapies. They are delivered by trained practitioners who work with people over a short or long term to help them bring about effective change and/or enhance their wellbeing."[3]

—BRITISH ASSOCIATION COUNSELLING PSYCHOTHERAPY

Leading Idea: therapy differs from the medical (illness) model of health care

THIS BOOK INTRODUCES THE thinking behind an approach to a relational therapy rooted in human value. We are shaped by the value society places on us. It is rooted in the assumption that human beings have high value; often to each other, often in our sense of self but always and ultimately to God.

We will draw on this idea as we explore the big quest to revalidate and endorse us that we look for wistfully in the dramas that play in our lives. That very quest works its way through core hungers of the soul that express our longings and we will look at what happens when these are blocked. A major focus for where blockage occurs with these strivings is in the unconscious mind. So often human problems arise from disturbances, frustrations and inner conflicts which show up:

a. In the way people **r**elate to others
b. In the way people experience themselves incarnationally as **e**mbodied
c. In the way people attach **m**eanings on situations in their lives and lack of purpose
d. In the way people exercise **a**gency or find the whole idea of finding their voice challenging

These areas of human functioning will serve as domains through which we can offer reparative work.

In the relational integrative therapy we now describe, it enables a therapist to dig down through all the recurring cycles in which people become trapped in patterns from which they cannot break free. Through vulnerabilities that clients develop or ways that they cannot help themselves, the goal is to find recover and restore the valuable person. Two humanities draw near; the other comes close and connects with a therapist in a profound way.

Through our lens, we will seek to show how the quest for validation of our personhood is a matter of fundamental drives, how this emanates from deep within our humanity and how it plays out in life, especially when disregarded.

COVID-19's Long Tail

This book was written amidst the disruption posed by the pandemic. Social experience is inscribed in our interior beings. How do we think psychologically about the new forms of experience that the virus has generated? What can be emphasized is summed up in the theme: Valuable Personhood. It is this that COVID-19 seemed to detonate in its existential threat to humankind.

For millions, COVID-19 was an experience of a world falling apart. Profoundly life threatening as it was for people in their bodily existence, it was destabilizing in their emotional and spiritual existence. Surely this void and crisis could never be a place of growth and change- it was too malign! Even those who had not lost someone directly to COVID-19 may have grieved other types of losses, ranging from time with loved ones to meaningful employment to a sense of a just world.[4]

Grief can get stuck. In its 11th revision, The *International Classification of Diseases* described prolonged grief disorder, a pervasive yearning for the deceased that persists past six months, coupled with emotional numbness and difficulty functioning.[5] Twelve months or more must have passed since the loss. Prolonged grief disorder was approved by the American Psychiatric Association for inclusion in the fifth edition of its *Diagnostic and Statistical Manual of Mental Disorders* (DSM–5) and a 13-item scale has been validated for measuring the condition.[6] This includes the bereaved's yearning for the deceased, emotional pain, difficulties engaging in life and feelings of numbness or meaninglessness.[7]

Questions of meaning inevitably arise. Why did God or the universe send this punishment? What could the deceased have done to avoid getting sick—counterfactuals that have no answer. One prominent theory of why grief arises is that it is not, in fact, about the severing of an attachment but about the shattering of our conception of the world.[8] Everyone has an assumptive world, a basic view of how the world works and their place in it.[9] This belief encompass the idea that the world is basically benevolent, that life is meaningful, and that *the self has worth.* Death, especially traumatic death, can rupture these core beliefs. The universal experience of bereavement called for grief literacy at the community level to try to build capacity to support one another in times of loss.

The self having worth? What is the basis for that in psychological life?

> "It felt I was being treated as a person of no value, no worth."[10]

The Metaphor of the Body and Ideologies of Mental Health

Mental health had come of age for such a sad time. It became acceptable to discuss in both private and public worlds, boosted by celebrities and Princes. Weaknesses were allowed to be discussed.

If the subject of mental health was no longer taboo, as death and sex had once been, its opposite was now no longer off-limits. "Mental illness" as a concept has been much debated along with its implication that problems in the mind should be defined medically utilizing metaphor of the body.

There have been many signposts to reconceptualizing counseling as a healthcare profession. Use of the words "healthy" to signify fulfilment in partner relationships or family ecological activity is one such example of linguistic saturation. In order to raise both status and public esteem, the counseling profession has lobbied hard for parity with healthcare professionals rather than being poor relation.

In therapy, the aim is that of deeper exploration of the mind. Are people in need of psychotherapy ill? Disease is both a category of thought and representative of a range of bodily impacts. We project parts of ourselves that are damaged and fragmented. The notion of illness is related to our general construction of nature. Medical interventions provide for expulsion of unmanageable parts of us.

It is akin to the racist imagery of the alien in our midst, in effect confronting hated parts of the self. Health care allows deviance to secure the boundaries of "normal" society. A society knows what it is by where it draws the boundaries. Nature and culture provide a dichotomy, a reservoir filled with meaning. Harvard sociology Professor Talcott Parsons was a major figure in the development of the sociology of health and illness. His work reflects the times in which he wrote but his core ideas remain central to medical sociology.[11] His 1951 book, *The Social System*, argued that being ill was not just a biological condition but performed a social role.[12] As a functionalist in sociology, Parsons saw illness as initiating the patient playing out the role of "sick person." Marxist sociologists detected the role of commercial gain in the capitalist approach to profiteering from pharmaceuticals; feminists argued that a woman is not allowed to play the role in the same way. She must just get on with it![13]

The medical model began to be impacted by holistic influences. Sickness came to be considered not just a disturbance in the self-contained arena of the body but a consequence of what we eat, where we work, the degree of exercise and emotional responses to or patterns of thinking about life. The shift from a biomedical to bio-psychosocial medicine was marked by change of talk from "treatment" to "health promotion." A person was not an eating disorder project, an entity wearing a label or to be regarded as merely the objects of our care. Nevertheless, although it has come from a different stable, the notion of well-being and mental health has been on the agenda for a long time.[14] Even spirituality is widely regarded as an essential dimension to medical care rather than being different.

It was a contemporary of Sigmund Freud, Emil Kraepelin who sought to create a taxonomy of mental illness. Kraepelin believed that all mental illness was genetic or physiological in origin, and his *Compendium of Psychiatry* (1883) became psychiatry's foundation text. Doctors could treat minds as well as bodies. Today, mental disturbance is most commonly viewed through a medical lens.

Is Counseling a Department of Health Care?

For all that counselors might share an agenda of working to improve mental health, this is fundamentally a different mode of activity. It has been subject to professionalisation and become a discipline with definitions and boundaries in contrast with a medical model of treating sickness. Ways of working as a counselor or psychotherapist differ fundamentally from others in the field. The task of a counselor is to work in a structured and way in depth with people. This means:

i. Addressing causes and not just symptoms of distress
ii. Facilitating well-being and subjective states as distinct from sickness and pathology
iii. The centrality of the relationship between counselors and those being helped: the interaction between two people hinges on the quality of that relationship.
iv. Seeking to bring, not a quick fix but a deeper layer exploration of what is troubling someone and giving rise to problems and tangles that someone is finding hard to untie
v. Seeing someone as a client you are working with in a temporary alliance rather than a patient who is the subject of a medical intervention
vi. A talking therapy not prescribing drugs
vii. Working with a prescribed Code of Conduct that regulates professional activity
viii. Working with a given theoretical basis from which emanates a distinctive approach

The term "counseling" includes a wide array of definitions. Is it a department of the larger psychological enterprise? The linked term "counseling psychology" has a strong association, particularly in the US, with humanistic and existentialist thinkers such as Abraham Maslow, Carl Rogers and Rollo May "who argued for the need to see human beings in a holistic manner, rather than a collection of psychological parts."[15] The American origins of the counseling movement are linked with Rogers who could not claim to be practising psychotherapy as he lacked a medical qualification. In the UK, counseling and psychotherapy largely developed outside the psychology profession. What was emphasized was not medical intervention but a therapeutic relationship. The quest for understanding and meaning was central not application of a scientific approach.

Prepositions are important here. Working with clients rather than doing something to them is the essence of counseling. Both professional counseling and pastoral counseling approaches seek to help people to live well, to flourish in the face of difficulties. Both claim to be addressing fundamental human concerns. Both emphasize empathic engagement with the world of those in pain. Counseling usually carries the idea of working in depth rather than helping someone through an immediate issue. The so-called "third force" in American psychology (in contrast with behavioral or psychoanalytic approaches) was based on humanistic assumptions rather than being faith-based.

Chronic levels of distress and concern are becoming normal. According to the charity, Mind, one in four people will experience a mental health problem of some kind each year in England. One in six people report experiencing a common mental health problem (like anxiety and depression) in any given week in England.[16] Therapy is hugely important in social life. Mental illness is arguably the biggest social problem in the UK. Approximately a third of families have someone who is mentally ill. The World Health Organization estimates that mental illness accounts for roughly 40% of all types of illness.[17] It is though worth asking, "Did COVID sparked a parallel wave of mental illness—or is such widespread suffering a natural response to the months of isolation, uncertainty and daily death counts?" Maybe we were mischaracterizing the challenges of living.

To be seen as a normal person who is responding and reacting in an understandable way rather than someone who is sick is profoundly liberating. The healing art involves immense skill. Despite what we will advocate in these pages, it is abundantly clear from the weight of research evidence that it is the strength of the working relationship, the therapeutic alliance that changes lives rather than a particular technique. Giving value to people in this way through a relationship of mutual regard and on equal terms as far as possible (allowing for inevitable power imbalance) is humanizing.

The relational integrative therapy we now describe enables a therapist to dig down through all the recurring cycles in which people become trapped in patterns from which they cannot break free. Through vulnerabilities that clients develop or ways that they cannot help themselves, the goal is to find recover and restore the valuable person.

Endnotes

1. At that time we called it a "mode." We have since learned that this is too bold: an integrative "framework" only becomes a "model" when it is activated in an actual counseling process by a practitioner who has made it their own.
2. The closest is probably Faris, A., & Ooijen, E. (2012). *Integrative counselling and psychotherapy: A relational approach.* Sage.
3. The British Association of Counselling and Psychotherapy. (n.d.). *What is counselling? About therapy.* https://www.bacp.co.uk/about-therapy/what-is-counselling/.
4. Portland Institute for Loss and Transition. (n.d.). *PI team.* https://www.portlandinstitute.org/faculty.
5. *ICD-11.* https://icd.who.int/en.
6. Prigerson, H. G., Boelen, P. A., Xu, J., Smith, K. V., & Maciejewski, P. K. (2021). Validation of the new DSM-5-TR criteria for prolonged grief disorder and the PG-13-Revised (PG-13-R) scale. *World Psychiatry, 20*, 96–106.
7. Verdery, A. M., Smith-Greenaway, E., Margolis, R., & Daw, J. (2020). Tracking the reach of COVID-19 kin loss with a bereavement multiplier applied to the United States. *Proceedings of the National Academy of Sciences, 117*, 17695–701.
8. Millman, E., Lee, S. L., Neimeyerc, R. A., Mathis, A. A., & Jobe, M. C. (2020). Modelling pandemic depression and anxiety: The mediational role of core beliefs and meaning making. *Journal of Affective Disorders Reports, 2.*
9. Harris, D. L. (Ed.). (2019). *Non-death loss and grief: Context and clinical implications.* Routledge.
10. Salman Rushdie during a psychology-based interview on *Shrink Rap*, May 12, 2008.
11. Collyer, F. M. (2012). *Mapping the sociology of health and medicine: America, Britain, and Australia compared.* Palgrave Macmillan.
12. Parsons, T. (1951). *The social system.* Free.
13. Milton, D. (2004). *Talcott Parsons and the theory of the "sick role."* https://kar.kent.ac.uk/62743/.

14. Jahoda, M. (1958) *Current concepts of positive mental health.* Basic.
15. Strawbridge S., & Woolfe, R. (2003). Counselling psychology in context. In R. Woolfe, W. Dryden, & S. Strawbridge (Eds.), *Handbook of counselling psychology* (pp. 3–21). Sage.
16. Mind. (n.d.). *LGBT+ mental health.* https://www.mind.org.uk/information-support/tips-for-everyday-living/lgbtiq-mental-health/about-lgbtiq-mental-health/.
17. Layard, R., & Clark, D. M. (2015). Why more psychological therapy would cost nothing. *Frontiers of Psychology, 6,* 1713

Introduction

History and the "Here and Now"

"Some people cling to hidden attachments of which they are generally unaware. . . . [T]hese false and hidden motives could prevent them from entering God's presence. . . . [T]hat which they cleave and cling lies so deeply buried that they are not even conscious of it."

—JOHANNES TAULER[1]

Leading Idea: an approach to therapy that is relational, holistic, attuned in terms of social realities and integrative. Therapists need to work "here and now" (top layer) of current client experiences but also with their history

"An officer is a miserable creature. Each envies his colleagues, bullies his subordinates, and is afraid of his superiors: the higher up he is, the more he fears them. I detest the idea of having inscribed on my collar how much I am worth, as if I were a sample of some goods."[2]

THE WRITER IS THE young Sigmund Freud, complaining to his colleague and mentor Josef Breuer about compulsory national service in the Austrian Army, in a "filthy hole working on black and yellow" as he put it; black and yellow being the Austrian colors. It is intriguing to ponder what would have been the outcome of pursuing this line of thought and bringing the struggle to realize our value into Freudian psychodynamics. The reaction—against how much he is worth being inscribed on his collar—is a strong one. He detests it. It is the Protest.

It is such experiences of reaction against being put down and made to feel insignificant that are highly instructive. These experiences serve as data; a window on what is going on in the psyche that reveal how humans are wired up. What though is the pathway to the inner world that experiences of being insignificant and devalued illuminate? Are they located in unconscious responses?

The perspective of this book builds on that. What will be developed in these pages is an approach to therapy that is relational, holistic, attuned in terms of social realities, and integrative.

Picking up the last word first, when it comes to counseling models it is common to use the term "*integrative*" in the sense that it brings together ideas and understanding from different approaches into one user-friendly and effective therapy. We shall be using the term in two contrasting ways:

i. Our approach to therapy is integrative in the sense that while the primary orientation is psychodynamic in the sense that we look to exploring the unconscious and root causes, we will be attuned to whatever seems most helpful with individual clients rather than be equipped to move solely in a particular theory of the inner world. Models of therapy such as CAT or CBT for example, although very useful and providing some good day by day coping strategies, are not focused on deep-seated long-term issues. This can work for many if you do not need to look at wounded history or behavioral/relationship issues. Some deeper analysis can, however, be beneficial in allowing people to explore issues in their past and hopefully resolve at least some of these issues and find some relief from trauma or root causes. Ways of looking at the field and systems within which therapeutic interventions take place can also be enhanced by use of Gestalt therapy.

ii. Our approach to therapy is also integrative in that we are attuned to the centuries of reflection in the faith-based traditions of Christian theology and pastoral psychology which have most definitely not out-lived their usefulness. Every approach to therapy is rooted in presuppositions about psychological functioning and a way of being human. How the human spirit imagines itself was not invented by Sigmund Freud. It seems clear that human functioning needs to have some orientation to what is beyond ourselves.

The perspective of this books, and the course that it underpins, is that biblical faith traditions have very rich resources to draw on which provides an important and wholly justified correlate with what can be learned from psychological theory and practice. This is not offered here in the sense of an "applied theology" as if the conversation only goes one way. Our approach rather is one of dialogue between two very different fields of discourse and study. Theological reflection and the social science world underpinning the study of human beings can talk to each other. It is a two-way street.

Where they can meet is around the value of people which is both a deeply theological idea *and* a social science construct that does heavy lifting. It is a stance linking together ideas in this book as:

i. The value of human beings is a working assumption in ethical frameworks that seek to promote the equal respect and non-discrimination that informs best practice and law. We treat people the same or aspire to as worthy of respect. That humans should be treated in a certain way is a theological idea about those made in the image of God;
ii. The value of human beings is also a psycho-social dynamic driver. We are hard wired to pursue this in our lives: high value is a powerful motivation. Where this is not forthcoming in our social or interpersonal world, something happens inside that dents our sense of self.

The approach to therapy here is that it is *sociologically attuned*. Most counseling models developed in the last century by white middle class men. Our approach seeks to incorporate issues of race, gender and categories of disadvantage into the heart of the model. It does this through analyzing how responses to what is going on in a client's social world form part of their identity. Their social experience is part of the story of their lives. Social scripts merge with interpersonal dramas in a way that is patterned in the unconscious. The deep impact of cultural identity reaches deep down inside.

The approach taken here is also *relational*. This also has two distinct focal points:

i. *Humans are relational.* We are defined by where we stand in connection with others. Our counseling theory is not about an individual psychology. Our own inner world does not stand by itself but is inextricably entwined with others with whom we stand in close relation. We have a social brain. In what will be a theme of these pages, our valuable personhood is formed and reformed as we interact with others. We flourish in relationships or are damaged in relationships which are a screen for our inner lives

ii. *Our work is relational.* At heart is an empathic relationship between the client and therapist within the therapeutic boundaries, the purpose of which is to help the client make sense of their situation and to find ways of making changes for the better.

Another focal point is that our work is *holistic* in its view of what makes us human. With reference to ultimate questions, we ask about how people are wired up and what is the source of distress. We look at people through a lens of being a mind-body—spirit continuum. Recognizing the complexity of human behavior makes us want to probe emotional blockages rooted in an unconscious realm that break surface through negative thought patterns and anxiety that so often have people in their grip.

Endorsement's Inner Quest (the Validation of Personhood)

The "engine" behind our approach to human functioning is the drive to be recognized, endorsed, and validated. Therapy means we seek to find the valuable person, recognizing that there are many aspects of ourselves that are often in conflict. Which departments of our very being are of high worth, such as need drawing out, re-framing and cleansing? It is surely the whole, the totality of who we are that is valuable and capable of living of a worthwhile life if we can be free of the blockages that cripple us and might also prevent us from being oriented to the divine realm beyond ourselves.

Our primary pursuit is to be a worthwhile person living a worthwhile life that matters because we matter. For that will deliver a life with meaning, significance, and purpose. This is argued here to be a primary motivation and not a secondary conceptualization. The value and worth of people is more than a principle of moral action and duty, calling us to a description of "this is how we 'ought' to live."

What will be developed as the foundation for this therapy is that this is how we ARE. It belongs to how we are wired up, to our innermost responses to external circumstances that declare "excuse me, I am a human being." The urge to count, to be endorsed and live a life that matters is a major force. It shapes how we pursue relationships, family, career satisfaction and adventure that bring approval, significance to our lives. This primary impetus we fulfill through meeting soul-hungers:

- I belong (*relational connection* and the power of place)
- I want (pursuit of desire, whether for sex or power that is a deeply *embodied experience*)
- I matter (valuable personhood, longing for *meaning*, worthwhile, significance, and purpose)
- I will survive (some sense of hope, the future and getting through, evoking our inner resources as *responsible agents*)

These soul-hungers are conceived psychodynamically, as fundamental motivations that play at an unconscious level and generating energy towards fulfilment outside ourselves. We are constituted by our loves, by our longing to be significant, to connect, and to be able to see a future. These ways of reconfiguring forms of fundamental impetus in human functioning are often in conflict; such as when desire for someone or something is incompatible with moral imperatives of the community one belongs to, or there seems little hope of reaching goals we have set for ourselves. They are refracted through four aspirations in human action, four lenses to help us discern clues to what is going on deep down. These will be four domains in which we can work fruitfully.

- **Relational**: Psychology is not to be understood as appertaining to human beings as entities in themselves. Cognition involves re-cognition. Relational disruption brings the need for repair and restoration. The therapeutic relationship is fundamental to the healing work.
- **Embodied Personhood**: Our "embodiment" is the most fundamental fact about us and it is through our physicality and social location that we encounter each other. Our identity is mediated through embodied experience be it emotionality, physicality, sexuality or disability.
- **Meaning**: The drive to find meaning for our lives is very powerful for us human beings. This is a coherent understanding of our lives that "makes sense," but also—a calling that fulfils us, a purpose that gives us a reason to live, a way to cope with pain, a *story* to inhabit.

- **Agency**: More than fulfilling physical urges, we need to know that we matter—that we are *noticed*. We can be robbed of our agency by others. We can though move beyond the script handed out to us and take responsibility for our own lives. Voice and choice are possible.

Redemptive Repair: Working with the Model

Problems and challenges in human functioning can arise from any direction. Those that lodge deeply and form part of us will usually have been embedded in the unconscious arena where root causes grow. The approach taken here is based on a post-Freudian theory of mind in that the content of the unconscious goes beyond life and death drives as psychoanalysis conceives. The central impetus of the unconscious is not the discharge of bodily needs but to be someone who, through connection, longs to discover that they matter. Desire, relationship, hope and significance are expressions of this.

If we take a systemic view of human beings and the distress that agitates, we can break into the system at many different points. Working with where a client comes in need will not usually make us begin with blockages and problems at an unconscious level. It may well be that difficulties in family or in the workplace, with anxiety or depression will highlight negative thought patterns that are not helping. But emotional knots and the effect of such things as trauma will take us to deep-seated causes. The difficulties people experience in their connection with others, in their relationship with their own bodies, how they interpret their own existence and try to make sense of it or reasons why they might be complicit in blocking their agency, invariably will have root causes that need to be explored. When people repeat patterns of behavior that surprises even them or when clients act out their pathology and dysfunction, they are expressing their unconsciously held conflict.

We will explore sources of healing, about which Christian theological reflection down the centuries has much to say. This leads to spiritual transformation and can be summarized in terms of:

i. **Resonance**: Discerning what themes are playing under the surface (and which the counsellor might feel in themselves) so as to hear the potential for harmony.

ii. **Repentance**: Acknowledging realistically where people need to take responsibility and admit tricky self-deceit, letting God down and often destructive behavior to others.

iii. **Re-membering**: Allowing fragments of our broken world experience and fractured memories to be re-framed and gathered anew. "Re-membering" comes to be about the members of ourselves and body of memory brought into wholeness like pottery shards.

iv. **Reconciling**: Looking at patterns of relating that have served as a screen on which to project the divided, alienated self thus seeking harmony between different parts of us.

v. **Recollection**: Meditation and prayer in a condition of all truly wakeful and deep modes of living, and hence indispensable for our transformation.

vi. **Re-valuing**: Grasping how being diminished, facing indignity or indifference impacts clients so they flourish: recover agency, dignity purpose, and worth, and affirm their story.

Explorers seeking the truth of what lies within have to travel into the deep regions and encounter many obstacles to the impulses and loves that dare not speak their name. A safe guide is essential.

Central to the healing process is that the therapist seeks to form a good, boundaried relationship. The relational space between therapist and client is broad enough to cover the relationship of self to self, the relationship of self to others, the relationship of self to context and self as a spiritual entity. It recognizes the existential realities of human existence, learned behaviors and childhood wounds alongside other things that influence the way we act and feel that make that a sharp experience.

Our emphasis here is integrative. There is a process of moving between different approaches to the interior world of the client that need not be in one mode only. A psychodynamic core means the therapist is attuned to deep seated conflicts someone might have to probe the inner place from which emotions might arise. Most obviously there are the problems and challenges of everyday life someone faces. These need to be addressed as they are troubling. Wounded history and emotional experience will fight back, however. Behind so many daily challenges, ghosts walk and stalk

An Integrative Approach

This book presents an approach to therapy which seeks to align counseling theories and Christian faith. There are numerous versions of both.

We offer a theoretical foundation by presenting a theologically rooted picture of issues foundational to people's needs, to human being and becoming. We will draw on Christian theological tradition that is deeply rooted in biblical reflection as well as human experience. We will also draw on social science and psychology inputs that have described our situation from different perspectives situated in the life and times of human beings. These represent different disciplines with their own way of speaking, vocabulary and traditions. Lining them up so a dialogue becomes possible is no straightforward task. There is a growing tradition, not just of these two disciplines in themselves but in how psychology and Christian, specifically biblical, faith have something to say to each other.

A point of intersection is needed where these different roundabouts of reflection meet. A critical correlation might be where Christian faith and social science have something profound in common. A point of intersection is provided by the value and worth of people conceived as an active principle of human action which functions both on the biblical landscape but which is also a major player in the social and interpersonal field. This entails re-positioning human value as more than an ethical ideal; as a dynamic in the way people interact with each other in society. The notion of human value is not easy to pin down. It is not though self-referencing. We hold our value with others in mutuality.

We will draw on this idea as we explore the big quest to recognize, revalidate and endorse us for which we look wistfully in the dramas that play in our lives. We will note how that quest works its way through core human hungers that express our longings and what happens when these are blocked. A major focus for where the blockage occurs underlying "Why I am hungry" is in the unconscious mind. So often distress arises from disturbances and inner conflicts which show up:

i. In the way people *relate* to others
ii. In the way people experience themselves incarnationally as *embodied*
iii. In the way people attach *meanings* on situations in their lives and lack of purpose
iv. In the way people exercise responsible *agency* or find exercising their voice challenging

Problems and challenges in human functioning can arise from any direction. Those that lodge deeply and form part of us will usually have been embedded in the unconscious arena where root causes grow. The approach taken here is based on a post-Freudian theory of mind in that the content of the unconscious goes beyond life and death drives as psychoanalysis conceives. The central impetus of the unconscious is not the discharge of bodily needs but to be someone who, through connection, longs to discover that they matter. Desire, relationship, hope, and significance are expressions of this.

If we take a systemic view of human beings and the distress that agitates, we can break into the system at many different points. Working with what a client brings will not usually make us begin with blockages and problems at an unconscious level. It may well be that difficulties in family or in the workplace, with anxiety or depression will highlight cognitive negative patterns that are not helping. But emotional knots and the effect of such things as trauma will take us to deep-seated causes. The difficulties people experience in their connection with others, in their relationship with their own bodies, how they interpret their own existence and try to make sense of it and reasons why they might be complicit in blocking their agency, invariably will have root causes that need to be explored. When people act out their pathology and dysfunction, they are expressing their unconsciously held conflict.

This approach is a theory of dialogic change. A therapist seeks to work holistically: looking and listening for disturbance and formulation in each of the four dimensions and why it arises. The meeting point of relevant social science and theology is a place where these different discourse structures can align. Though full weight is given to the value of the human on theological and ethical grounds (people matter!), the belief by the therapist and often client that God is in the client's story and consulting room can be explored. Some sense of transcendence, spiritual growth and growing as a person emanates from power of dialogue in depth for transformation and the power to change. There are specific sources of healing and growth available through power of biblical reflection as we look for the valuable person and endeavour to draw out the impact of unconscious mental forces.

Although our approach looks at what transpires between therapist and client occurs in a field of interaction and the healing process can begin anywhere in that field, according to what the client brings, the focus for the approach outlined here points towards reaching to what is out of view:

the unconscious mental and emotional life where root causes of distress so often arise. It is not a case of insisting that therapy must commence there as invariably, what has gone on in the background will not usually be uppermost in someone's consciousness. Nevertheless, a therapist in this model will want to be looking through the windows of relationality, embodiment, meaning and agency to explore what has given rise to the distress. If not, the underlying distress will fight back so to speak.

This approach to counseling is integrative. It offers its own depiction of human functioning that combines theological ideas with multiple social science reference points. Notable amongst these are the impact of systemic factors and the weight of scripts handed to us that are internalized.

Systems thinking is an essential perspective in contemporary therapeutic perspective. By this is meant more than family systems. Systemic practice and awareness is coming to the fore in social work training though less so in counseling education. This is a deficit as it is not possible to leave behind the impact of culture and race that shapes us from day one producing different versions of ourselves. It can no longer be acceptable to look at an individual psychology on its own as if culture and reciprocal interaction is irrelevant to a standard model of a generic human. Sociology will need to be brought into the picture as the systems of social ecology bring sharply different weight to people's experiences.

The approach we take here is holistic, seeing a client as the whole person they are. So we set up two contrast poles. The first is between short-term and long-term work which can be framed as being between cognitive work on beliefs and thought patterns that are giving rise to a great deal of anxiety *and* work on hidden dynamics well below surface giving rise to emotional and neurotic blockages.

A therapeutic model endeavours to work at two levels. These levels represent contrasting polarities akin to the difference between north and south poles. The North Pole, shall we say, is the external reality that the client has to deal with, the shape of things of which clients are conscious. This must be addressed for it will be the presenting domain for which support and help is requested. There is also a South Pole; a deeply hidden conflicted domain that may lie deeply hidden and usually deceptively camouflaged.

This polarity can be characterized in different ways. It is misleading to label it as contrasting *thought and emotion* since there are few purely cognitive processes. A theory of emotional cognition obliges us to view so many cognitive conclusions as laden with feeling and affect (career aspirations, education choices, art appreciation images of beauty, romantic attractiveness or political worldviews, for example, that are rooted in emotive experiences shaping likes and dislikes).

It is misleading also to characterize this polarity as being between *surface treatment and depth*. Cognitive processes have deep roots. How someone responds to life is often shaped by emotions and experiences that supply a stock of perceptual ideas about he or she thinks about the world.

It raises the question of what exactly we mean by "depth"? Here we refer to layers below the level of what is going on consciously in current life of clients rather than that of which they are not clients.

The contrast in approaches to therapy based on cognitive work and beliefs in contrast to a deeper layer is essentially one of *time frames*. Short term interventions are framed as being for a set period, often 6–12 weeks that are not targeted at sorting out the deep-seated inner world of the patient but offering something that can help for now and that may address the mental models that are faulty. Conflicted inner states are clearly an issue but the impact of what is going on now is a better place to offer therapeutic intervention. Often a reason for that is pragmatism. Intense pressures on health service budgets force reduction in time that can be permitted for therapy with each client.

These different ways of working are usually regarded as constituting different constructs; engaging with different aspects of client experience. The appropriateness of a construct might depend on:

i. Do you go deeper or do work with what presents in the exterior world of the client?

ii. Do you deal with thought patterns or probe emotional blockages with hidden power?

iii. Do you deal with the here and now or seek to address history? The images that such representation conveys are more than metaphors such as working with mirrors or archaeology. They are images of therapeutic work that have emotional potency.

iv. How much time do we have? What are the practicalities of embarking on treatment?

v. What resources are available from very busy mental health professionals for help?

vi. Do we go for something that seems to have an evidence-base and power to change?

The Top Layer

What level of therapy is appropriate will depend on the goal of therapy. Are we giving a solution, a short-term "cure" characterized by relentless positivity that transforms the power of negative mindsets? Or are we able to name the hate, shame and worthlessness that lie deep down so often? It is a criticism of cognitive models of therapy that they can address world of "the world of the here and the now"; leaving clients able to think more positively about their situation. That is a gain worth having. Yet experience shows it will be relatively short-lived if root causes are not addressed and negative material named. It is important that appropriately focused therapy is directed where most needed.

The therapist is obliged to address how clients presents and the aspects of themselves that are agitating. That may be all they have time for sadly. Such a reality constitutes the top layer.

The contrast pole is the deeper work of what is usually characterized as psychotherapy. Going deeper reflects the interplay of external realities that are pressing alongside inner realities. Very often, those realities are shaped by distress or trauma. Childhood experiences are one aspect of this but then so too are subsequent traumatic events that have wreaked devastation on the inner world and how the exterior world has been felt and held. Whether or not the trauma happened in childhood or a later experience, the unconscious memory of that event reverberates strongly with the result that there is no result and no resolution. People have got stuck.

The top layer is the arena of conscious action and often turbulent thoughts

It is a mistake to see the more cognitive processes contrasted with "deeper" areas for therapy as segregated states. They are interwoven aspects of our existence. A skilled counsellor can oscillate between what is going on at a surface level that may be causing considerable agitation but then addressing root causes and conflicts that may be driving that agitation in the first place.

To view the contrast as segregated states can easily pitch students and counsellors into labels and silos of knowledge which generate taking up positions. Cognitive therapies can be regarded as quick cures administered by official health professionals. Psychotherapy can be seen as costly and an approach that misses the point rather than helping people understand themselves. Arguably, what will benefit our clients is that we can speak the language of different types of therapy. Integrative approaches can work if they speak the same larger theory of human beings. To harmonize, they need to meld at the level of a culture of enquiry rather than be solution-focused.

Another polarity is between an individual psychology and a person considered as part of a field of interactions. It is the contrast between a system and what can be termed a "monadic" view of what goes on within a person in themselves. This is a major question and divide. Do all problems originate from within an individual or do they arise through interaction with the systems of social life? Following on from the Enlightenment, the classic neoliberal theme is that of individuals pursuing their own needs. Mapped on to that is the tendency in our cultural climate to be a customer, issuing likes or dislikes and engaging with others on market terms. The contrast "north pole" is that mental health is not just about individuals but from social pressures on people.

What happens in between the poles? This is always a relevant question in any analysis of a field, whether it is the social field or a force field as might be analyzed in physics. In psychotherapy, there is me, there is you but there is also the space between. What happens in the linkage between two interacting entities is of huge interest. Something takes place between a person and the social field in which they meshed. Something takes place when therapist and client meet and form a strong healing bond. A polarity between the present (here and the now) and a deeper layer is not neutral.

Our approach here is integrative. We espouse a relational form of therapy that is holistic in that the client comes with who they are and what may be troubling them. It is our task to offer a working relationship that can stimulate transformative change. A client will not, however, come with whatever may be problematic all labelled as cognitive or psychodynamic. They may almost certainly be confused but also fragmented. Ambiguity is likely to be the hallmark of their present dilemmas.

There are different ways of performing an integrative therapy.

In the approach taken here, therapeutic help operates by four principles:

i. It is performative, tailored to the needs of the client and actual clinical issues. The agenda for therapy is not rooted in what a therapist brings but in what a client brings. A therapist is a catalyst for transformative change: to invoke Carl Rogers, this is "client-centered therapy."[3] The very use of the word "client" rather than "patient" denoted the role of the individual in seeking help and overcoming difficulties. Clients are in the driving seat and bring what is troubling them. This must not be construed as being surface and therefore superficial. Such an approach can go deep and result in profound change. The starting point is those aspects of life that the client is conscious of and which may well be generating some anxiety.

ii. It is concerned with the deeper layer, root causes; the level down broadly corresponding with the unconscious area of mental life. A client may well want to talk about what is bothering and deeply unsettling. It is in the belief that people are so often conflicted that to offer help to the hurting to bring about lasting, profound change, requires work that is in-depth (as all therapy must be) and which operates at a core level of human functioning. The sources and causes of distress need to be addressed or the problems will only reappear.

iii. It is concerned with social realities that shape the experience of being-in-the-world that the people we seek to help live out from day to day. This lived experience is central to the identity people have, moulded as they are by invisible forces beyond their control. Rogers refers to the desirability of counseling students having some knowledge of clients within their cultural setting. "Such knowledge needs to be supplemented by experiences of living with or dealing with individuals who have been the product of cultural influences very different from those which have moulded the student."[4] He did not pursue that thought, however. Humans do not live in a vacuum. We play out our dramas in our life and times.

iv. It is rooted in the approach to the transpersonal that is represented by the tried and tested reflection of Christian theology which offers a critical rigour rather than a "fuzzy" spirituality.

This is part of what it means to be working in the unconscious (in other words explore what is going on at an unconscious level). Very often, it is a mistaken premise that mental disorder in say black people (bipolarity) is the result of an individual pathology. Gaining competence in such social experience as gender, what it means to be able bodied or not or race and culture are important realities. They not just about delivery of service or best practice but deeply—layered identity.

Yet an organic process of tailoring the help needed to the client may well have to recognize that someone might not have the capacity for deeper work, be ready to confront the blind-spots within themselves or probe from where difficult emotions arise.

Working with the unconscious involves a number of different well-tried and tested routes, mostly entailing some form of interpretation of what is being acted out. Amongst these is working with transference, interpreting the current relationship between therapist and client as feelings or desires for another person are redirected to therapist. This is the royal road to the unconscious—"who do I remind you of?"! Evaluating this transference has been seen as central to psychodynamically oriented techniques.[5] Staying in exchanges of transference requires necessary focus to do its work.

A way of representing the different levels of treatment lies in history. Wounded history dogs people and societies. There is a powerful impetus to know and not to know at the very same time. That is true of societies when as they are reluctant to face a difficulty history; perhaps that of complicity in genocide, mass murder or systematic abuse of children. It is also profoundly true of people as an individual entity (if such a person exists). One thing psychoanalysis has been very good at it is in working with immense fluidity in repressed knowledge. People can fight hard not to acknowledge what deep down they know. Others seek to make sense of the darkest chapters of their lives.

The "here and the now" is the reality that is present to the person in pain. He or she is aware of being baffled, being perplexed, being in a state of anxiety and feeling unable to resolve the problems that life is generating. It may be that there are relationship problems. Maybe financial or family pressures are holding someone in a vice. Maybe a lack of resolution has led to depression or anxiety.

Yet so many of the problems of life have deeper causes. There is a past as well as a present. Wounded history affects us and shapes us profoundly. It might be a baffled awareness that complexity lurks deep down;

it might be a realization that how we are in the world shows up a conflicted state of things. "Why do I react like that?" is a recognizable sigh. The mystery of our existence is inseparable from the enigma of our past.

History bleeds into the present and indeed the future. We live in a continuum in which earlier versions of ourselves are a very present reality in times of trouble. In psychotherapy, time travelling is an essential capability performed by both client and a person-helper. History is still here.

The therapist has to reckon with the power of the unseen. As the contours of the present come into focus, the vagaries of what is happening is surely a sign of deeper issues that may be troubling. History has us all captive. The good news is that we do not need to be hostage to it. For there is also a future. The therapist must know how to go downstairs but also go on the roof as it were.

Label-Lite

Performing an integrative therapy must do justice to the top layer and the deeper layer in the basement. A therapist must be attuned to both realities.

In social experience, labels are laden. They matter profoundly. Labels create a power hierarchy. Labels point out who are the acceptable people and who are not. "How do you feel about being labelled? What labels matter to you?"—these are important questions to probe. Different visible aspects of ourselves represent different identities for how people see us though we may protest profoundly about being put in a box which is then wrongly labelled.

Yet in psychotherapy practice, labels must be utilized with great care, as in diagnoses and modality.

Diagnoses—the medicalized language of disorders and symptoms can create a false distance between what someone is going through and the reason for their distress, whether it's trauma, abuse, poverty or prejudice. Telling someone as an established fact that they have a mental illness according to the latest diagnostic tool can put someone in a sealed box for life. The imposition of potentially stigmatizing labels must be undertaken very sparingly. Diagnosis is but a descriptive term.

By way of example, one very vocal and high-profile critic of the standard Diagnostic Manuals in psychiatry is Allen Francis. A former author of DSM-4, he contends that millions of people who are really no more than worried well are being diagnosed as having a mental disorder and receiving unnecessary treatment. Francis argues that stigmatizing a healthy person as mentally ill leads to unnecessary, harmful medications, the narrowing of horizons, the misallocation of medical resources and a shift in responsibility for our mental well-being away from our own naturally resilient brains and into the hands of Big Pharma, who are reaping huge profits. DSM's flaws are not reason enough to abandon diagnosis though, in his view. Criteria help determine if someone's problems are the result of a physical illness.[6]

An alternative view to psychiatric diagnosis is that of the "Power Threat Meaning Framework (PTMF)" that asks not "What's wrong with you?" but "What's happened to you?" This constituted powerful artillery in the anti-psychiatry movement. Emotional distress, unusual experiences and many forms of troubled or troubling behavior are understandable against the backcloth of someone's person's life and circumstances, the cultural and social norms we are expected to live up to and the extent of our exposure to trauma, abuse, injustice and inequality.[7] We will return to questions of meaning and power when we visit "Meaning-making" and "Agency" in the approach we take to counseling psychotherapy. Diagnoses can be helpful if used sparingly and do not imprison people in a category.

Modality—whether the type of counseling adopted is incompatible with others is a vexed question while integrating faith and the world of psychotherapy adds a further layer. Underlying philosophical assumptions might very well be incompatible. Employing a "pick'n mix" eclecticism cannot just proceed by way of elements extracted from their origins and mixed at whim in a cocktail at the expense of the integrity of the theory as a whole.

There are broadly five main schools of psychology that provide formats into which therapy can fit:

- *Psychodynamic*: Explaining human behavior in terms of unconscious processes below the radar such as desires and fears, which we are not consciously aware of.
- *Behavioral*: Explaining human behavior as determined by the environment, by conditioning.
- *Cognitive*: Explaining human behavior in terms of rational processes, that our thoughts determine feelings and behaviors

- *Humanistic*: "What is it like to be this person?," the self-actualization that needs to be fulfilled and which emerges most obviously in person-centered counseling.
- *Gestalt*: A field theory about the way in which people engage in shifting scenery of figure and ground to make sense of their experience in a way that stresses personal responsibility and a focus on the individual's experience in the present moment. Within the therapist–client relationship, the "here and now" (what is happening from one moment to the next) allows self-awareness to lead to personal growth. Self-awareness can become blocked by negative thought patterns and behaviors.

The question is whether these are such different ways of operating that they cannot be combined. Is one committed to one mode of doing counseling that excludes other ways of operating? It is beyond the scope of this book to weigh different merits of each, given their history. Our approach incorporates aspects of Cognitive Behavioral Therapy (CBT), Gestalt, and Person-Centered aspects around a Psychodynamic core. A particular distinctive is to integrate a theological perspective.

Mahrer suggests that theories should only be integrated if they share the same larger theory of human beings.[8] These various approaches invoke perspectives on human functioning that are hard to reconcile. They resonate with the distinction between qualitative and quantitative methodology, often characterized as different ways of seeing the world, different ontologies. Yet one salient fact trumps the various methodologies. It is that the person in pain in front of us may have different aspects of themselves but fundamentally is a unity; there is one of them. A client does not present with parts of themselves sticking out that can be labelled as requiring CBT, person-centered or psychodynamic interventions. Labels become things and get reified. We deal with one client at a time in a fragmented unity; clients that long to break free from the stories that have them chained.

It is useful perhaps to remove the capital letter so as to de-centre the modality. Helping the client to address the challenges that are pressing upon daily life may well involve core beliefs and cognitive processes in what used to be called "left-side brain" work. That does not mean our modality is purely *cognitive*. Equally, we can address deeper vulnerabilities of emotional experience, trauma or the ways client might be unable to help themselves without labelling it as "*psychodynamic*." At times, a therapist will work in a *person-centered* way so as to set up the working relationship between them. Yet the working partnership could be preparatory to various schools of counseling thought. Aaron Beck's 1979 text on a *Cognitive Therapy of Depression* emphasized the personal bond and Rogerian skills of warmth, empathy and genuineness.[9] There has to be a distinction between forming the conditions for exploration of human dilemmas and the exploration itself. Operating in that modality means we set up the foundation of the working alliance but does not have to entail the linked assumption that all the resources are within to be self-directed.

A flexibility can be deployed that goes with moving between different ways of working. If we track our clients into the arena of root causes, we are entering the zone of psychodynamics. Behavioral therapies, which attempts to replace dysfunctional thoughts and reframing them with more adaptive beliefs, do not always allow for the emergence of the frightened, terrified parts of a person to emerge and restored holistically between body and mind.[10] Psychodynamic perspectives do not have a monopoly on working in depth and seeking to unravel Oliver who is twisted.

With all these approaches helping clients become aware of their internal self (working model) is key to understanding why they react and behave in certain ways. Though languaged differently, it seems possible to tailor intervention to the need of the client, especially with regard to what is happening in the "here and now" of the client's world. Some interventions will be more appropriate than others. While recognizing the vital need to work in the unconscious domain of root causes and in the transference with client, the therapist in our approach will utilize different modes as needed.

Ways of working which are valid in their own way can help someone move forward. They can also point quite significantly to unconscious processes. For example, why are negative thoughts being generated? What lies behind rigidity of mental constructs that constitute a poor self-image or relationship difficulties? If the cognitive dimension is an overflow of the deep inner world of the client, then very often therapists will find themselves confronted with self-defeating behaviors. A person-centered approach may help to resolve difficulties someone has. By helping someone see their situation as a field of shape-shifting perceptions, Gestalt therapy can be of great help. All these approaches tug at unconscious processes and seek to draw them into the light of day.

Later, we will consider the concept of resonance and how human encounters can take place under the surface of things. The top notes are an essential dimension of the music but they are supported by notes in the minor key or further down the scale that underpin the melody. In an account of the social world by Hartmut Rosa called "resonance," the quality of a human life cannot be measured simply in terms of resources, options, and moments of happiness; instead, we must consider our relationship to, or resonance with, the world.[11] Practitioners in different modalities might not be able to meet at the level of labels. Different silos and trainings might prevent it. However, the various approaches *might* meet if we get behind and under the labels. Some forms of therapy are useful in combination with others.

Therapists need flexible capability. The top-layer, the "here and now" of the client can be addressed in various ways. Flexibility can tailor the intervention and response to what is going on in the circumstances the client is grappling with and how those raise questions about the internal self who is battling away. Therapists can adapt according to what is breaking surface and agitating someone.

What is being advocated here though is the need to work at the deep level that so often undergirds client distress. No one awakes saying to themselves they will repeat harmful behaviors. Like miners who have to go down a long way to uncover and bring coal or minerals to the surface, psychodynamics is a particular focus on working *in* the unconscious, not just *with* it.

For many, the ability to oscillate between the two layers organically is a question of resource of time and money. To go deeper into psychodynamics will inevitably involve longer time and expense. A Brief Therapy that is solution-focused may be what is needed to help the hurting recover.

Multiples studies show that when therapy takes place, there are changes revealed in brain imaging.[12] More than three-quarters of those who have therapy report being emotionally better off.[13] This is amply demonstrated in clinical trials using the same methodology as is used to test medical interventions. Counseling and psychotherapy have a high success rate that is borne out in evidence.

Psychotherapy produces greater improvement than no treatment. But are all talking therapies equally effective? Studies have shown that there is little difference in effectiveness in therapeutic approaches, despite the obvious contrasts in approach.[14] Certain therapies may be useful for one type of problem but not so effective for another. Research indicates that desensitization and modeling are useful for some fears and phobias in a way that psychoanalytic approaches are not. Addressing core beliefs may benefit from some short-term cognitive work in a client-centered way.

The goal is that the valuable person, often buried beneath life's rubble, can emerge.

PART ONE

Deep-Seated Reasons

Unconscious Influence

Chapter One

At 3:00 a.m.

Avoiding the Void

"Drugs and alcohol are not my problem, reality is my problem, drugs and alcohol are my solution. . . . I will relinquish all else to ride that buzz to oblivion. . . . I look to drugs and booze to fill up a hole in me."

—RUSSELL BRAND[15]

Leading Idea: We need to be able to sit with the void that people experience.

1

The world is asleep. But you are awake. It is dark, so dark that without streetlights or someone stirring nearby, you can hardly make out where the ceiling is. Or come to that, the floor is difficult to discern. Disintegration is the order of things visible and invisible.

Sometimes you feel you could disappear anyway and you think the floor might swallow you. You feel you are teetering on the brink of a black hole. You are at serious risk of coming apart at the seams.

Your body has been shifting position. Now you are in transition of a different kind; from one stage of stage to another. Half the people who complain about abruptly waking up in the night stir at around 3:00 a.m. in the morning.

There is not a sound to be heard except what comes from the noise in your head. It is the sound of haunting. They used to call this "the devil's hour," mockingly inverting the time when Jesus died, at 3:00 p.m. It was said that demonic activities are at their highest at *3:00 a.m.* The "witching hour" comes from the poem "Night, an Ode" by Rev. Matthew West back in 1755, but two centuries before that, the Catholic Church forbad activity at this time as part of emerging fears about witchcraft—a moral panic if ever there was one. Then there are the ghosts.

More people die between *3:00–5:00 a.m.* than at any other time. Not for nothing is this the graveyard shift. For many it is the time of maximum darkness within and without: the slide into the false consciousness that is the beginning of psychosis.

PSI experiences—consciousness that seems to go beyond the ordinary constraints of space-time—predominate in dreams at this time.[16] So do encounters with apparitions and of a sensed presence[17] It coincides with the 3:00 a.m. peak melatonin period or the immune system being weakened and its impact on the brain which is modulated by time of day.

Suicides are more likely to occur between midnight and 4:00 a.m. than during the daytime or evening, peaking at 2:59 a.m. In contrast, the mean suicide rate per hour was 2.13% between 6 a.m. and 11:59 p.m. When six-hour time blocks were examined, the observed frequency of suicide between midnight and 5:59 a.m. was 3.6 times higher than expected. "These results suggest that . . . just being awake at night may in and of itself be a risk factor for suicide."[18]

When the circadian rhythm, or internal sleep clock, is disrupted, the risk of developing depression increases. People experience depression differently. Some people experience significant increases in the severity of their depression symptoms. Others may experience increased feelings of isolation, hopelessness, and emptiness at night. There is nothing but you and your thoughts. You are lost.

We feel our humanness keenly, the reality of our situation that can be described as a threat to our existence—existential. We are in danger of disappearing down a dark hole, of slipping into the void.

The experience of depression varies. Some people experience significant increases in their depression symptoms at night. They may experience more symptoms, or their symptoms may increase in severity. Night-time depression can also create or worsen insomnia, by keeping you awake longer or making it more difficult to fall asleep. Some people may experience an increase in the severity of their depression symptoms.

Others may experience increased feelings of isolation, hopelessness, and emptiness at night. In the daylight hours, it's easier for some people—especially those with mild or moderate depression—to keep themselves busy. Work, school, or social activities act as a distraction during the day. But at night, there is nothing but you and your thoughts. You are coming apart at the seams. Disintegration calls with an ugly voice.

At 3:00 a.m., there seems less with which to defend ourselves. Much that we use to fill our lives is absent. What though is this void over which we are suspended and how do we name it and face it?

2

The void is the inner, inescapable reality of existential life for humans. It is the dread black hole over which the self is suspended. Witnessing the unreachable void is a sacred task for counsellors; staying with the client's meaning and meaninglessness is vital for therapy. Experiencing it is a reality gnawing away even at the well-defended. Meaninglessness stretches tentacles our way.

The "Void" has been discussed within Freudian Psychoanalytic theory looking at the abyss. It speaks of a place of awful abandonment stemming from childhood infancy, described sometimes as "the yearning for the breast." Other theorists such as James Loder and Paul Tillich speak to a place of feeling disconnected from God, "yearning for something better." This is evident when we experience a loss of a relationship for example or death of a family member. Loder believes God does not leave us there as the Holy Spirit comes to us finds us and heals us in what he describes as "a transforming moment."[19] Tillich believes that existential anxiety is at the root of it all: "Neurosis is the way of avoiding non-being by avoiding being."[20]

The Void lies at the unconscious state or though sometimes pressing into conscious realization, for the most part there is not enough of an awareness of what is happening within. Until clients come to the point of realization or desire for change, they remain in survival mode; hanging on, hanging in. Therapists are called to sit with the void people experience and be a soul-friend to many.

In situations of loss, a psychic void leads to people going to extremes searching for external soothing and identification. Voids are the places in the psyche where our sense of meaning and coherence is lost or obliterated. In the void, we may not know what to cling to, or feel able to cling to an intimate partner or parent. This can become an unbearable and unavoidable feeling. Conversely, sitting with the void and facing into our greatest fears about loss, abandonment, rejection and even death, can be both instrumental and fundamental to personal growth and clinical development.

This is the starting point for this book as it is common human experience born out of our createdness and maybe our fallenness. It is the threat of looming loss that leers in experiences of many forms of mental illness, depression and, at the most extreme, suicidal thoughts. The breakdown of intimate relationships or death of a partner is likely to trigger such emptiness. Separation anxiety of this sort bites us to the core. The core uncovers the void. Enduring loneliness such as many felt who lived an isolated existence even before social isolation became exacerbated because of COVID-19. In 1971 in Britain, some three million people lived alone. Forty years later it was nearer eight million. The invisible bonds that knit people together had been progressively weakened and cut; replaced only partially by internet connection. A decline in attendance at church, youth clubs and other forms of voluntary association has created a fragmented society that creates emptiness for many. "Existential Loneliness" is a new concept. The sense of emptiness and void is a deficit within each person, not a lack of meaningful relationships. Has our deep sense of something missing been miscast as an interpersonal problem? Loneliness is interpreted invariably as meaning a lack of human connection but in an existential sense it runs much deeper than that and is a fundamental part of modern human existence. Michael Shreiner argues that "the more freedom you have to direct the course of your life the more will this feeling of being separate gnaw away at you. Here we see the appeal of all caste systems. If your role is clearly defined for you and you are completely sure of your place within a society then you feel like you are a part—not apart."[21]

Loneliness is the subjective aspect of objective isolation. Loneliness is felt where there is no significant relationship or where connection has been lost with a loved one. The fear of loneliness is that we are and will be in lack. It is both present reality and presentiment that we will feel the need of something in our lives that will bridge the divide to each other and even to our own selves. Is it always negative? Are we in suspension, waiting for delayed response from those who populate our clump of the world? Higham suggests that we misidentify ourselves as separate entities: that we are looking for a direct relationship with the source of belonging and affirmation.[22] So where can we find authentic connection?

The sources of existential dread that often leers at people through night (and day) have been discussed and debated since literature began to be part of the human enterprise. This seems to be common human experience. "Life has meaning"! That is what a successful human life asserts, often in the face of its contradiction. Faith stands at the opposite pole to the meaningless of the void.

"The majority of patients are bedevilled by a lack of meaning in their lives," declared Professor of Psychiatry Irvin Yalom.[23] Our profound need as human beings is to inhabit a coherent, meaningful universe. "Why am I here? Where am I headed?" are fundamental questions to human existence and lie at the heart of existential therapies. We will encounter this when we explore meaning-making.

For now, it is worth noting that the void and a sense of emptiness seems never far away; the sense that something is missing. This has been the focus of both philosophy and the major religions. "To live, conscious of the inevitability of suffering, weakness, age and death, is impossible" added Siddartha Gautama, the Buddha. "We must free ourselves from life, from all possibility of life."[24]

It is both interesting and sad to reflect on the experience of the brilliant German Friedrich Nietzsche. He wrote about the looming void in western civilization but also he lived it. The dominant characteristic of Nietzsche's life was that of the lonely self, battling on in order to make sense of life.[25] When humanity realizes that it has lost God, universal madness will break out.

In his work on Nietzsche Walter Kaufmann has this to say: "to have lost God means madness and when mankind discovers that it has lost God, universal madness will break out. . . . We have destroyed our own faith in God. There remains only the void. We are falling. Our dignity is gone. Our values are lost. Who is to say what is up and what is down? It has become colder and night is closing in."[26]

"*There remains only the void.*" Is that the consequence of the loss of faith or an interior collapse when we lose our hold on life and are overwhelmed or demoralised?

Most contemporary people who have rejected God would probably not say they that are in a "void." But, when humanity becomes the measure of all things and cannot escape the subjective arbitrary nature of our own judgements, this too is living in a kind of void.

Leo Tolstoy—brilliant and profound nineteenth-century Russian novelist—experienced constant inner restlessness and existential anxiety. His former wild life left him feeling empty. Increasingly, he pondered what meaning did his life have that the inevitability of death cannot destroy? This represented a profound spiritual crisis that the great writer experienced shortly before his fiftieth birthday. Lost was any passion for his work as he came to dismiss as meaningless the eternal fame he had once dreamt of. With his greatest works behind him, Tolstoy could not muster any sense of purpose As his biographer Henri Troyat remarked:

> Was there anymore healthy, better-balanced life in the world than his? Everything he had ever wanted when he was young he had obtained, and in the prime of life, . . . and yet, he was not happy. Or rather the form of happiness that had become his lot did not content him and he wondered whether there might be some other kind.[27]

"I would be deep in problems of estate management," he writes in his autobiographical wrestling "Confession," "and a question would come to me. All right, so you have 1350 acres of land in the government of Samara and 300 head of horses: so what? . . . I told myself, 'Fine, you will be more famous than Gogol, Pushkin, Shakespeare, Moliere, and all the writers in the world—then what?'"[28]

The despair Tolstoy felt at that time was being shared by a good many intellectuals in Russia in a movement of nihilism. He drew inspiration from the peasants who seemed to have a simple faith in God. From that time, his mind felt lighter. "Everything came alive, took on meaning."[29] For Tolstoy, faith was the antidote to despair as a sense of meaning that connected the finite with the infinite.

It is not a fad of nineteenth-century intellectual nihilists. Susan Sontag was a brilliant twentieth-century American writer, Marxist intellectual and film maker. She sought lover after lover but when they left, as they all did, what remained was a gaping hole inside her. After what Sontag referred to in her diary as "the last phone call from one of them, she went into the now-familiar diary mode of self-reflection, lamentation, exhortation and crisis support. '*Let it hurt*', she wrote bitterly, while also convincing herself that she had been wasting her time with Nicole the previous few years. '*I knew that. Susan became unbearably needy. In her loneliness, in her post-operative shock, in her fear, she was greedy for company, insatiable. She simply could not bear to be alone.*'"[30]

The personal fear of loneliness was mirrored by her need for artistic nourishment, which found such a fertile, instructive and lucid outlet in her essays. But, as she entered her fifties, Sontag found that her melancholy and loneliness began to become more intense. She felt physically exhausted, and was having problems concentrating. Her friend Sigrid Nunez writes of a period when Susan's "chronic irritability and discontent shaded into something darker. She found herself crawling back into bed soon after getting up."[31] Susan saw a neurologist who told her she was suffering clinical depression, at midlife. "Always when I saw her now she complained of being lonely, feeling rejected, abandoned. Sometimes she wept," Nunez writes. Her loneliness was intense in the months of her illness.[32]

The London Times wrote in his obituary about their most celebrated columnist, "Bernard Levin was the most famous journalist of his day. Prolific, controversial, passionate, versatile, maddening, enthusiastic, sometimes irresponsible, always courageous, he was recognized instantly in the street by people of all ages."[33] In May 1978, Levin had visited the "Festival for Mind and Body," a fair at Olympia, and reflected on the need for a new spirituality in a society of which he was commentator.

> Countries like ours are full of people who have all the material comforts they desire, together even with such non-material blessings as a happy family, and yet lead lives of quiet, and at times noisy, desperation, understanding nothing but the fact that there is a hole inside them and that however much food and drink they pour into it, however many motorcars and television sets they stuff it with, however many well-balanced children and loyal friends they parade around the edges of it, however much contentment they place between it and, their own consciousness, it aches.[34]

Russell Brand once commented:

> Drugs and alcohol are not my problem, reality is my problem, drugs and alcohol are my solution. . . . I will relinquish all else to ride that buzz to oblivion. . . . I look to drugs and booze to fill up a hole in me.[35]

At night we have visitors—anxiety, shame, distress, pointing with unbecoming honesty to the void. It is from the black hole at the heart of this void, from which emanates a mocking laugh at 3:00 a.m.

3

Our struggle to fill and face the void constitutes the starting point of this book.

We are a being that cannot come to terms with itself. Yearning to express ourselves, we do not want to be what we are. Concealed behind a thousand ideals, the lonely self harbours innumerable contradictions in its inner being; unsure where to go to be free from them or to untie the knot. Who is this who asks the question? Who is it, so conscious of wonder, so tortured with lonely questions of existence? Who is this who even dares to pit itself against the vastness and claim significance?

Kierkegaard's book, *Sickness unto Death*, can be regarded as one of the key works of theistic existentialist thought—a brilliant and revelatory answer to one man's struggle to fill the spiritual void and sense of abandonment.[36] It was conceived as an antidote to despair and a powerful psychological insight into faith (which at heart introduces openness into uncertainty). Whether believing in God or no, how do people cope with the void when it calls to them—as it surely will? Kierkegaard spoke of how human beings limited and diminished themselves to avoid catching a glimpse of the "terror, perdition and annihilation that dwell next door to any man."[37]

The range of what people do to avoid facing the void are as varied as the human enterprise. Desperately, clinging to whatever we have we will hold to avoid the dread decomposing of ourselves. For the Void is the presence of absence. It is not quite the same as a sense of cosmic emptiness because it is full—full of toxins, acids, and negative things. We are threatened with being sucked in like a black hole from which no light can escape. Though a place in our psyche, space has collapsed and the darkness closes in. Our experiences can often misrecognize absence as only Void. When we touch Emptiness, we feel it to be *only* Void. It is from such ontological misidentification that therapeutic potential can arise.

It has huge resonance with the hugely evocative children's fantasy *The Never Ending Story* in which "The *Nothing*" is the main antagonist. It destroys gradually through its power to absorb.

Many will have experienced what it is like to stand by a bridge. You look down. You feel the urge to jump. It is inexplicable yet tantalizing. Why would you do such a thing? You shudder and walk away. Such is the call of the void, *l'appel du vide* in French. Most ignore it, but not everyone succeeds. It threatens our sense of control, of order, of meaning. It insinuates absence as a threatening place.

That is why we fear it. The void will claim us.

Freud theorized disintegration through the controversial concept of the death instinct. It never, however, found real acceptance in the psychotherapeutic community. Where there has been childhood trauma—when the "no-thing" space becomes a horrifying black hole. Abyss calls to abyss, the despair as a "sense of broken reality" caused by the juxtaposition of her hollow, empty persona and the "devouring black hole" of an internal world.[38]

The end of one relationship or form of addiction generates a crisis which requires replacement with another addictive behavior. Nothing satisfies what has become a biochemical need. They may go from drinking to gambling to sex addiction until they address the underlying problems of trauma, shame, and emptiness.

The experience of eating to fill the void is both literal and metaphorical. In contemporary society we are consumers of everything. Food (and drink) help fill the stomach of our physicality but both have always attracted meanings that go far beyond into the second stomach. The appetite for meaning, love and value is less readily filled.

Fail to consciously face our emotional void and we will be addicted to throwing things into the Void, hoping to fill it up: strategies that works but temporarily. Drugs, relationships, work, things all can be used to cover over the experience of void but they are transient distractions. Self-destructive behaviors such as alcohol, unhealthy eating patterns, obsessive actions or recklessness will multiply harms to yourself and others. You are vulnerable to being controlled by others, taken advantage of.

To face the voids you carry in your heart and soul requires honesty as well as courage. If something is missing, broken or empty inside of you, there is no person or thing that will fill it. To sit with the void in another life is to be a soul-friend, clothed and filled with the spirit of empathic solidarity.

Schopenhauer referred to the void as the "bottomless abyss of its heart," and that no worldly satisfaction could fill its infinite cravings.[39] People generally regard feelings of emptiness and loneliness as distinct from themselves and cling to the illusion that their inner void could be eradicated, avoided, or filled. They can spend their lives trying to do so, perpetuating endless internal conflict. Twelve-Step Programs are founded on the premise that cravings and inner emptiness cannot be filled through addictive be-havior, and that relief is spiritual. Bill Wilson, the founder of Alcoholics Anonymous wrote to psychoanalyst Carl Jung who replied explaining that alcoholism was a spiritual problem—"a spiritual thirst of our being for wholeness, expressed in medieval language: the union with God," which he believed to be the answer.[40]

People eventually discover that they cannot run or hide from themselves or their feelings. However, support is essential to endure our confusion and depression long enough to permit real change, especially. The existentialists encouraged individual decision-making and determination of values that require us to go out on a limb and not be enslaved by social pressure, internal should's, or fear of abandonment. Similarly, Twelve-Step programs urge action and personal accountability—living a moral life, taking daily inventory, and making amends.

This is about the fracture of the human soul. We pride ourselves on rationality but live with pain and distress. Learn to look past the messy culpability and see people who deserve a chance to heal.

Skilful guides are often needed to help us face such an unsafe entity within our own psyche and hold us steady. This is where the therapist comes in. For you also have experienced it.

4
Naming the Void

There are different ways of thinking about the void that is the starting point for validation of the self, whether endorsement through career or relationship, the fundamental human project.

The void is a negative place. Like the Bermuda triangle it is replete with wrecks: the living remains of ways, places and people who hindered rather than healed. The void is made up of destroyed or pulverized forms; the empty, lonely feelings that stem from holes in the heart. Such holes might be fresh wounds like a breakup, death in the family, or losing our job. Sometimes they are signposts to something deeper, like a lack of connection with family growing up, a childhood trauma, or hurt caused by the living and the dead. The void was generated by something destroyed which has not been grieved and healed. Understanding the void calls us to an education about our inner feelings. How can we conceptualize it?

It is not the same as cosmic loneliness, the enigma of trying to end the emptiness that arises from whether we have a place in the scheme of things. In the cosmos, there is no empty space. Even the places between heavenly bodies are filled and fizzing. The same is true for our human-scale embodiment. But emptiness as many experience it is open, creative, full of possibility and swirling patterns, not the unsafe place that preys on the insecure, full of negative thoughts. That is the restlessness, a hunger that can drive addictive behavior.

Fragility is everywhere. We live a fleeting life in a world marked everywhere by disintegration. Such is the void. There are many candidates for the threatening negativity.

Guilt and Shame

The quest for just deserts, for justice and resolution (both in right relationship to God and others) is a major theme of life. The vindication of good is not for morality plays only. It is our personal and group story. Our own sense of guilt reflects inner knowledge that someone must pay—often us! As Kant probed in his moral argument for the existence of God, the invoices are often addressed incorrectly in this life. Guilt yields to a theological lens on why and how we feel bad about behavior. Shame is usually given a different account, often related to falling foul of community norms which sets up a deficit. The reduction of shame is a major driver in social settings of honor cultures. Suffice now to note that the swamp that needs to be drained is often full of what has been brought into the interior world. A sense of the eternal is often heavily compromised by the internal.

The effect of internalized shame is to cause us to doubt our worth and lovability. It alienates us from others and crucially, in self-rejecting ways, from ourselves. This critical self-evaluation can be projected onto others. Low self-worth and shame sustain our childhood beliefs that if we were perfect and didn't make mistakes, we would be cherished and accepted. Shame and emptiness can create a sense of isolation and rejection. Maybe this is what stirs at 3:00 a.m. as the void activates feelings of abandonment and shame from childhood.

From a Christian theological perspective that emphasizes what it means to be relational (as our approach here seeks to pursue), there is a conundrum. How do I end up finding myself alienated from others, given I could only exist in relation to others? One answer is that I am alienated because I am fallen from grace and that this reflects messy realities of the human situation as the man and the woman chose to do and to be. I am and will be in alienation as long as I live, move and have my being. There are intriguing resonances here with the work of some depth psychology that purports to uncover deep longing for a return to archetypical experiences of paradise. Enter Stanislav Grof.

Birth

Arising from lifelong research into psychedelic drugs, Stanislav Grof constructed a comprehensive framework out of the broad range of experiences triggered by LSD in patients and research subjects. Grof's theory of the human psyche creates a space for a greater understanding of our inner selves. His seminal book, *Realms of the Human Unconscious*, was first published in 1979 widely acclaimed as shedding light on many fundamental, but mysterious human potentialities.[41] Grof's theory of the human psyche was an exercise in transpersonal psychology and supposedly opened ways to a greater understanding of our inner selves at a deeper stratum than previously accessed.

His followers claim that Grof's work has revolutionised psycho-dynamics, taking the biological and biographical perspective of Freud and integrating it with Jung's work on the archetypes that structured human behavior. Patients moved back through childhood experiences, often traumatic, to the original trauma—that of intense engagement with birth. An intensity was encountered in a distinct sequence that moved from "undifferentiated unity with the maternal womb, to an experience of sudden fall and separation from that primal organismic unity to a highly charged life and death struggle with the contracting uterus and the birth canal, culminating in an experience of complete annihilation . . . followed by an experience of sudden, unexpected global liberation."[42] According to Grof, this was a liberation characterized by a strong sense of re-birth but also universality. It was a fundamental human experience. That reliving one's birth was accompanied by profound spiritual and existential crisis, ultimate meaninglessness of life, a narrowing of mental horizons, hopeless alienation, a sense of going insane and an encounter with death.

Is this dark hole we are being sucked into at a primal level what troubles us at 3:00 a.m.?

Death

The great American writer Ernest Hemingway frequently observed that the many tasks and projects people embraced constituted a strategy of defence against death, an ultimate nothingness that haunted him.[43] It might be thought to be contradictory to this that he engaged in persistently reckless behavior but maybe he was flirting with the void that eventually sucked him in. He took his own life in 1962 from a surfeit of despair. When some imagine their deaths (including the non-religious), they project themselves into a future self which experiences an eternal silent darkness. When we die, what is next is *nothing*; death is an abyss, a black hole and end of experience; eternal nothingness, the permanent extinction of being.

Nevertheless, is this the void that haunts and leers at 3:00 a.m.? Is this empty abyss ultimate darkness? How shall we handle the threat of disintegration, of coming apart at the seams?

Many philosophers have objected to the notion that we fall *into* nothingness, to remain there eternally. Larry Josephs, an AIDS patient, wrote, "I hope that when the time comes to face death, I will feel stronger, and less afraid of falling into an empty black abyss."[44] Some have written about positive nothingness, a long night of sleep. The great religions have much to say about this and most claim that death is not the end. Hope and resurrection characterize the Christian response.

The threat of ceasing to be and becoming one with the nothingness is the ultimate fear of losing oneself, of disappearing. It must be said that such anxiety is less obvious in the full light of day. The well-defended personality has fortified itself all too well. It is at times of heavy assault on the defences—or perhaps at 3:00 a.m.—inchoate dread that is part of the fabric of being looms and leers.

Primal Scream

Or perhaps the void points to difficult experiences in childhood that need to be re-lived? Originally published in 1970, the Primal Scream was the brainchild of Arthur Janov who worked with 63 patients during his first 18 months. One early session included a scream emitted by one of his patients, after Janov encouraged him to call out, "Mommy! Daddy!" In Janov's account, the patient subsequently announced that he could "feel."[45] Twenty years on, the "New Primal Scream" took the theory further, showing that repressed pain is bad not only for mental but also for physical health.[46] Many emotional and social neuroses can stem from often seemingly trivial childhood incidents, let alone major trauma. Things going wrong in earliest years can create serious mental, behavioral and health issues. Illness is the silent scream: releasing the primal pain can lead to healing and even a change of identity. We have to relive our childhood to recover. Many have heard of Arthur Janov because of his famous clients, such as John Lennon, to whom he sent a draft of his book.[47]

Clients reported how they gazed into the abyss and it molested them. *The Primal Scream* is about untwisting yourself, "creating yourself anew." Maybe this is therapy gone mad.[48] Maybe the void points to causes of distress that need rooting out?

Separation Anxiety Disorder (SAD)

Separation anxiety is a normal part of childhood development. It is usually temporary: commonly occuring in babies between 8 and 12 months old, it usually disappears around age two. However, it can appear in school years and also occur in adults. One-third of children with SAD will be diagnosed with mental illness as an adult.[49] Such anxiety is identified when a child is exhibiting behaviors such as extreme crying, clinging to parents, not engaging in anything that requires separation, failure to interact in a healthy manner with other children, refusing to sleep alone or nightmares.

It could be the result of a family history of anxiety or depression, overprotective parents, problems dealing with their peers, moving to a new home, changing schools, divorce or death in a close family. Lingering effects might reveal themselves as excessive distress about being away from home or loved ones and a nagging worry about losing a parent or other loved one. Or a child might be tormented by constant worry something bad will happen that will result in separation from them.

These things rear their ugly head in adults as they follow you through life. Adults might show unusual distress about being *separated* from a person who might be moving away or excessive worry that someone will come to harm. It is not unusual for separation anxiety to be manifested in adults who never experienced it as a child. Separation anxiety is an anxiety disorder much as agoraphobia and panic disorder. *DSM-5*, the American Psychiatric Association's diagnostic manual for mental health conditions defines separation to include a heightened fear of being alone or needing to know where a spouse or loved one is at all times.[50] The writer Graham Greene begins his "long journey through time" with a public school education in childhood. Unhappiness in a child, he wrote, accumulates because he can see no end to the dark tunnel. The thirteen weeks of a term might just as well be thirteen years.[51] Maybe deep-seated phobias and anxieties of this kind are what troubles people at 3:00 a.m.? Maybe this is the SAD void they fear they will be sucked into.

Attachment Anxiety

The haunting deep-seated anxiety often stems from a lack of appropriate parental interaction. With an absent or unresponsive mother-figure, there beckons the slide into disintegrative nothingness of a black-hole. Awareness of deep distress arising from a missing parent reflects John Bowlby's work on attachment theory. Bowlby studied intense responses of children during stays in institutional settings and delineated observations of protest, despair and detachment.[52] When a young child who has formed an attachment with a mother-figure is separated unwillingly, distress will ensue. If placed in a strange environment with unknown people, that will give rise to acute anxiety. Protest against absence is followed by despair at lack of return of the object of attachment with the child eventually losing interest and becoming emotionally detached. In this way, separation experiences could become pathological. Missing someone who is loved and longed for generates fear and anxiety. Bowlby probed why the distress arises to begin with. The result was Attachment Theory as conceptual architecture explaining responses to separation. He refers to how fear of darkness leads a child to feel alone. This had been the starting point for Freud's theory of anxiety generally; not dark so much as absence of someone you love and being alone.[53] Maybe loss is the fear of death, the threat of dissolution. A deep longing to belong or feel important seeks to cover up nothingness and loneliness we experience. Is this primeval darkness the void that haunts people at 3:00 a.m.?

Alienation and the Validation of Self

More might be said. "Today, the experience of nothingness is simply a fact: many of us have it. . . . [W]hat shall I do with it?" Michael Novak, in his "Experience of Nothingness" shows the paths by which the experience of nothingness is becoming common among all those who live in free societies.[54] Nihilism has European connotations. Novak, however, articulates this experience of formlessness in an American context. For him, recognition of how widespread the experience of nothingness must be acknowledged if the courage to be means anything. Such alienation from life and even from ourselves has been widely discussed amongst existential philosophers. It has been much discussed by theologians, such as Paul Tillich whose *The Courage to Be*[55] signposted how contemporary people might overcome the problem of anxiety that besets the human condition. It has strong echoes of Genesis 1:2 and the formlessness from which creation originally sprang.

Suspended over the chaos might well be universal experience. In his powerful treatment of Karl Barth's theology, Berkouwer wrote of the nothingness which was excluded by God's creative act.[56] The chaos and darkness were passed by but confronts us still as a reality. "No creature is 'nothing'; every creature is 'something' but something at the edge of chaos, secure but also endangered."[57]

Barth is quite clear that God did not create the chaos. More recent perspectives on chaos theory or quantum physics will question that as swirling energy patterns and extremely strange behavior of particles seem to represent both birth and backcloth for form, shape and an ordered world. Yet disorder is never far away; dissolution and disintegration are ever present threats to our existence.

Such is the antithesis of life. Such is the void over which we are suspended. It is of the nature of humanity that we seek not only existence but purpose; not denial of our personhood but affirmation. The conditions of life in which we might fall apart at any time are not hospitable to humans. The void seeks to claim us but it can never name us for we have been named by God.

> And the earth was without form and void; and darkness was on the face of the deep. And the Spirit of God moved over the face of the waters. (Gen 1:2 KJV)

Chapter Two

Am I OK?

Endorsement's Quest

"Comfort, comfort ye my people."

—ISAIAH 40:1

"I'm not what I think I am, I am what I think you think I am."

—CHARLES COOLEY[58]

"I did love you. I just couldn't show it."

—JUDY GOLDING[59]

Leading Idea: Endorsement is the central human quest. The impetus to seek and find the face of another who will welcome us and who recognizes us lies at the heart of human experience and avoidance of the void. It underlines that humans are shaped by ultimate concerns, not just a body, and is ultimately spiritual.

At heart of human functioning is a quest for an answering echo. It is a search for the validation of self, for recognition of high value.

Highlighting the dramas played out in everyday life, Eric Berne proposed that his triad of ego-states was far more observable in everyday life than the theoretical construct of ego, superego, and id proposed by Freud.[60] A key philosophical foundation of Transactional Analysis (TA) relates to the worth of human beings. The best-selling practical guide to TA, suggests, "I'm OK—you're OK."[61] According to a standard training text, "the most fundamental assumption of TA is that people are OK. This means: you and I both have worth, value and dignity as people. I accept myself as me and I accept you as you." This is said to be a statement of essence rather than behavior. The authors say:

> At times, I may not like nor accept what you do. But always, always, I accept what you are. Your essence as a human being is OK with me, though your behaviour may not be. . . . I am not one-up to you, and you are not one-up to me. We are on the same level as people. This is true even though our accomplishments may differ. It is true, even though we may be of different race, age or religion.[62]

What this worth and dignity is and from where it is derived is not made clear, except that it is claimed to be equal in status to that of others, and hence a universalist claim.

The key move of our approach to therapy here is to reconceive the pursuit of high value from being an aspiration to being a fundamental impulse in the dramas through which human beings play out their existence. There is a wide gap between regarding the search to be a valuable person as an ethical concern as if would be ideal and obviously beneficial if only people were treated this way *and* between seeing this quest as a driving impetus in human affairs. Where it is present, people flourish. When absent, a sense of self is eroded and the human spirit withers somewhat.

Pursuit of a high value that comes from endorsement can be described in a multitude of ways and across varied landscapes. The quest for such recognition can be labelled "comfort, reassurance, approval," seeking agreement or just "love." It is a defence against the void, the smirking vacuum.

It might be a renowned statesman such as Winston Churchill whose quest to seek approval from his distant father shaped him profoundly. It might be a fulfilling job; a neighbor who now has no family but who receives welcome and validation from a dog who wags a tail enthusiastically. We have to find that somewhere, be it family, career or pets. We respond to the "welcome of the universe," to being seen and heard, involved and included and being dignified. This goes deep: to feel safe and secure within is a prime impulse and is linked to perception of how we are doing in life.

We are highly motivated to seek validation because of intrinsic knowledge of valuable personhood. Such awareness is patterned into our primal awareness and has deep roots. It lies within unconscious impetus and is relational. Psychically, this begins in mother-baby interactions, sustained and developed in multiple social transactions. But it is also deeply theological, reflecting our existential situation. This quest is spiritual. It is a place where theology and social sciences can meet.

One access into this idea is through "recognition"—the struggle people have for the recognition of their person by others. Recognition has a long running in social philosophy. Following a lead from Hegel who categorized recognition "as an egalitarian blending of love and esteem,"[63] the German theorist Axel Honneth theorizes recognition as the basis for morality. Denying recognition to people hurts them not because it restricts freedom to act but because of the positive understanding of themselves they have arrived at inter-subjectively.[64] A categorical imperative to recognition is required because in their wish to achieve recognition for themselves, people must give it to others.

This dialectic lies at the heart of social experience as well as the turbulence of emotional life. It generates a variety of interpersonal effects. The phenomenology could include feelings of isolation and detachment, distrust, stigmatization and being different from others that survivors of childhood sexual abuse experience.

In numerous cultures, for instance, shame may be an effective response to the threat to one's social self, defined as a self-conscious emotion, experienced when a core aspect of the self is judged as defective, inferior, or inadequate.[65] Such negative social evaluation is experienced as a child transformed into a negative self-evaluation, which can manifest itself as "there is no sense of 'I.'"

Most human cultures set store by gaining confidence in the approval of our family. It starts with our immediate caregivers, the wider family or the village. Then come teachers and school or college experiences before the quest for validation takes us into the workplace or finding a family of our own. Humans are naturally social creatures. We thrive in community and most have a strong desire to belong in that community and seek validation from it. The workplace becomes a strong focus. "Produce, produce, produce" is a restless imperative, a defence to avoid against both void and destitution. In contemporary society, social media has become a major source of social approval. How many "likes" we have complements how many fish we have caught as the measure of life. The comparison is just too compelling. In a variety of ways, we need to be told we are doing well.

With our social brain, the search is on from the outset. "Comfort us. Approve of Validate us. Affirm us. Confirm our existence. Endorse our personhood. Recognize us. Include us. We are valuable."

Social valuing is hugely important to people. The pursuit of value as a motivation takes us from concern for honor, status and legacy to social esteem, reputation and tokens of recognition. This is a standard observation in social psychology, for example Tajfel's Social Identity Theory where self-esteem is in dynamic relationship with group identity.[66] Yet where does this emanate from? A case can be made that these are species of a drive for personal value that is a vital element in human flourishing. It comes from an internal need, sustained or eroded by group processes. Pursuit of a high value seems a key ingredient of biographies, varying through the life-course but arguably central to what it means to be human in both healthy personalities and pathologies. Psychoanalytic politics offers an example of how this motivation is competitive, a zero-sum game. In the Wednesday society, the members sparred for position, descended into acrimony or vaunted their originality—yet such praxis did not impact theory. Individual biography can be charted against the drive to accrue social value which reacts with devaluing circumstances and interpersonal put-downs as well as systemic factors that distribute worth in capitalist society. Behind the ceaseless fight for tantalizing recognition is the internal struggle to be valued by peers, by history and oneself.

Amidst the complexities of the interior world, the unconscious activities of the mind should include the desire to be valuable, to count and be of worth. Distorted neuroses may be a lot to do with blocked attempts to extract significance and value from our world. Repression may or may not be a disguised factor in pathways towards fulfilment but rejection is an experience that bites people to the core. Core challenges reveal the strength of unconscious influences in human action as the subject is often in the grip of forces that are past all understanding. Yet as a specific content domain in its own right, this core aspect of human identity has been insufficiently theorized as *the* driver.

This is surprising as the importance of, for example, the experiences of Victor Frankl, the psychotherapist who went to Auschwitz, would be widely recognized, despite being very much outside everyday experience.

"It is very difficult for an outsider to grasp how very little value was placed on human life in camp."[67] Frankl contended that psychotherapy denied the spiritual side of our humanity. He quotes, with approval, the aphorism of Goethe: "if we take people as they are, we make them worse. If we treat people as if they were what they ought to be, we help them to become what they are capable of becoming."[68] Frankl also showed that the moral worth of the individual was not only vital to retain, even in hell, *but that this translated into psychological reactions.*

> Under the influence of a world which no longer recognised the value of human life and human dignity, which had robbed man of his will and had made him an object to be exterminated, . . . the personal ego final suffered a loss of values. If the man in the concentration camp did not struggle against this in a last effort to save his self-respect, he lost the feeling of being an individual, a being with mind, with inner freedom and personal value.[69]

Social Life

It is vital to understand the routes through which experiences of devaluation are triggered in psycho-social worlds. There are essentially three. Circumstances that erode a sense of value and by implication, a culture of recovery boil down to the Protest against being treated with:

i. **Indifference**: The need to be heard, to be taken seriously, and to be recognized and given attention. "Attention must be paid—even to a salesman."[70] Being heard communicates that I am worth listening to. "I am not an agenda!" "I feel treated like dirt by the system."[71] Clients react negatively to not being seen or voice not heard.

ii. **Indignity**: *At the interplay of indignation* and dignity lies the assertion of a valuable self. "I am worthwhile." A narrative about the effects of constant rejection after being laid off from work shows this aspect: "I can't describe it. It's just like, it is like, the end of the world. I'm not ready for retirement; there is still a lot of work in me. There's no one to blame. It's just gone. That's it. Thrown on the scrap heap at 53."[72] Clients react negatively to being rejected, set aside or being subject to invasive handling.

iii. **Inferiority**: The reflex against demeaning talk or being put down, that calls for appropriate respect for a valuable self and affirmation.

> "When people say things I feel small. They make me feel I'm not worth very much."[73] Clients react negatively to being belittled and made to feel two feet tall in social encounters. This humiliation can be construed as a form of inequality—made to feel less than, written down and diminished. Erosion of our value calls for response.

These factors are a major source of distress. Together with other human strivings, they represent a powerful impetus towards worthiness in such forms as purpose and significance and the need to be a worthwhile person, living a worthwhile life. It is the backcloth to the approach we take.

Racism, class, gender, disability, ageism, religion, culture, etc. have functioned as streams which convey the social transmission of value in a way that assigns lesser worth or value to many. Against this dialectic, we react in some way. The pursuit of validation is central to core human strivings or hungers of the soul that generate a need for fulfilment and resolution. These soul-hungers connect directly with the four lenses of the REMA approach and could be languaged as:

- I belong (*relational connection* and the power of place)
- I desire (pursuit of desire, whether for sex or power that is a deeply *embodied experience*)
- I matter (valuable personhood, longing for *meaning*, worthwhile, significance, and purpose)
- I will survive (some sense of hope, the search for security, the future and getting through positively such that we can flourish that evokes our inner resources as *responsible* agents)

Such human hungers are refracted through invisible social and cultural systems. We only understand the individual within these that impact how individual identity is generated and functions.

The dominant pursuit of value-in-oneself may seem obvious yet it is not up there amidst the panoply of mental driving forces that form the seed-bed of psycho-dynamics. Neither is it a regular topic in social psychology. One could have a sense of identity without that being grounded in worth. The two categories are not coterminous. Are we psychologically structured so as to require a strong sense of value within which to live and move and have our being and do our best work? What does it mean for human action that we seem compelled to live as if we had high value or we wither in its absence?

A sense of value is an environment that promotes human flourishing. The impetus to realize our value and protest in its breach seems to be a fundamental drive. There are many things people do to try to discover a sense of value and then negotiate it throughout life. We are miners, working at the lead mines to uncover the silver of recognition so that value can be extracted. We are hunters, in pursuit of social value from others and "value-in-oneself" internally. Sometimes, these are opposed.

Freud said he could catalyze neurosis into ordinary unhappiness as a pessimistic norm. By contrast, Abraham Maslow argued that psychology should also include the study of healthy personalities. He described what he thought healthy personalities should be like. Self-actualizing individuals enjoy a reasonable feeling of worth and respect and do not for long have crippling feelings of inferiority or worthlessness.[74] How much value is the psyche endeavouring to realize? This is both personally and culturally dependent. The drive is to establish a stasis of a valuable self and be validated. That will assume various shapes, often expressed as a status quo of respect, dignity and significance.

Maslow's hierarchy is problematic. Self-actualization does not entail the importance of holding value-in-oneself with others, relationally. Neither does it show why the need for comfort and love is often prized above being well fed and materially secure. A better account is surely needed.

If we are to construct human functioning this way, the question to ask therefore is how far the impetus towards valuable personhood is spiritual in nature. Endorsement's inner quest is a major player in social experience or interpersonal distress that clients have faced. Its dramas elide a range of psychological reactions to do with feeling less-than, denigrated or even worthless. There may well be a cosmic dimension in the need to know that we matter that affects what our psychology is like. There is something within us all that longs for recognition against all that negates and threatens; that rises above eternal self-preoccupation towards that which is eternal.

Whatever else should be included within the term "spiritual," a reverence and wonder at the natural world (what theists call "creation") is usually deemed to be fundamental to it as is the reassuring sense of belonging and "our link to the ultimate source of meaning and purpose in human life."[75] Yet it is precisely that connection to a realm beyond the disjunctions of material and temporal reality with which our valuable personhood resonates. The UK Royal College of Psychiatrists suggested that "spirituality is identified with experiencing a deep-seated sense of meaning and purpose in life, together with a sense of belonging. It is about acceptance, integration and wholeness."[76]

Chapter Three

Why Am I Hungry?

Strivings of the Soul

"It is important to realise the developing human person as a desiring creature, fundamentally constituted by his or her loves."

—BRUCE HINDMARSH[77]

"Our wealth has grown so great and yet our greed grows greater: However much we have, still more we'll covet later."

—OVID[78]

"I try and try but I cannot stretch life far enough. Every member of our family feels isolated, however friendly we may appear to be."

—SOFIA TOLSTOY[79]

Leading Idea: Four core hungers often in conflict conceived psycho-dynamically.

i. The pursuit of relational connection—I belong
ii. The pursuit of embodied desire—I want
iii. The pursuit of meaning and significance—I am worthwhile
iv. The pursuit of hope and agency—I will survive

THE PREVIOUS CHAPTER REFLECTS why we are hungry in the first place. An internal demand is set up within the psyche for endorsement, for recognition. This imperative is *a* and even *the* core driver. Here, we introduce the concept of core hungers in human action that create longing and belonging.

Let alone students of counseling models, these core hungers will be familiar to anyone who has lived very long in this world and contemplated the mystery of their own being or experienced life. They will be familiar to anyone who poured their souls into their phone—both lusts and longings.

The essential point to grasp is that these core hungers not only take us by hand and heart and propel us towards fulfilment and resolution, they also create conditions for existential anxiety and the inner void because these cries of the human heart are so often frustrated, in conflict and unresolvable.

Desire will be familiar to anyone knowledgeable about Freud, and of course their own heart. It goes under the name of libido and in psychoanalysis, it denotes a sexual energy that goes far beyond the intimate act to a lifegiving creative force that powers just about everything. In reflections from religion and literature it has a long much longer pedigree, usually passing under the name of love.

It can be argued, indeed, that all these fundamental impulses and core hungers that propel human action can be costumed as forms of love. A meditation on the different types of love—including the self-love of narcissism would surely encompass all of life's projects and endeavours. The hunger to be significant and worthwhile, usually against devaluing circumstances, could be seen as a clamoring to be highly regarded and interesting. The hunger to have and to hold is both to possess and to give. The hunger to be connected is always in relation to someone or somewhere else but at heart is love of roots that will nurture us. The hunger to have hope is for love of our own survival—and us—against vicissitudes of life that would undermine it—especially the ugly monster Thanatos.

The Greeks had different words for all these type of love.

To suggest that the pursuit of high value is a strong motivational driver in human action necessarily obliges us to think about how the core hungers are configured. The history of psychology is replete with projects to categorise mental structure.[80] One thinks of Freud's endeavour to re-classify the drives into those aimed at self-preservation and those aimed at sexual satisfaction (subsequently elevating aggressiveness into a rival to libido in his *Beyond the Pleasure Principle*[81]). Once the structure and mode of the unconscious had been explored, psychoanalysis could attempt to provide a picture of the whole mind. The primary instincts were described as sex instincts, the aggressive instincts but also the ego ideal that served to protect the conscious self from unwelcome intrusion from below.[82] Freud's contemporary William James described an instinctive theory of motivation—an inborn pattern of behavior around play, shame, anger, fear, shyness, attachment, modesty and love. Though the drive theory of motivation seemed successful, achieving certain goals to assuage unmet needs did not account for why we might eat even when not hungry. Food feeds the soul.

These hungers and loves are fundamentally relational, not self-referential, formed in relation to someone and something else, even at the level of wanting to possess things or people by bringing them into our orbit. This is not just about self-esteem. Augustine recognizes self-love as the foundational sin. The tussle between love of self and love of God is central to the human situation, given that within love of God as the ultimate good turns us inside out to love our neighbor.

The sigh to love and be loved and to feel that we matter is as core as it gets to the human situation. As Augustine also said in his powerful analysis, our hearts are restless until we find ourselves in God.

Relational Connection and Security (I Need to Belong)

There are belonging needs. Humans are inveterately sociable, wanting security. Inclusion and belonging are friendly to each other. Being out in the cold is damaging. Developing a sense of well-being and belonging is vital to education. It affects the mental health of children and the staff who work in and support schools. Belonging is crucial for cultivating a sense of participation in a community, family or couple relationship. Love and belonging go together like a horse and carriage.

The urge to belong goes to the source of what make us human. Despite the Pandemic that forced distance upon us, people are as swayed as they ever by the desire to maintain relationship and build community: at work, in voluntary organizations, military regiments, in villages, in towns, in cities, in regions and classes. They belonged to the club, the sports team, firm, unions or a worship place. Relationships fill the human story, the search for secure intimacy drives personal life. We are made with an ache to love and be delighted in. What is it about us that we have yearned for a completed life, to be enmeshed in a web of belonging, build communities and a city that will live forever?

There are families and friendships where intimacy is a skill to be acquired. And there are communities with a task, with which we fill our days as we trade and exchange with those across our world. But to experience purpose without community is barren food for the spirit. In a sophisticated culture the explosive power of falling in love would never die. For the great majority of those around us, the answer to life lies in fulfilling relationships. Ye this too creates a profound tension. If we are born to communicate, what ultimate mysteries lie behind the many misunderstandings that dog our lives? Learning to understand the mystery of a different soul that enriches us, the otherness of another is a life-long project—for many, it is *the* life-long project. We are compelled to penetrate the mystery of a different soul that enriches us, the otherness of another.

Yet belonging makes and breaks us. Trust is built up slowly as a sandcastle. But the tide destroys it with one destructive moment. We were made for community and without it we die. Fearing vulnerability, we are lonely inside castle defences; fearing commitments we long for intimacy. We were made for closeness and hungry for depth. Rather than healing and soothing places, for many relationships are war zones where destructive forces raged violently. Such are the contradictions!

Embodied Desire

Within the big tent of desire dwell many ghosts and demons, sexuality and lust. Yet desire is fundamental to embodiment such that it would be unthinkable without it. Attachments systems are developed through embodied states, most obviously through the physicality of hugs by care-givers.

Libido came first. The theory of drivers of interpersonal and social processes was given contemporary shape by Freud giving primary importance to the sexual drive. Psychoanalysis, and with it, the twentieth century edifice of talking therapy, was based on the idea that surface phenomena were insufficient on which to build a theory of human behavior. Through exploring the logic of dreams, Freud had proposed to investigate the inner workings of the human mind. Rooted in desire, the archaeology of the drives, the dark underworld of conflicted human emotion and above all, human sexuality became ingredients of a new orientation in our thinking.

Introducing narcissism into the range of libido became part of a project to re-classifying the drives into those aimed at self-preservation and those aimed at sexual satisfaction. Narcissism muddied the waters. Love of self and love of others differ in their objects, not their nature. Freud hesitated for a long time to elevate aggressiveness into libido's rival.[83] Nevertheless, narcissism is a key concept in the way that "natural" desire turns towards self-love.[84] Someone might identify with one who is absolutely loving, namely his or herself or construct a delusional system based on grandiosity. Self-desire is an active ingredient of megalomania and god-like ambition. Libido is invested in oneself.[85]

Yet ambivalence is a common emotion. Love and rage for the same object occurs in the same person. However, thus began the analytic pre-occupation with destructiveness, returning to a dualistic scheme as outlined in *Beyond the Pleasure Principle*. Two warring drives henceforth became Freudian orthodoxy. What lives wants to die again. Psychological activity is essentially pervaded by conflict. There is a fundamental division in mental operations, repressing energies from repressed material. The new map of mental structure included ego as province of mental activity.

According to psychoanalysis, desire originates in the experience of the infant making the demand of the maternal Other in order to satisfy its need. The intricacies of communication takes place in the most intimate settings: between mothers and their babies; between lovers; in the unconscious bond of two people—in the consulting room, where two individuals sit alone in one room, looking and listening, breathing and dreaming. Both for Lacan as well as for Freud, desire is the subject's yearning for a fundamentally lost object. It is the latter's account though that has framed the architecture of desire in the modern consciousness. Sexuality is the fundamental expression of human desire. He was quite clear that sexual desire had its origins in infancy.

> It was essential to Freud's theory from the outset that sexuality is not some simple, unitary biological force that springs into being fully framed at birth or for the first time in puberty.[86]

In their radical work on Freud's original conception of the unconscious, both Melanie Klein and Jacques Lacan theorize how human needs become transformed by unconscious projections into human demands and desires. For the latter, what is important is the tension between the pre-symbolic and symbolic registers and the inevitable disappointment that the desired object must have for us.[87] Klein sought to understand these processes in the infant (i.e., pre-symbolic stage). How do we deal with the frustration of a desired object being unavailable (or withheld)? Her theory of unconscious envy represents an instinctive human response to the frustration of needs and desires. This "quest for the breast" is her object-relations approach to psychoanalysis given that the first object to be envied was the mother's breast. In this primary envy, the infant equates the mother to the breast, a "good object" rather than seeing the mother as a person in her own right. For Melanie Klein, envy stems from intolerance to frustration, and it is one of the most primitive and fundamental of emotions. Desire, human destructiveness, and self-destructiveness are closely linked.[88] In their own eyes, someone has an ideal version of themselves that becomes vulnerable.

Definitions are important. Is the desire to possess another and take them into oneself, the same as the desire to have power over them? Is desire for sex the same as the urge to reproduce or nurture? As Freud and others have made central to their scheme, desire (in the sense of self-gratification) is a powerful urge when it is thwarted. A wide range of human problems stem from this. The neurotic tangles people get into invariably are the result of seeking to fulfill desire in complex ways.

The soul-hungers are entwined. One writer, LaCugna, has spoken of sexuality as "the dynamism that takes us beyond ourselves towards another, creating the possibility of 'genuine communion among coequal persons.'"[89] Desire and connection are fundamentally related but often in conflict.

However we theorize desire, it is clearly described in the living traditions of biblical text. Desire is a recurrent theme. Augustine perceived that the capacity for union with an infinite God meant that the human person is insatiable. Our thirst for God is never quenched. The soul is in the image of God "insofar as it is capable of him and can participate in him."[90]

The Pursuit of Meaning and Significance—I Matter

> Everyone is born ok. . . . [T]here is a profound difference between the intimate worth of our existence and any evaluation of our behaviour. Our being is unquestionable, our actions may not be. . . . Whatever we do, every life has its own unique value. Clients are helped to restore this belief in themselves as intrinsically worthwhile."[91]

Though difficult to classify the impetus to be valued and to feel valuable, the need to feel one is worth something is central to what it means to be human. Organizational or interpersonal approaches that give value to people rather than devalue them tap into an aspect of the human psyche that responds to a sense of worth. There is an underlying value, the site of conflict, of action and reaction that can be tapped into. But how are we to speak of such an impetus?

Amidst the complexities of the interior world, the unconscious activities of the mind should include the desire to be significant to be somebody, to count. It might come via family, from career or achievements that enable us to make our mark and leave legacy. Distorted neuroses may be a lot to do with blocked attempts to extract significance and value from our world. Repression may or may not be a factor in disguise of pathways towards fulfilment, but rejection is an experience that bites people to the core. Core challenges reveal the strength of unconscious and automatic influences in human action or as the subject is often in the grip of forces that are past all understanding.

A sense of significance can emanate from a worthwhile projects we are involved with. However, a sense of value that depends on income, talents and achievements, will oscillate according to the un-predictability of circumstances, testing how far a sense of "*I am acceptable—full stop*" is embedded within the psyche. We are hostage to those who hold a negative opinion of us.

Hope, Security and the Exercise of Responsible Agency (I Will Survive)

The question of hope is, to some extent, the province of existential psychology, an approach that is concerned with self-authentication and the search for meaning. Its remit is "you" rather than on the symptom. Human beings have a capacity for self-awareness, to make rational choices and to develop to their maximum potential. In line with most existential philosophers, we must continually re-create ourselves: the meaning of things constantly changes. Responsibility and freedom are its main concerns. A therapist such as Yalom will point the way to life-enhancing experiences against the backcloth of ultimate concerns of life: death, freedom, meaninglessness and existential isolation.[92] "Try to grasp something by which to live. Feel something, find something and you will be someone." This is not rooted in the inherent value of the human. The question of how I exist in the face of uncertainty, conflict, or death does not focus on external devaluing forces but one's inner choices.

For Victor Frankl in Auschwitz, what about human liberty? Is there no spiritual freedom regarding behavior and reaction to any given surroundings? No choice of action? "Every day, every hour, offered the opportunity to make a decision, a decision which determined whether you would or would not submit to those powers which threatened to rob you of your very self, your inner freedom; which determined whether or not you would become the plaything of circumstances, renouncing freedom and dignity to become moulded into the form of the typical inmate."

Anyone, Frankl asserted, "can even under such circumstances decide what shall become of him—mentally and spiritually, may retain his human dignity even in a concentration camp. Dostoevsky said once 'there is only one thing that I dread: not to be worthy of my sufferings.'"[93] Psychological observations of the inmates showed that only the men who allowed their inner hold on their moral and spiritual selves to subside eventually fell victim to the camp's degenerating influences. Any attempt at fighting the Camp's influence on the prisoner had to aim at giving him inner strength by pointing out a future goal to which he could look forward. We can only live by looking to the future.

We are more future-oriented than past—oriented though anchored in that strange sea. A version of psychodynamics to excavate subconscious forces from childhood often misses the power of purpose. These factors are well described in biblical texts about which the wisdom of the ages has reflected.

Frustration

We have looked at four main channels through which the central aim for value and endorsement is worked through: relational connection, embodied desire, meaning and significance, and the hope of exercising agency and security. These factors are inextricably woven together. Relational connection is very much an embodied experience—either generated from physicality or from the particularity of social location. Invariably desire is relational but also yields to meaning and significance derived from investing in objects or worthwhile pursuits such as careers. Hope and security are bolstered when one belongs, reinforced through bodily health or the self-preservation of worthwhile pursuits. The longing for connection is for secure relationships to nurture us. The longing for worthwhile-ness is a longing for meaningfulness (significance), the pursuit of desire is a deeply embodied experience for us and the pursuit of hope ("I will survive") evokes our inner resources as responsible agents.

What happens when these are blocked? In psychodynamics, being conflicted is the central feature of neurosis. Conflict is deep-seated and invariably exists below the conscious levels of the mind. Conflicts in early childhood arise when a child seeks security and love yet are lacking. Such frustration sows the seed of much disturbance. In an account of a genuinely human existence, Stephen Neil suggests that the great enemies of the internal life of humanity are fear, frustration and resentment.[94] The causes of being conflicted are seen under these headings.

- When belonging and relational connection is thwarted, the outcome is insecurity and isolation.
- When the hunger for embodied love is unfulfilled, the frustration will generate disturbance.
- When meaning and significance is frustrated, the result is a strong feeling you do not count.
- When the impetus towards hope and agency is blocked, this leads to depression and often despair.

Frustration is the largely unconscious animus in mental tension arising from such inner conflict. All these aspirations become blocked at some point. The result is frustration and disturbance. We might aver that we are divinely loved (1 John 4:16). But which part of us is high value? What about the aspects of ourselves that might be seen as negative or problematic—the hatred and rage?

CHAPTER FOUR

The "I" in the Eye

Identity and Valuable Personhood

"An identity is who or what a person or thing is. Your identity is how you define who you are; it is also how others define you (and these definitions are often not the same). That's why we talk about self-esteem and probably don't always realise how important it is to health and wellbeing."[95]

Leading Idea: A sense of self is embedded in our identity. "Valuable personhood" encompasses the struggle to realize worth against what erodes it. The effects of this show up in therapy.

REMA IS AN INTEGRATIVE, relational, and holistic approach to understanding human experiences which represent four interconnected aspects of human life: one's need for Relationships, Embodied personhood, drive to Make Meaning, and need to find Agency. REMA focus on the wholeness of personhood. As an integrative and holistic model, it places a significant value on spirituality and personhood—what it is to be human—but also interacts with socio-cultural contexts.

So what is personhood? Here is one definition. A person is "the kind of entity that has the moral right to make its own life choices, to live its life without (unprovoked) interference from others."[96] It is a Xhosa proverb. "I am because of you." Persons depend on other persons to be persons.

Theories of human nature, personhood, and the self have had a long running in the history of western philosophy. There have been many ways of arguing for metaphysical underpinnings for what is often been characterized as a philosophical anthropology with a focus on the basic constituents of the unified self. Pre-Socratic philosophers through to thinkers of the present time have something to say about a developing story of what it means to be human, and how we understand ourselves as persons. Being human encompasses what all humans share—a pattern of living with traits such as biology, emotional, rationality that set them apart from other living things.[97] Some headlines were:

- Plato: Human personhood defined by a capacity to think and rational thoughts.
- Augustine of Hippo: Humans are soul and body, relating to other persons and God.
- Thomas Aquinas: Nature not existence determines personhood. Humans are persons because of their ability to participate in community.
- Existential philosophy: We are defined by how we act.
- Contemporary ideas such as characteristics for personhood (e.g., linguistic and operational).

As Descartes observed, possessing a good mind is not enough.[98] What is crucial is how the mind applies itself. Living bodies without reason are not persons in this view. For the subsequent philosopher John Locke, personhood includes a conscious awareness of self as self. A person is defined as a thinking, intelligence being that can reason and reflect. Locke argued for consciousness as criteria for personhood: consciousness is essential to thinking. Personal identity is linked to the survival of consciousness after death rooted in a criterion of personal identity through time. John Locke argued that personal identity is a matter of psychological continuity. He considered personal identity (or the self) to be founded on consciousness (memory): not on substance of either the soul or body.[99] In a more contemporary mindset, physiological attributes do not equate to personhood.

The perspective of this book is that it is fundamental to who we are as human beings, that created by a relational and trinitarian God, we relate and look for relationship within ourselves, with the divine, with humanity and with the created world. Framed in the divine mirror points us in this direction (Gen 1:26). Our relationships are outward as well as inwards. We do not stop being a person though when we are no longer able to relate. While people are physically located in time and space, humans are impacted by the effect of relationships and the environment on their developing sense of self. The language of self and the self-psychologies, neurobiology, attachment theory and developmental psychology fit well with this *relational* anthropology.

Our humanity is *embodied*. The approach here pays close attention to the body as a prime site for therapeutic work. It is an arena for client history and can be read and interpreted. Spirituality and sexuality are at the core of our being, which both touch and affect us within our fleshly bodies at a profound level. This is crucial to being human. We take seriously the transpersonal dimensions of human life and the embodied nature of feeling and memory.

Meaning making is more than a cognitive capacity by which we reflect on our lives. Narrative and telling our story is crucial for humans, both our individual stories and the bigger metanarratives with which we identify and by which we explain who we are. This view is compatible with a biblical view of mystery by which we know that we do not know and are content. The relational connection with God, with others, with the world, means we can hold on to an ultimate sense for our existence. Meaning and trust are closely related.

Agency is the capacity and need of human beings to feel in charge of themselves, to be able to have impact and significance in the world, and to make a difference. It can be in tension with our need for relationship. Agency is closely related to hope; we act as human beings, in the hope of achievement. Our sense of self and of our social identity is bound up with our agency, our capacity to do something and to act out of a sense of capacity to be creative.

These provide the four domains in which we will engage in reparative work with fragmented people. They represent ways in which hungers of the soul work out in everyday life and shape who we are.

Identity and Its Complexities

Identity is a sense of "who," the subject in our experiences who emerges from our inner states and interpersonal relationships. Interactions with parents and peers shape our sense of self-states. An integrated sense of who we are both as fully embodied and fully relational is vital to our approach.

Identity is hugely political issue in contemporary society. Identities are essential to the significance of significance. They give each of us a sense of ourselves, of our grounding in the world and of our relationships to others. Who we are, a defined sense of identity is given to each of us by the specific circumstances of our lives and the particularities of personal experiences. Our experience of self does not come from the inside alone. The self is shaped by our culture.

One of the dilemmas of our time is that, instead of society, we have been left with transient groupings of individuals who come together only to best pursue special interest claims based on identity or ask for recognition. Authentic association is based on subjects forming voluntary groups to purse common undertakings. They associate, not because of who they are, but because of what they want. It is based on differences tolerated because of a shared, universal foundation. Relativism shattered that foundation giving rise to a deep intolerance and indifference to others: to groupings based on different identities. The shift towards identity politics reinforced the sense of a more fragmented society in which the old social bonds had snapped. Many sections of the working class found themselves politically voiceless at the very time their lives had become more precarious, as jobs have declined, public services savaged, austerity imposed, and inequality risen. Those who feel left out, dispossessed and voiceless have clamored to make their needs known.

In his *Multiculturalism and the Politics of Recognition*, Charles Taylor, the Canadian social philosopher, underlines the way in which the notion of recognition, developed by Hegel as intrinsic to core humanity raises dilemmas in the public arena. "The development of a modern notion of identity has given rise to a politics of difference."[100]

The politics of identity—to create new struggles for recognition—is a key driver. The roots of contemporary identity politics lie in the new social movements that emerged in the 1960s to challenge the failure of the Left to take seriously the issues of racism, homophobia and women's rights. Struggle for black rights in America, in particular, was highly influential in providing a template for many other groups to develop concepts of identity and the importance of organizing. Squeezed between an intensely racist society, on the one hand many black activists seceded from civil rights organizations and set up separate black groups. In the 1960s, the struggles for black rights and women's rights and gay rights were closely linked to the wider project of social transformation. Disability came into sharp scrutiny also as it was argued that society disables us. Eventually, the promotion of identity became an end in itself; to which an individual's interests were inexorably linked. The question people ask themselves today is not so much "In what kind of society do I want to live?" as "Who are we?" The two questions are intimately related. Any sense of social identity must embrace both and offer solutions. In his book, *Identity: The Demand for Dignity and the Politics of Resentment*,[101] the demand for recognition, Fukuyama says, is the "master concept" that explains all the contemporary dissatisfactions with the global social order. The quest for equal and inner dignity, the human desire for recognition and respect, has become hugely important, especially for those that were marginalized. The enduring question of "Who am I?" is a vexed issue in personal life and politics. It is not just about race and ethnicity. Ever deeper questions about "How I look?" relate to "Who I am?" and are basic to explorations of race. The identity I have is determinant of my experience of the world. How would looking different affect my life experiences and outcomes? How has it affected them until now? Outward appearances are fundamental to how others perceive us, and by extension how I perceive with and engage with the world.

What is recognition? The social psychology of G. H. Mead hypothesized that the intuitive sense of human individuation is a developing process by which the person can form an identity through interaction with others who recognize that identity and offer approval and the means for expansion of the circle of social environment. This is the "looking-glass self." As consciousness of human identity grows, subjects are dependent on conditions for recognition afforded in that social environment.[102]

One example that comes up a great deal, especially amongst young people, is those who pay close attention to their on-line body image. There is a fascinating and often troubling interplay between the social gaze of unknown others and the internal mirroring of that. It enables many to feel a sense of achievement and the validation of self: indeed, a high value in their world. Though allowing new forms of human interaction, including online counseling, the internet inhabits the dark side of the moon in addition to its sunny face. The dark web is a space where evil smurks, where electronic denizens wait to pounce, where identity theft and cyber-bullying is rife and where trolls leer and smear. Even routinized social media offers a space for harm and for the kind of abuse that is no longer tolerated in public discourse or on the TV.

Identity is loaded with almost unbearable tensions on a contemporary scene. Take gender and race.

Unquestionably, these are controversial and unsettling times for issues of gender and sex. What is a man? What is a woman? The term "sex" refers to male or female biology: sperm or eggs whereas "gender" was the cultural overlay shaped by society that affects roles and behavior. The growth of Second Wave feminism in the 1960s saw gender differentiated from biology on the grounds that male bias interpreted gender differences as being biologically determined. This was now seen to be historically convenient and a cloak for power. Discrimination became illegal. Biology was banished. Now, debates about sex and gender are deafening and often vitriolic. Gender seems to include identities that do not corresponds to biological sex. The primatologist Frans De Waal stresses that gender dimorphism is patterned in the unconscious and hence generates bias.[103] Or the view can be taken that gender identity is malleable, fluid.[104] Transgender people, by contrast, usually argue that they have an inherent gender identity that has been mischaracterized hitherto. Biology is back!

- "Now I am free, free to be myself. I am happy" (a transgender woman).
- "One of my guiding principles is doesn't hurt any of us to treat and honour people with respect as they see and experience themselves" (a clinical psychologist).[105]

Patently, the experience of race is also sharply debated. Psychological research has studied the devastating effects of racism. Most standardization samples can skew the generalizations we make about human behavior—comparison groups were often western, educated, industrialized, rich, and democratic (WEIRD).[106] As racial awareness increases, for a counsellor, finding your way through your own stance relates to one's own bias and privilege can make empathy difficult. Fragility might arise from guilt as counsellors come to see themselves in the therapeutic process. Building multi-cultural competence can help as can being able to use system-centered language to describe the systemic and structural factors that support racism.[107]

Identity is therefore a very loaded term. It depicts an inner sense of who I am which can be distinguished from the more obvious facts about me. My physical characteristics or my social relationships—father, partner, son, colleague and what I do—are increasingly being seen as not those that define us. With gender identity, that has generated new and often acrimonious debates, there is an "inner sense" of who I am that usually trumps the external markers. How people go about forging their identity gives rise to enormous political contention on the contemporary scene. Maybe the outward markers of me are accidental and do not reflect who I am? Maybe they are imposed on me by others, be they family or society and do not reflect my true self. If I believe myself to be a woman, then that is what I truly am, regardless of the body I was born into. This is the claim.

The approach we are proposing allows external factors *to do something*—to have a full part in both shaping and constituting the human person in need of soul repair. The methodological innovation is:

i. To show that the tension between social structures/systems and agency reflects the way that external and inner worlds meet and often collide or collude. The essence of this tension is one of felt value by the client and a capacity to assert this against the backcloth of what is going on in their lives that evokes distress. It is about worth as intrinsic to psychic structure.

ii. The weight of social factors such as gender and race systems is brought into the model of human personhood: they form the invisible unconscious and a latent capacity to respond to them with protest. These social factors are species of human devaluation or erosion of worth. Reaction against them— "excuse me I'm a human being"—belongs to the human DNA.

iii. In the clash between external and internal worlds, it is the capability to respond with discovery of our worth and dignity that supplies energy towards endorsement, for change and growth and to find the valuable person. This is a profoundly theological project.

The struggle to realize our value against the many factors in social life that erode it is fundamental. Rather than say the saga of the Oedipus complex, it is this dialectic that lies at the heart of human functioning. It forms identity within our social location. There are strong psycho-social assaults on dignity (one of the prime ingredients of value) that come from poverty and injustice.[108] Going to a foodbank can be stigmatizing for some. Being poor relative to the standard of the day will create harm because it affects that sense of self that relies on high value in order to flourish.

In the interpersonal arena, rejection due to a partner's emotional unavailability might trigger anxiety as a reflection of our unworthiness.

This might create low esteem and result in being needy, clingy, lacking self-control. This can be languaged as a Faulty Working Model internalized as an adult.

I See My Worth in Your Face. "Thou God See-st Me" (Gen 16:7)

This statement in Genesis by the servant girl Hagar is deeply instructive. She is escaping the hostility of Abraham's wife Sarai. Then comes an encounter with God; One who knows and sees her fully. In that encounter, she affirms that God somehow knows all about her and sees who she is. It is in the gaze, in the act of seeing and knowing that human identity is formed and cradled.

The concept of identity today is roughly equated with the soul, a lasting aspect of the self that transcends both the physical characteristics and social relationships in which the self finds itself. In Christian theology, we do not "have" souls, we "are" souls. Souls change through time. Concepts of suffering as in the writings of Irenaeus in the second century suggest that this world is a divinely shaped sphere of soul-making.[109] The world is the best of all possible worlds because it allows humans to fully develop. Creation is incomplete, as humans are not yet fully developed. To experience evil and suffering is necessary for such development.[110] Origen too responds to the problem of evil by casting the world as a schoolroom or hospital for the soul.[111] Creation is incomplete.

This approach to soul-making is challenged by the seeming reality that many evils do not promote spiritual growth but are rather destructive. Keeping the human spirit intact is an immense challenge. Yet life crises often provoke positive change. This may because of the plasticity of the brain. By adulthood once development is completed, the brain resists change.[112]

Dostoyevsky's presents an argument in his novel, *The Brothers Karamazov*, in which Ivan Karamazov presents an account of incredible cruelty to innocent people and children to his theistic brother Alyosha. Dostoyevsky's work, polyphonic in nature, shows that the love Christ showed to all, the final stance in the novel, is the only good. In the face of evil it is the beauty that will save the world.

The birth of recognition is an act of vision, of being seen. As Object Relations psychotherapists tell us, mother-baby transactions are vital to bring emotional circuitry to life. Later on in life, this will be shaped (for better or worse) in the social gaze. This has theological resonance. We are made in the mirror. The human soul is seen by God who calls it into being. It looks back at God and has life.

The Value of the Client

> Acceptance means valuing others because they are human.[113]

A set of ethical values are now considered essential to the operating codes of many arenas of social life. To take one example, ethical statements that began to operate in health or psycho-therapy reflected these assumptions. The fundamental values of counseling and psychotherapy included a commitment to respecting human rights and dignity. The principles that those values shaped emphasized the need to value the human. This is embodied in a culture of respect for a client.

"Value" is a driver in some psychological processes yet a content area that psychology has yet to conceptualize adequately. Best practice both in the medical and the psycho-therapy models recognizes, for the most part, the importance of respect for the patient/client. Some of the newer psychotherapies too hold the value of the person as being a key assumption to their paradigm. Lacking is a conceptual formulation that can draw up the dots of important human experiences, experiences that are recognizable yet which do not fit easily into the psychological lexicography.

The notion of a sense of self is commonplace in contemporary social psychology. Yet what we are calling attention to is a particular way the self is held, "a valuable self" that refuses to go second class, a valuable self best glimpsed through the prism of its opposite.

There are to be sure some usual suspects in any treatise arguing for a growing humanistic approach in the talking therapies and the medical model of distress of which evidence-based practice is but one.[114] Nevertheless, some deconstruction of professional ideology seems important in defence of valuing the human and preserving the voice of the individual amidst the systems of our time.

Gradually, the task of the counsellor has been seen as facilitating a therapeutic encounter which is more than a collection of skills and strategies. An effective counseling relationship came to be seen to include two core qualities—acceptance and understanding.[115]

With his emphasis on person-centered counseling, Carl Rogers proclaimed the importance of "unconditional positive regard."[116] This is respect for the client,[117] aiming to maintain a relationship that is as free as possible from value judgements. Clients should not be blamed or condemned. While they may not be helping themselves, strategies they have adopted are an effort to manage lives and emotions. This does not mean that clients cannot change or that the therapist should collude with self-destructive behavior. Clients should be given respect; experiences should be given credence and emotions validated. We should, argued Rogers, distinguish carefully between the behavior of the clients and clients themselves, who are "valuable because they are human."[118]

Empathic understanding, trying genuinely to see the world from the perspective of the person in pain in front of us, was not only seen to be important as a basis for practice. It was part of the therapeutic process.[119] It was liberating; people in pain can become active in their own healing and be empowered. Best practice came to be unthinkable without such acceptance being a core value. It implied paying attention to people, conferring upon them a high value. The point is that this applies to everyone. It would not be acceptable for some to be treated ethically and others not. In short, the working assumption is that people have a dignity, a dignity that should not be assaulted or violated.

Humans are moral agents to whom is owing a different standard than being property. They are also personal agents who require a high value to be recognized and affirmed.

How deep does this go?

Chapter Five

Models of Mind

Revising the Unconscious

"For from within, out of the heart of men, proceed evil thoughts, adulteries, fornications, murders, thefts, covetousness, wickedness, deceit, licentiousness, an evil eye, blasphemy, pride, foolishness. All these things come from within and defile."

—Mark 7:22

Theorizing the Unconscious

Wounded history has powerful roots and bequeaths a dangerous legacy. It does not only arise in early childhood. It can just as dangerously arise in traumatic events that have taken place later on. Psychodynamic practice is especially equipped to delve into the deep places. Client-centered approaches have a strong emphasis on a therapeutic relationship in which blockages in both conscious and unconscious life can be addressed and the hurting move into a better place. But this is a very different focus from working IN the transference so as to read the projections that are taking place. CBT can play a useful role in exposing negative mental representations and damaging beliefs. But this is a different focus from the conceptual space and time accorded to unconscious influence in negative areas such as rage and hate accruing from different parts of ourselves needing addressing.

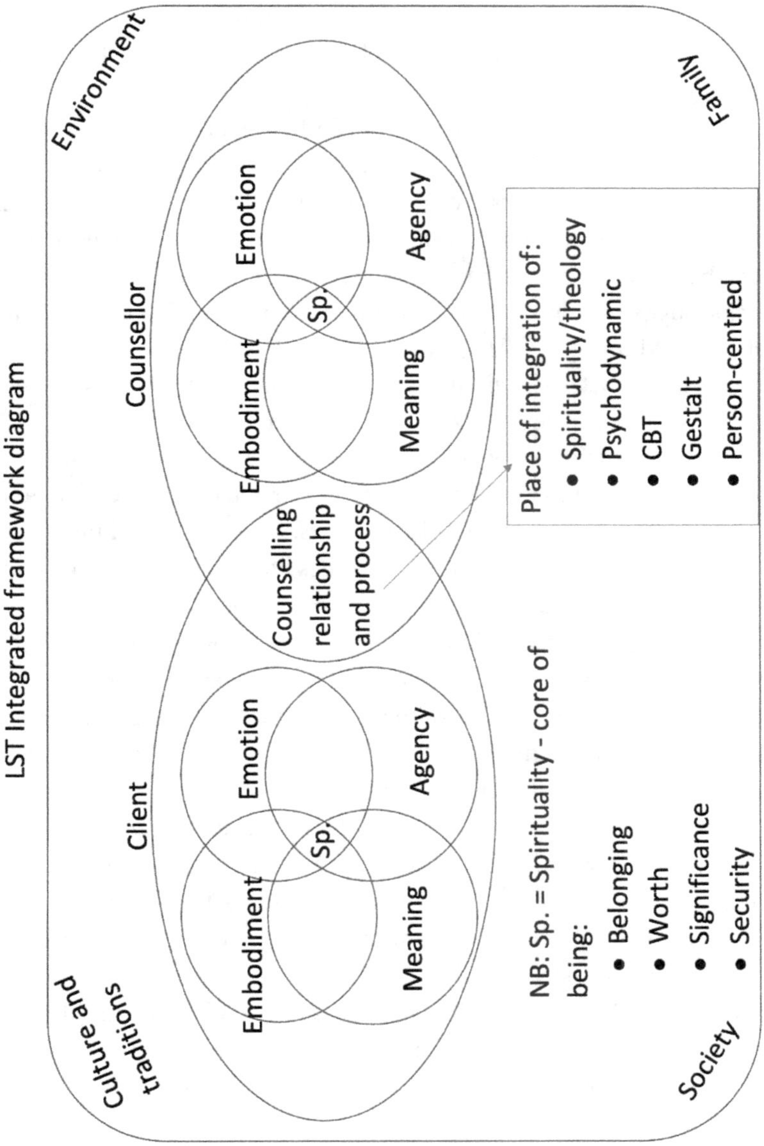

Integrated multidimensional LST framework[120]

The perspective of this book is that the human unconscious should be redefined in order to encompass the human pull towards longings and belongings, towards worthiness, and towards the imperative of hope. These are manifestations of the primary drive towards endorsement, the pre-eminent drive of the human soul. This impulse is profoundly theological but at the same time is shaped by social facts. Hence the pursuit of validation.

For the classic view of unconscious influence articulated by Freud, the primary drives of love and hate arose from bodily forces that are secreted into mental events. What though are the psychic origins of an impetus towards endorsement, towards recognition and questions of purpose? These human givens become a strong part of fundamental drives. As Freud suggested, once bodily demands become mental, they constitute what he called the "id."[121] They originate in physical drives. It is this picture of instincts that was revised in psychoanalysis and needs to be revised further to take full account of the human person and its dilemmas.

With a particular view of human nature, the psychotherapist Erich Fromm asks how human needs such as love, relatedness, meaning and connectedness are met by particular societies. Accepting that human nature is shaped by social conditions, he probes how much alienation from our essence society requires. Relevant for our approach here, Fromm suggests that the desire for interpersonal connection and fusion is the only way of overcoming the separateness that is the fundamental challenge of human existence.[122] Love that permeates the universe was there all along, waiting to be discovered. But how much of this derives from a deeper layer of reality: the unconscious mind?

Early psychotherapy was held in the conceptual straightjacket of mind and body dualism. Our minds are like a steam engine; a pressure is built up that needs to be released. The deepest layer—the id is on the level of the beast; eros and thanatos have somatic sources. The human drive bubbles up from physical locations—from mouth, anal and genital areas. It was Melanie Klein who liberated psychoanalysis from the mind-body problem. Love and hate emanated from the mind, not the body. Sexuality is a trickle down from the mind and relatedness rather than emanating from the body.

Freud's own theory of the drives went through profound evolution. He sought to differentiate two ways that the mind worked. One was the strong and imperious impulse towards gratification: the pleasure principle. The other was the subsequent developmental process by which the ego postpones wants and wishes: the reality principle. Maturity followed this path most of the time.[123] Such was developmental experience. But how did these trade-offs between conscious and unconscious demands relate to the content of these contrasting domains?

That perspective on human nature leads us to orientation through society and seeking endorsement from others rather than fulfilling our instincts. Lacking fixed drives, we seek validation through our choices as existentialists have stressed. This can bring an unbearable burden. In the twentieth century it lead to surrendering our freedom to totalitarian regimes who will make choices for us. In the twenty-first century, the anxiety of freedom leads us to being the only species that destroys its own ecosystem.

If we aim at relief of symptoms rather than insight about root causes, we are less likely to be interested in the unconscious. Philosophers had sought to follow the words of the Delphic oracle "know thyself" but inner resistances had blocked the way. As Heraclitus had observed, the soul is a far country which can neither be approached or explored. Can we ever know it though or is the unconscious the great unknowable except by the methods of psychoanalysis? How does it work?

Again and again, human subjects give voice to an intriguing question, a question that in the arena of battle comes across as completely baffling. It might be because the individual has been recruited to act in settings of racism in which devaluing social inferiors seems normal behavior. Later on perhaps, and only with reflexive insight, someone might come to see their earlier stance as being deeply perplexing. Why on earth did they think like that? Before feminist critique became normal, how did we come to be shaped by attitudes and behaviors that were deeply patriarchal or misogynistic? However did ageing or disability come to be labelled with unconscious disdain?

Or why is it that individuals can be overwhelmed with unsuspecting personal forces that devalue other lives? It may be stepchildren behaving like monsters when Mum forms a new relationship; somebody falling in forbidden love or a flood of emotions coming from nowhere that is deeply disruptive. A client encounters a strong resistance to admitting hostile feelings towards a dead parent or indeed verbalise feelings at all. Repression of deep-seated material can be potent indeed!

Humans have always tried to find ways to address the inner life. Christianity had done this for 1,600 years through theological reflection and mysticism but was sharply questioned in the Enlightenment.

Many approaches to counseling do not focus on the unconscious. Dr. Aaron Beck, the founder of Cognitive Behavioral Therapy shared the perspective of humanist counseling theorists such as Carl Rogers and Abraham Maslow that attention should focus on what the counselee is bringing that is clearly distressing them. Deeper-layer work is secondary. We should focus on immediate issues.

What exactly is the unconscious? Not everyone accepts that this is a particular layer of mind. It is a mysterious area that shows up in everyday life when we encounter a depth psychology underneath our behavior. There is a life we are not conscious of, a hidden force that comes through the cracks. It is an aspect of our reality that we cannot immediately connect with and access as it lies just over (or under) the horizon.

Though Freud's concept of the unconscious will continue to invite comment, it seems beyond dispute that common to human experience is the sense that we are a stranger to ourselves. The reason why we do and say things or react in a certain way is a mystery to our own minds invariably.

Core challenges reveal the strength of unconscious influences in human action as the subject is often in the grip of forces that are past all understanding. For the unconscious is not just another aspect of our minds; a version of ourselves that we only have to discover and surface for all to be well. It is a swirling mass of contradictions and conflicts that can at times seem at odds with our own interests. "Part of me wants this; part of me wants that" often reflects a divided self suggested by R. D. Laing.[124]

Freud did not invent the unconscious. Nietzsche, his contemporary, had spoken of one's own self being well-hidden from one's self. The pressure of unconscious forces had been grasped by philosophers such as Schopenhauer and indeed any writer who had spoken of being a mystery to oneself. Overcoming the resistances that the self puts up to self-discovery was not a new thought to anyone who had grasped the reality of biblical insistence that the heart is deceitful above all things.

Freud's contribution was to chart the forces that shaped the hidden mind. The Freudian unconscious supposed a mental structure consisting of three layers (conscious, preconscious and unconscious). The dynamic flux involved with that structure is supplied by two mental forces—libido and Thanatos, life and death instincts. Mapped on to this theory of instinctual forces are three psychological entities. The id is present at birth and consists of our most primitive urges propelling us towards gratification. Reality in how we navigate life is supplied by the ego which is mostly conscious in being able to mediate between competing demands of the id, the external world and the superego (a servant of three masters). It is the superego that is a breakaway continent from the ego and represents the moralistic constraints of parents and social mores.[125] Eros and thanatos (love and death) constitute the two main drivers of human functioning that emanate from the unconscious. The analyst brings insights into messages from the unconscious that need to be decoded and brought into consciousness. This is a profoundly interpretative exercise. Would we ever get it right?

A formative idea in psychoanalysis is that of repression. Why should the hidden mind put up such a fight or set itself against its own recovery? Resistances will be generated that need to be discovered by the analyst and prized open. Painful truths might be experienced by the client as being unbearable. Losses might need to be mourned. Cracks in the client's depths arising from relationship fissures need to be addressed though not necessarily by reparenting by the therapist in the form of a substitute relationship.

We have to become aware of how our neurotic responses derive from the inner depths, notably the way that desire is at the heart of the earliest relationship. Life is about managing two major dynamic forces motivating human personality from the unconscious, the reification of sexual energy, and the urge towards death—eros vs. thanatos. Consider though the thinking subject, the me that is writing these words or a reader receiving them. This is complemented by the consciousness to have a thought or emotion about that thought. This facility of mind is that of reflexive self—awareness. It could be labelled, "the Interpreter." It enables the self to inhabit itself self-consciously. But there is a deeper layer dimension of the self; the source of emotional reactions that spring, surprisingly from the underground network of roots.

A different map of the soul is provided by Carl Jung's investigation of the psyche (soul). He drew upon comparative studies in human culture, myth, and religion. His articulation of a map of the human soul through the study of himself and others tries to describe the psyche in all its dimensions and explain its internal dynamics.[126] There are some notable features.

Ego lies on the frontier; the border between what we know and what we do not know: the conscious and unconscious. It is what people tell themselves to maintain continuity what we understand at the moment, of our experience of being human. Ego is shaped by memories, traumas, emotions, and what we sense in our bodies as both current and genuine.[127]

In the conscious realm ego is expressed by persona. Persona is the face that individuals display to the world. It is a mask worn for people to see; we offer what our families, friends, and associates expect. Even those closest to us never get to see the "true us," only the part of us that we allow them to see. Persona is the mask we show around us.

For Jung, the personal unconscious is alive with complexes. These are related groups of emotionally charged ideas, thoughts and images which gather throughout one's life. Negatively charged complexes (such as traumatic childhood experiences) disrupt the psyche, which can lead to mental illness or neurosis. Complexes are autonomous and exhibit consciousness of their own. They also bind a certain amount of psychic energy and have a will. The goal of the unconscious is to bring those complexes into the conscious.

The shadow is the opposite of the persona and carries unwanted shameful, unacceptable parts of our psyche. These become parts of a person's nature contrary to society's customs and moral convictions. These parts are buried deep within, hoping they will stay undiscovered. Whatever parts of the personality have been suppressed because of cognitive or emotional dissonance fall into the shadow. Introspection can, to some extent, bring the shadow into consciousness if tracked deeply enough into the realms of darkness and coldness. Shadow is highly selfish, wilful, unfeeling, and controlling, with the intent of fulfilling personal desires for power and pleasure at any cost.

The anima and animus lie in the personal unconscious, opposite gendered, unconscious figures in our soul. For men, the anima is a feminine figure; for women, the equivalent is the animus, who is masculine. These subjective personalities represent a deeper level of the unconscious than the shadow; they are more "other" (outside of self) than the shadow. Anima and animus reveal the features of the soul and lead into the realm of the collective unconscious.[128]

Jung saw the collective unconscious as the fundamental basis of the individual psyche. Whilst the personal unconscious makes up lives past which was at some point in the conscious, they may have been forgotten or repressed, the content of the collective unconscious has never been conscious and is not acquired but inherited. The collective unconscious has two main aspects:

i. Archetypes—These are patterns that help to form our understanding of unconscious ideas.
ii. Instincts—These are the innate biological drives that determine our behavior.

Both archetype and instinct are related. They exist side by side as reflections in our minds. Archetypes and Instincts exist independently of the individual psyche and contain universal recognized, inherited aspects.[129]

The approach we take here though is that we should seek to listen to the unconscious, to endeavour to draw out what is causing dysfunction or conflict deep down. Unconscious motivations may well be contributing to the roots of dysfunction. What is being acted out; what are the messages from the unconscious that are shaping behavior. This makes us work psychodynamically. It does not necessarily make us Freudians in the psychoanalytic world of thought and practice. The main goal of psychodynamic therapy is to bring unconscious material into consciousness and enhance the functioning of the ego, helping the individual to become less controlled by inner drives and conflicts.

It is well known that early Freudian psychoanalytic theory evolved both in his own hands and in the hands of subsequent generations of theorists. Prominent among these is object relations theory, a variation that put less emphasis on biological based drives and greater importance on interpersonal relationships. In this awkwardly named approach, objects are usually persons, parts of persons (such as the mother's breast), or representations. The primary object is the mother. A child's relation to an object (e.g., the mother's breast) servers as a template for future relationships. Melanie Klein, whose name was chiefly associated with this variation at the outset in her seminal 1921 book,[130] argued that "objects" can be both external such as a body part and internal, replete with emotional representations of an external object (e.g., good breast vs. bad breast). Her focus in this work was not Freud's oedipal construct in relation to the father but the first months of life where the mother, or significant care-giver, is vital. The prime driver of in personality development is the warmth of contact and the need to form relationships rather than the release of sexual pressure as bodily drive. Melanie Klein's later work stressed the phenomenon of splitting where human functioning is driven by sub-personalities of ourselves that come to the fore at different times. Despite being disowned by Freud, she has been highly influential in her insistence on the role of mother and first months of life.

There are pressing reasons to bring what is unconscious into the light of day. It might be the need to surface difficult memories that have been repressed. It might be repeat behavior such as when someone keeps falling in love and never finds their way to a more sustainable relationship or when someone finds a partner who once again abuses and treats them badly. It might be a litany of medically unexplained symptoms—all too common in the literature on conversion disorders. There is no obvious biological cause to what Freud labelled hysteria but which today may be seen as trauma.

The Content of the Unconscious

Patently, there is a good deal more going on in our minds than we aware of. This is a side of our reality that beckons to us and yet which seems unfathomable. It is the arena of root causes and emotional blockages, of deep-seated fears and desires as well as being a repository of trauma.

There are various ways open to us that we could use language to describe and name. The unconscious could be labelled as layers of sedimentary rocks, moving down though subsequent accretions to earliest substrata laid down in the first months and years. A biological metaphor could be used to speak of deep roots of our personality. We might also consider the unconscious as a cupboard in which various phenomenon are placed such as:

- The impetus towards desire be it sexual or power over the object of desire
- The impetus towards connection and belonging
- The impetus towards significance and worthiness
- The impetus towards hope and continuation

As discussed in chapter 2, these are manifestations of what is arguably the central imperative towards endorsement and validation, which a baby will seek to extract from mother or caregiver.

Into the cupboard as well must go experiences of emotional cognition which were positive and affirmingly warm. However, events that gave rise to fear and trauma must also be recorded as they will imprint on the deep personality and potentially cripple adult mental life. What after all is the origin of besetting fears?

In that interior space lurk ghosts, things that frighten, nameless terrors and the origin of phobias. These are apprehensions about the world that stem from a time when the developing child is unable to use language to name and claim safe space.

In the deep interior also lies the source of addictions.[131] Beyond genetic predisposition, the early childhood environment is where the neurobiology of the brain's reward pathways develop. This is where emotional patterns are wired into the unconscious that lead to addiction. So often, addictions reflect an emotionally empty childhood, making it a relational rather than a medical problem.

Amidst the complexities of the interior world, the unconscious activities of the mind should include the desire to be valuable, to count and be of worth. Distorted neuroses may be a lot to do with blocked attempts to extract endorsement from our world. Repression may or may not be a factor in disguise of pathways towards fulfilment, but rejection is an experience that bites people to the core.

It is not so much drives and instincts that lie at the deepest layers of personality but emotional experiences, usually pre-language, or something that happens that is too deep for words. The impetus towards security is not directed to *something* to make us safe but *someone*. Eclipsed by object relations, the content of the Freudian unconscious needs to be revised.

In that interior space, deep down in the cupboard lie adult experiences also that might well latch on to primitive echoes from the earliest times. Adult traumas, however repressed, do have a life of their own though and do not have to have resonance with childhood for the fresh content (maybe from war, terrorism or abuse) to be pushed down and kept well hidden in case it comes out for malicious play. The cupboard must be securely locked. The unconscious contains all sorts of significant and disturbing material which we need to keep out of awareness because they are too threatening to acknowledge.

The unconscious mind acts as a cupboard indeed of primitive wishes and impulse mediated by the preconscious domain of mind. We have no idea what is stored there. For the unconscious contains all sorts of significant and disturbing material which we need to keep out of awareness but which need to surface if it is disturbing now. In that cupboard argued Freud is our biologically based instincts (eros and thanatos) which represent primitive urges for sex and aggression.[132] Our primitive urges do not reach consciousness because they are unacceptable to our rational selves.

The interior of the cupboard is a timeless zone. It is like Narnia. Time stops still and if entered, one is confronted with the originating terror, rattling its chains as if it was but yesterday. It could be said that primeval urges and fears have been tamed by adult life and a civilised world. But fears and desires are real enough and are a strong part of the foundations of personality. The challenge is not to solve the contents of the unconscious but to work out why all this matters. And who is the person, the speaking subject, whose unconscious it is?

The burgeoning science of psychology doubted this concept of mental processes operating at an unconscious level. The concept of the unconscious mind defied objective description and was difficult to test in the laboratory. In curious parallel with Freudian ideas being discredited in many quarters, cognitive psychology began to describe unconscious processes, such as procedural memory.[133] To an unconscious domain of mind is attributed automatic processing[134] The role of the unconscious in human behavior is shown in implicit processing in social psychology formats.[135]

Psychodynamics focus on unconscious processes that by-pass conscious activity. The task of Freudian psychoanalysis is the recovery of the unconscious and to bring drives to the surface. Although the idea of the unconscious came to be superseded by research into how the brain functioned, what Damasio calls the embodied mind,[136] key assumptions became part of the currency of our time. The unconscious nature of mental processes, the peculiar mechanisms they obey and the instinctual forces that are expressed in them"[137] are concepts that became taken as read. We later grasped that matter and energy are not to be put into different boxes as Freud supposed.[138] Nevertheless, "it does provide a roadmap of all the right questions, the kind of questions that personality psychologists have been asking ever since."[139]

However, empirical research in psychology has taken the concept of the unconscious beyond what Freud could theorize. The idea of how the conscious adapts to information processing differs from the psychoanalytic concept. Our mind operates at optimum by delegating much high level processing to the unconscious[140] which is clearly a sophisticated domain, not the Wild West. The unconscious is not now regarded as a single entity but a collection of systems and modules that gradually come to operate below the radar of consciousness. Endemic in human functioning seems to be an unconscious language processor that, as Chomsky argued, allows us to decide whether or not a sentence has been correctly formed.[141] There is another system that lets us recognize faces with remarkable efficiency. This adaptive unconscious is an information processing tool that operates for efficiency in human functioning not repression. All in all, the concept of the unconscious has been vindicated though in more advanced ways than Freud hypothesized.

The mind creates experience. But we also have awareness. Through language we become conscious of mental events. It is a curiosity that when the mind wants to find what consciousness is, it finds itself. Consciousness experiences itself as a conscious subject. Internal self-reflection is fundamental part of being human. To know ourselves as replete with valuable personhood is a quest.

But turn to a technological way of describing the contents of the unconscious: the story from neuroscience. Neuroscience shows us there is something going on in the brain we are not aware of.

The advances of neuroscience that have transformed psychology show that whatever has happened to us is patterned into our neural circuitry. It is literally, the way we are wired up. This is a story about biological systems that are complicit in emotional regulation and our relational brain.

The unconscious mind as conceived by psychotherapeutic pioneers was a place where instincts were formed from the bodily impulses, that were then translated into dynamic action though often repressed. Though the three-brain theory (higher cortex, mammalian and reptilian) has been debunked, conceptions of the brain that demonstrate deeper layers find support from neuroscience.

The unconscious seems to be making a come-back despite Freud's varying fortunes. Perhaps it is true that "psychoanalysis still represents the most coherent and intellectually satisfying view of the mind."[142] But will that perspective extend to a spiritual impulse? Is that included in the unconscious?

Psychoanalysis speaks of parts of ourselves trying to reach into deeper consciousness such as when the therapist feels something different than what seems to be going on in the room. Analyzing what is known as counter-transference can be very illuminating a possible link with the unconscious. Deepest parts of ourselves though are intrinsically connected with how the brain is organized for emotional experiences but also spirituality, however that is defined. Experiences of consciousness itself go beyond purely mental functioning. Mind has constructed a self-world model of how things are organized, how the world is. Perhaps spirituality can go beyond this.

Chapter Six

Revising the Unconscious

Wired for Belief

"To the psychologist, the religious propensities of man must be at least as interesting as any other of the facts pertaining to his mental constitution."

—WILLIAM JAMES[143]

THROUGH THIS BOOK, WE have been considering the notion that the impetus towards valuable personhood and of high worth is a fundamental drive. This shows up in the consulting room in the patterns of relating, in a desire for embodied connection, in significance and meaning and in the necessity of hope. In the present chapter, we will argue that what can be labelled a "spiritual" impetus is also rooted in a fundamental drive and is not just the product of culture and language.

These impulses are entwined. They converge because the spiritual dimension within the human operating system "not only provides answers to life's explicitly religious questions but also, more fundamentally, shapes perceptions, attributions and affects in the construction of subject experience including experience of human suffering."[144] In short, the quest for value and meaning is central to a spiritual sense of life. Human beings look for a high worth that is very closely associated with what is beyond ourselves. The impetus for both emanates from the human unconscious. Fundamental lenses on the nature of human existence entail the intersection of psychological and spiritual realms.

As will be evident in the next chapter, the impetus towards high worth cannot be attributable solely to early attachments. There are many who will not have had positive experiences in their formative emotional history who nevertheless have a capacity to believe that they are loved and worthwhile. Arguably, psychology and spirituality are one and coexisting rather than two different entities.[145]

In *The Ego and the Id*, Freud described a revised mental topography.[146] His structural analysis proposed a theory of mind beyond psychological theory of the day. The new map consisted of:

- Ego (the self)
- The id (the source of impulses, of life and death drives, eros and thanatos)
- The superego (that mediates between the two)

In psychoanalysis, the superego was a dimension that went all the way through the mind. The ego faces outwards to the external world via language, activity and perception but also can face inwards. There is the coherent ego and defences of the mind that serve as agencies of repression. Large parts of the ego are unconscious. The task of bringing material into consciousness is an enormous struggle against deeper layers of the mind where fundamental drives that control us make their demands.

For Jung, the unconscious is not as Freud supposed a dark, primeval place of unruly impulses but sophisticated. Inside lie hidden memories of a whole race of people. Primordial images—forms of behavior from ideas, images and memories are represented by what Jung termed archetypes represent those memories. These are ground level themes—all big ideas in science and religion go back to this. Jung's ideas represent a close link to mythology and religion. The human unconscious elides a myth-making level of the mind in common we all have in common.

There are, he suggested, very broadly two halves of life. Until age 35, our focus is on making our own way in the world, distinct from parents. Over age 35, the emphasis shifts to reconciling different aspects of ourselves towards unity. Looking inwards, bringing opposites into balance is the goal of therapy as we seek to listen to what our unconscious is saying. In the journey towards wholeness (individuation), it is the function of consciousness to translate these into a reality for the client.

We never lose the connection between mind and body. We can speak of a bodily ego. Linked with this, there is much more interest these days in a physical map of brain consisting of:

- Cerebral cortex (frontal lobe, parietal lobe, occipital lobe)
- Limbic system
- Amygdala

The question is where do we locate the spiritual impulse within the psyche?

A proposition that there is a spiritual impulse within human experience comes as no surprise. Within major religions and within philosophy, history and literature, the search for the spiritual has been spoken of for century after questing century. On the contemporary scene, a revival of spiritual awareness has been inconceivable in a former time when it was widely assumed that religion was dead. But it is not the old-time religion that has been stirring. The children of the secular generation have not been turning to the church to satisfy hunger but to unconventional, DIY faith. Spirituality was taking off in a world built on technology, progress and pragmatism; where gurus were management consultants and advertisers. The idea that the physical universe is all there is had been too confining. A spiritual dimension insisted on creeping through the concrete. The people were rediscovering that they were a spirit and not just a body, a mind, a sex instinct or a worker. Sensing a reality greater than the material sphere of rational knowledge and of this world, they were hungry to experience it. The land of the spirit has been widely noted and widely trailed.

The origins of the religious sensibility are perplexing to historians. What is based on? Is the spiritual impulse hard-wired into our brain? Is the sense of something "more than meets the eye" a response to human smallness and weakness amidst cosmic insignificance and indifference? The sense of something beyond the material and empirical world of everyday experience has been all pervasive, even though it has been expressed in a range of belief systems, traditions of numinous beholding and diverse communities of belonging offering spiritual support to the faithful.[147]

There are various maps of mind. Different options are available for the structuralizing of spirituality:

i. As an aspect of depth psychology that connects with a transpersonal realm.

ii. An aspect of the ego that also picks up on literature and artistic sensibility.

iii. An antenna that can relate to what is beyond ourselves and even God.

iv. Languaged in different ways but one example is "the human spirit."

Another approach might be to speak of spirituality holistically. We are whole people, not souls awaiting liberation from the body. The spiritual realm is not a department of our being but the totality of our complex entirety.

The spiritual core seems to be pointing to a deeper consciousness, a side of reality of which we are unaware until we encounter it. Jung saw a spiritual dimension as part of the unconscious. In his concept of introversion and extroversion, Jung makes it clear that he refers to the conscious rather than the unconscious mind. The domain of the ego is that of the conscious, personal "I." Every conscious ego has its unconscious shadow that is hidden behind a mask, labelled by Jung, the "persona." This represents all the drives, desires and what may be at odds with social conventions. Growth comes as the personal ego accepts its unconscious shadow and integrate the aspects that are distressing and unacceptable. Thus connection with out true nature is established and connection with the collective unconscious; the higher self or spiritual soul as Jung saw it.[148]

The literature on this is truly vast and predates Jung by centuries. Biblical writers speak of the human spirit, the means by which we connect with what is beyond ourselves, with God. Our capacity for fellowship and communion with the divine distinguishes us from other sentient beings.

This has echoes of the powerful insight of the powerful insight of Calvin that the knowledge of God is given in the same instance as the knowledge that the human being has of itself. Calvin insists that without the knowledge of God there is no knowledge of self but without knowledge of self there is no knowledge of God. There is a reciprocity between self-awareness and knowing God.[149] An increasing recognition in psychology that there is a spiritual desire within humans aligns with this theological view.

It was Calvin's contemporary, the Spanish noblewoman Theresa of Avila, who founded the Carmelite profession of convent prayer and meditation and who wrote a guidebook for the spiritual life: the "Interior Castle." This classic work on prayer came about after a vision from Christ, picturing "the soul as if it were a castle made of a single diamond or of a very clear crystal, in which there are many rooms, just as in Heaven there are many mansions." In the centre of crystal castle is the Sun, or the King, who gives all the splendor and beauty to the rest of the castle. The closer we approach the centre, the greater the light. The seven mansions are more of a continuity (a gradual and imperceptible growth) rather than separate rooms.[150] Is, however, the deep interior of the soul akin to the inner mansion which connects with God?

One of the classics in the field of spirituality and psychology was William James' seminal work on the varieties of religious experience. He asserted that there is something within people that seeks meaning beyond the immediate concerns of life.[151] Harmony with the world beyond, the highest universe, is our true end and destiny but this is developed through prayer or inner communion with the spirit thereof.

The age—old spiritual quest has caught the attention of neuroscientists such as Andrew Newberg, who presents evidence from brain scan studies that prayer and meditation permanently change numerous structures and functions in the brain, values and the way we perceive reality. The benefit is strengthening neural functioning in specific parts of the brain that aid in lowering anxiety and depression, enhancing social awareness and empathy, and improving cognitive functioning. Newberg was a founder of the new interdisciplinary field called neurotheology. Evoking the title of one of his books, along with therapist Mark Waldeman, human beings are born to believe.[152] Newberg examined not only the neural activity of the religious brain, but also the effects of various religious beliefs and practices on human mental and physical health. Using an academic approach into what he calls "objective measures of spirituality," Newberg sought to explain the neuroscientific basis for why religion and spirituality have played such a prominent role in human life.

In one account of the interaction between religion and brain science, God is a hallmark of the very way in which we think.[153]

Or the work of Victor Schermer could be quoted, referencing Winnicot's suggestion of a "pristine ego," a spiritual core or "true self," a natural spiritual awareness in children that dwindles under the assault of a secular world view. This true self is covered over by the everyday ego, the false self that has to navigate the world.[154] Schermer examines ideas from religious traditions including Judeo-Christian, Hindu and Buddhist, and considers their implications for psychotherapy and personal growth. He draws in Jungian psychology, the later work of the psychoanalyst Bion—and how object relations theory connects with the theory of spirituality.

There is an expanding literature on spirituality as an important dimension of psychology though what is meant by the slippery "spiritual" is both varied and vague. It is a variation on the "God concept," the image people might have of God in their psyches that is usually unconscious and influential. The difference is that "God" refers to an overarching, sacred and indivisible unity as Christian theology has outlined over the centuries.

Larry Culliford, in his book about the psychology of spirituality, suggests that belief is a form of attachment.[155] People love whatever they feel bound to. Culliford argues that human beings are bio-psycho-spiritual in nature. This three-fold essence is one and indivisible. The mind-body-spirit scheme seems to have resonance with how people understand God—either the Christian vision of the Trinity or other conceptions of the divine. Health professionals, Culliford argues, pay attention to one or other of those aspects but invariably omit the third component, that of a spiritual dimension.

Truine concepts of mind abound. Another three-fold scheme of mental topography suggests itself.

Locating the spiritual impulse within the unconscious, a deeper layer of mind or self, has some parallels too with Hinduism where the atman, the breath (spirit), encapsulates a human essence that is transmissible to subsequent forms of life.

How to locate the spiritual impulse, what might be termed "the spirit" is a challenge to map on to secular models of mind, notwithstanding the prevalence of the mind-body-spirit tripartite scheme. From the point of view of biblical psychology, there is also "the heart" and it is from here, from deep within, that come the maelstrom of greed, desires and violence that parallel in large measure with the Freudian unconscious that must be kept securely under lock and key.

This book is prepared though within the Christian tradition, deeply influenced by a three-fold conception of God. Springing from conviction of the deity of Christ, the Trinity could only be developed in the second, third and fourth centuries using increasingly sophisticated conceptual tools that worked with such concepts as "persona" and "hypostases." One God with three persons: a multiplicity of divine centres of being within a single monotheistic identity (or a Father-Son diad mediated by the Spirit as some conceptions have it where the spirit is the relational principle). Emanating from that divine action, "thou God seest me" (Gen 16:13) is a profound spiritual sense of recognition that reflects humankind made in God's image, that looks back to mirror the divine.

What that spiritual impulse is and how we should describe it is of perennial interest. A lady might say her sense of the spiritual is very important to her; accessed through yoga-based meditation. Does that reflect a profound foundation of the human situation that we are reaching beyond ourselves? Is this located at the very birth of human identity and self-awareness that lies latent until developed?

A neuroscientist Mario Beauregard used sophisticated technology to peer inside the brain in a way that lead him to the surprising conclusion that spiritual experiences are not a figment of the mind or a delusion produced by a dysfunctional brain. Beauregard and O'Leary argue that the mind cannot be simply reduced to physiological reactions in the brain, exploring attempts to locate a "God gene" in some of us. The claim is that our brains are "hardwired" for religion.[156]

Deeper aspects of reality, of conscious life are becoming illuminated by the developing field of neuroscience. There is more to the brain than what neuroscience tells us. Just because nothing happens without a brain does not mean that the brain is all. Numerous advances are pointing us in a direction that is at odds with the materialist view of reality that believed matter and energy is all and that there is no spiritual dimension. There is an alternative view now proposed that the brain is not a self-contained information processor but a transducer for the realm of mind (akin to a microphone passing on sound and converting voice and volume). This might help to explain such phenomenon as blindsight (blind people being aware of objects in their environment that they cannot consciously see), mindsight (near-death experiences of congenitally blind people where they are able to see normally), terminal lucidity (a brief period of clear consciousness that sometimes precedes death in dementia patients), hallucinations and such diseases as schizophrenia could be explained by the inference that the human brain focuses and transduces consciousness rather than generates it.[157]

The focus for much of this work is intra-psychic: internal to the individual. It is necessary though to consider the interplay between personal and social psychology arising from social imperatives. This will be the focus of another chapter. How therapists work with religious and spiritual issues in clinical practice is a large issue that has been the subject of "The Churchill Framework." This sets out the core competence framework in dealing with such matters, including recognition, respect and reflexivity.[158]

Arguably, a latent spiritual awareness is integrally linked to a latent sense of value. It is reasonable to propose then that the theory of the unconscious can extend to the spiritual impulse. So what about the social contexts and invisible systems into which human beings are enculturated? Is that included as denoting activity that is largely below the level of conscious life and which is learned behavior and habits of mind? So much of human functioning involves us not having to think or do anything. It is automatic.

Chapter Seven

Revising the Unconscious

The Birth of Worth

"The less we value and accept ourselves, the more we are driven to work hard to ensure other people's affection, approval and acceptance. If you have not learnt to value yourself, you have to work hard all the time to be good enough in people's estimation."[159]

Getting Attached

Secure attachments are one obvious candidate for the inculcation of a sense of value. John Bowlby suggested that early separations from the mother, or mother-substitute, provoke anxiety and in some extreme cases, "de-activation" of attachment behavior or persistent lack of feeling for others. "Whenever young children, who have had an opportunity to develop an attachment to a mother-figure are separated from her unwillingly, they show distress: and should they also be placed in a strange environment and cared for by strange people, such distress is likely to be intense."[160]

Bowlby's proposals about attachment theory were shaped by psychoanalysis and a retrospective examination he carried out into the childhood experiences of delinquent adolescent boys. The study showed that these young people had commonly experienced a history of being taken into care and passing from one substitute mother figure to another. A subsequent report about homeless children underlined that for mental health, "an infant and young child should experience a warm, intimate and continuous relationship with his mother (or permanent mother-substitute)."[161]

In his original research about security of attachments, seventeen of "Forty-Four Juvenile Thieves" had suffered maternal deprivation for six months or more during the first five years of life compared with only two members of a control group. Fourteen of the juvenile thieves had what he termed "affectionless" personalities. Ages differed as did their crimes. Other factors could have been involved. Bowlby's conclusion was unequivocal though: "Prolonged separation of a child from his mother (or mother-substitute) during the first five years of life stands foremost among causes of delinquent character-development and persistent misbehaviour."[162]

Michael Rutter's review of maternal deprivation theory in relation to attachment patterns concluded that there were no persistent effects of separation distress but that patterns of response are established that influence the way the individual reacts to some later stress or adversity.[163] In short, it is the way children learn to cope with life rather than separation itself that causes delinquency.

- Secure attachment (c. 60% of population): Separation distress, quickly pacified on Mum's return.
- Insecure-Avoidant attachment (c. 20%): Not much protest on departure, no quick desire to connect on return.
- Insecure-Ambivalent attachment (c. 15%): Children protest, and cannot be pacified on return, clinging tightly.
- Insecure-Disorganized attachment (c. 5%): No consistent pattern of response—freezing, collapsing, going vacant, leaning against wall.

Psychologists gradually abandoned the notion of maternal deprivation leading to delinquency and violence but the importance of a pattern of dependable attachments has remained. The literature points towards the need for attachments but the possibility of attachments being met by other significant people. It does not have to be the mother who provides the primary attachment bond. Rutter suggested that a substitute will be an acceptable equivalent as long as a mother-figure is almost always available in the perception of the child. This is good news for families who have experienced the loss of the mother. The children need not grow up delinquent! To evaluate the role of attachment theory on this theory of violence, the case for attachment theory, as amended by Rutter, seems to be strong. Infants do form attachments that require a care-giver to be available to a young child in the first year. But it is the quality of the relationship, the sensitivity and interaction with the child that is paramount.

"When parents tune in to and respond to their children's needs and are a dependable source of comfort, those children learn how to manage their own feeling and behaviours," reported the lead researcher Sophie Moulin of Princeton University. "These secure attachments to their mothers and fathers provide these children with a base from which they can thrive." Researchers combed through over 100 academic papers and data on 14,000 children born in 2001 collected by a US longitudinal study.[164] Their analysis showed that about 60% of children develop strong attachments to parents, which are formed through simple actions, such as holding a baby lovingly and responding to the baby's needs. Such actions support children's social and emotional development, which, in turn, strengthens their cognitive development. These children are more likely to be resilient to poverty, family instability, parental stress and depression. If boys growing up in poverty have strong parental attachments, they are two and a half times less likely to display behavior problems at school.

By contrast, the approximately 40% who lack secure attachments, on the other hand, are more likely to have poorer language and behavior before entering school. This effect continues throughout the children's lives, and such children are more likely to leave school without further education, employment or training, the researchers write. Among children growing up in poverty, poor parental care and insecure attachment before age four strongly predicted a failure to complete school. Of the 40% who lack secure attachments, 25% avoid their parents when they are upset (because their parents are ignoring their needs), and 15% resist their parents because their parents cause them distress. "This report clearly identifies the fundamental role secure attachment could have in narrowing that school readiness gap and improving children's life chances. More support from health visitors, children's centres and local authorities in helping parents improve how they bond with young children could play a role in narrowing the education gap," said the Director of research at the London-based Sutton Trust which published the research.[165]

Secure attachment patterns—those who find it easy to get on with others, comfortable depending on them, those who have no worry about being abandoned or someone getting too close arise from home environments where they were sure of the support from their caregiver and do not worry about it.[166] This positive attitude carries over into other relationships in their lives. Avoidant patterns are those who are uncomfortable being close to others, who develop sometimes an angry self-reliance and cold distant attitudes to others, find it difficult to trust and difficult to allow oneself to get too close. They are nervous when anyone gets too close and often, love partners want greater intimacy that they feel comfortable giving. These come from homes where they have been repeatedly rebuffed in their efforts to enjoy contact, where mothers were not consistent in their affection or attention.[167]

Alternatively, those who find that others are reluctant to get as close as they would like, worry that their partner doesn't love them or won't want to stay, who can scare someone away, come from home environments where caregiver's behavior is inconsistent or chaotic. They are victimized at school and attempt to cling on to teachers and friends in a way that leads to further hurt feelings.

Recent studies have charted the similarity of patterns of relating between mother and baby—the need to provide protection, security and consistency—and intimate adult relationships.[168]

Parents with secure attachment tend to have preschoolers who are similarly secure in their attachments. Parents who are insecure-dismissing, insecure-preoccupied and insecure-unresolved are most likely to have children who show excessive aggression and conduct problems. There is a robust link in the literature between inter-generational repetition of parenting style, how a parent was parented and attachment patterns of their children.[169]

Strong associations between adult attachment deficits and those of their children have been found; for example, the work of psychologists such as Main and Goldwyn who sought to measure attachment patterns across the lifespan using the AAI (adult attachment interviews). "Cross cultural and inter-country comparisons of attachment patterns confirm that the modal type is that of secure attachment, typically around 55–60% infant-mother dyads showing the pattern."[170] This confirms findings that the incidence of children who could be growing up without experiencing a secure foothold on life is 40–45% of children in a given population! Do we wonder why there is an epidemic of depression, suicide and substance abuse in our culture!

There is a complex inter-relationship of factors that shape the experience of childhood. When the infant consolidates its attachment in the 2nd half of the first year of life, it experiences "stranger anxiety" that enables it to distinguish between its personal entourage and the tense world out there. Infants need other minds to develop normally. Without healthy emotional attachments at this juncture, the infant will find it harder to form emotional attachments later.[171]

In short, John Bowlby's work showed that the way infants learn to bond is a psychological process of connection. Nature is very economical. Children develop a working model of how life is. This schema shapes what they can expect and whether the world will be a secure environment where they will feel at home or bequeath to them an insecure foothold on life. Neuro-scientific research, which has advanced very rapidly over several decades due to new technologies, has confirmed this picture.[172]

Attention and affirmation—the very factors that generate a sense of value—are not luxury goods but a vital developmental need. Research on Romanian orphans left in their cot and deprived of responsive contact had a "virtual black hole" where their orbito-frontal cortex should be.[173] Studies show that positive looks from parents are a crucial stimulus to growth of a social brain.[174] Through positive messages written across the face of the significant Other, pleasurable biochemicals help brain development.[175] It is here we build a valuable self.[176] Someone lights up when we are around.

Secure attachments are the channel through which attention and affirmation generate the capacity of the infant self to assert its identity safely and the adult to feel valued in the world.[177] The evidence ultimately favoured those psychoanalysts (like Fairbairn and Bowlby) who asserted that attachment and lust are two independent biological needs.

Emotions are vital ingredients of secure those attachments necessary to bond with givers of care.[178] Emotions are vital to the development of empathy[179] but also creativity.[180] The ability to regulate emotional responses so they are less intense and not so overwhelming is an important part of healthy development. A child's ability to regulate emotions is crucial in building resilience, coping and social competence. The idea that early attachments shape a working model of subsequent relationships has been a vital component in attachment theory. The literature seems to confirm that experiencing positive affect or emotions from significant care givers helps to forge strong secure base from which to explore life. Positive experiences, especially of play, are vital for emotional regulation and the development of a healthy sense of a valuable self.

Parenting Styles

Parenting style matters hugely. A considerable body of research literature as well as practice points to the quality of the relationship between parents and children that is vital for positive development. The role of parents in responding sensitively to the need for soothing or stimulation enables a child to learn the fine art of self-regulation.[181] A responsive, warm parent-child relationship evidently fosters self-worth and social responsibility. Such responsiveness and support for the developing child will vary in its expression as the child grows; the parenting style needs to be modified and in any case varies across cultures, but the value and importance of engaged parenting cannot be denied.[182] Warm, responsive relationships between parents and adolescent children help to foster the kind of positive outcomes that will be important for society generally—such as the formation of identity and pro-social behavior. Attention and effective monitoring of a child's whereabouts is important as ineffective monitoring seems to be linked with anti-social behavior in middle childhood.[183]

Attention is a crucial conduit of value—especially the loving gaze of a biological mother, a "valuer," the face of one who is pleased to see you and calls you by name. This is a vital part of affirmation, which also has the elements of touch and play. These factors connect emotional circuits that are fundamental to the wiring of a healthy self. The capacity to assert a valuable self may depend on how much affirmation and attention has been paid. Such affirmation leads to the child and then the adult feeling that a secure place in the world is deserved. Supportive nurturing results in positive brain chemistry that continues into adult life.[184]

By contrast, deficits in self-worth may stem from a lack of valuing in developmental phases. What counts is a nurturing relationship. Where an infant scans facial expressions of care-givers and learns to read fear, anxiety or depression, circuits are connected that will bequeath an insecure foothold on life. The child and the child within the adult responds to the world with an anxious or an avoidant pattern. This not only shapes adult styles of relating but capacity to believe one is valuable.[185] The quality of a child's social experience flows from the mental property in which value is internalized.

Here lies the origin of much dysfunction. There are many walking wounded who have experienced a lack of warm contact and real understanding, or alternatively a parent who is violent, emotionally or physically. Such early relational trauma has impregnated any sense of worth they may have with pain.[186] It can lead to women handing themselves over to their fate as submission in the hope of protection or care.[187] Their spirit is all but annihilated yet still they persevere because it seems right.

Much domestic abuse appears to emanate from men who are disempowered and have been cradled in low self-worth. Their quality of social interaction is poor. Depression and poor quality relationships are partners in crime: lowering the barriers to poor health and lowering life expectancy. Lack of self-respect, compulsive engagement in relationships that wound us yet leave us hungering for further wounding are manifestations of a devalued self. We end up devaluing ourselves. Sometimes we look for people who put us down sexually rather than build us up—and this can be both damning for the soul but keep us coming back for more as moths are drawn to the light. Self-harming can be an ugly, dangerous infliction that gives us a buzz paradoxically and energizes us as we take back control of our own lives and write our own scripts on our bodies. Often it stems from an empty place within associated with a poor valuing of self.

Effective parenting as a reinforcer of healthy development evoking a sense of worth has been fundamental to the debate around early intervention. This has been brought into policy debates about child poverty. There has been a growing acceptance of the idea that outcomes for children are exacerbated by weak parenting styles which help to reproduce poverty.

For a strong sense of value and worth to grow, affirmation and attention must be linked with boundaries. In Adam Philips' study psychoanalytical study of excess, *On Balance*, he explains excess as a desperate search for limitations by a parental figure who will say, "no." Exaggeration is a strategy for gaining attention, to know that somewhere there is a restraining hand; someone to care for us.[188]

At around 12 months, fathers start to become important. Attachment patterns begin to form with Dad. Positive experiences, especially of play, are vital for emotional regulation and the development of a healthy sense of a valuable self. "My father never showed the least affection for any of us," recalled the son of the Iron Duke, First Duke of Wellington and hero of Waterloo. Little wonder that both boys grew up lacking in confidence and had to fight many personal battles.[189] The writer William Stryon was at times cutting and remote, often inspiring fear and loathing in his children.[190] Without their mother's restorative good nature, no one would have been able to endure it. Stryon said it stemmed from depression arising from the death of his mother.

The contrast is illustrated well in a statement by Bill Gates senior about the secret of family success. He reported that he and the mother of the founder of Microsoft went on "effective parent training" at the church they attended. "The thing that the people there taught us and emphasized, which is so central and so significant is that you should never demean your child."[191] The words of *The Help* capture well the ideal: "You's smart, you's beautiful, you's important."[192]

It would be pleasant to think of messy family life as cosy places where they are happy to take you in. Yet the internal landscapes of our time often show a different reality—huddled masses living with low self-worth.[193] As a child, how you think of yourself is crucial—whether you have a positive sense of a valuable self rather than a negative view. Adults become skilled in a strategy whereby a statement is made that seems denigrating but is wistfully ambiguous in looking for a loud rejoinder to the contrary. The very act of apparent collusion conceals its hopeful opposite.

A Mum lays into her son, nagging him left right and centre. Then he goes to school, white-hot. Surprise, surprise, he gets into trouble from hard-pressed educators! The fact that she had negative life experiences and an over-bearing father who shouted at her all the time means Mum is participating in an unhealthy re-cycling project. "There are days when the memory of my father's criticism starts to sink me and I lack the energy to rise above it."[194]

The daughter of the writer William Golding recounted how his children were put in second place to their parent's projects and had to work twice as hard for their parent's attention and approval. "I did love you," her mother said. "I just couldn't show it."[195]

In a study about the well-being of children, the UK was at the bottom of three dimensions, those of *Subjective Well-being, Behaviors and Risk*, and crucially, *Family and Peer Relationships*: *"The true measure of a nation's standing is how well it attends to its children—their health and safety, their material security, their education and socialization, and their sense of being loved,* valued, *and included in the families and societies into which they are born"*[196] (emphasis added).

"Children learn what they live. . . . If a child learns to live with criticism, he learns to condemn."[197] That is a commonplace observation and arises because a sense of a valuable self has been breached but not embedded. Children thrive with a sense of a valuable self. Without such internalization, a child may also grow up learning to collude with the put-downs and criticism. Children who do not fit into the academic mould can all too quickly learn to see themselves as failures, writing themselves off. "Being told I'm not as clever as my sister locks you into a self-fulfilling prophecy."[198] They may grow up to have little grasp of the connection between work and reward. Lack of respect from the outside world is paralleled by lack of internal expectation. With added components of verbal or physical violence, this is the cradle of a dysfunctional life. For well-being, you have to be connected.

In contrast to Maslow's hierarchy of needs, our psychological development is more basic to our needs than material satisfaction. As demonstrated by baby money tests, primates prefer safety and comfort to being well fed. Therapy can help us becoming conscious of how attachment patterns may have got stuck and thus move on.

In conclusion, this discussion underlines the role of positive relationships in our early emotional history to form bonding systems. Secure attachments plug into the need for value in our psychic structure that is vital to a positive meaning environment needed to work and function at our best.

The really interesting question about this is what happens in situations where there has been insecure or avoidant patterns of attachment? The marked absence of bonding will make for a difficult psychological history. Difficulties forming relationships may well ensue. Anxious patterns could arise in how people view their world as an insecure place. Yet invariably something that can be appealed to. Something can be mobilized within the person that, against unpromising beginnings, can come to feel that he or she is worthwhile and worthy of respect. It may well have to grow, be nurtured and defended (by caregivers, teachers or partners). But the capacity for potential sense of valuable personhood will very likely be patent or latent. This is a research agenda. It may well point to a capacity that is embedded in the human DNA; the capacity for love but also a spiritual response.

Chapter Eight

Widening the Unconscious

Unconscious Bias and the Devalued Self

"When I am low, the old internal dialogue kicks in. All that self-talk, all those negative voices telling you that you are not worth much or even rubbish!"[199]

"The loving eyes of healthy parents enable us to see ourselves as wonderful, special and worthwhile individuals, while the distressed eyes of dysfunctional parents create feelings of shame and worthlessness."[200]

The self does not exist in isolation. It is always entangled with culture.

Psychoanalytic theories are steadily falling out of favour within many American schools of social work. This lack of emphasis on psychodynamic perspectives deprives students of the rich developmental insight that can be of particular value in field placement settings like domestic violence shelters in which mother/child dyads are typically of clinical significance. For instance, in contexts of domestic violence, "in order to avoid unduly blaming women in contexts of domestic violence, clinical social work students interested in utilizing the theory of object relations in their work must employ an array of additional analyses that focus on issues such as race, financial status, and psychological effects of trauma."[201]

Our reaction to people is affected by age, skin color, ethnicity, height, gender and the way they dress. Behaviors and decisions are affected by our bias which happens outside of our control. It happens automatically and is triggered by our brain making quick judgments and assessments of people and situations, influenced by our background, cultural environment and personal experiences. Social stereotypes about certain groups are formed outside our own conscious awareness. When things are conscious we can attend to them but when they are not it means they can impact us and our relationships in negative ways. We may avoid people. What is unconscious determines much of how we psychically exist as human beings. A range of assumptions shape how we organize our world into social categories. The real meaning of most of the things we think, feel and do is outside of our awareness and determined unconsciously.

As these words are written, Wales has honored the first woman headteacher who was black.

Betty Campbell grew up in 1940s South Wales in Tiger Bay docklands with a growing desire to be a teacher. This was not encouraged by her own teacher. She was told quite clearly that the difficulties were insurmountable. A black, working-class woman could never reach the academic heights to which she aspired. This reduced her to tears but it made her the more determined to achieve. In time, she went to teacher training college and became the first black woman headteacher as well as black history campaigner. Betty Campbell fought for her childhood dream and succeeded, leaving an immense legacy and influence. Despite growing up reading fictional accounts about privileged white girls in a very English boarding school, Betty felt that people from that background were no better than she was. She had proved her doubters wrong.[202] The point to make here concerns self-belief; a belief based on a perception of worth. The moves seem to be threefold:

i. The social imperatives of class and race were both overlapping and immensely strong.
ii. Somehow, a childhood dream and aspiration grew that ran counter to this.
iii. At first, there seems to have been acceptance of these insurmountable obstacles (collusion?) Then comes the energy for the Protest and realization of her dreams.

The great majority of psychotherapeutic models seem to look at human functioning in terms of an individual entity with drives and impulses that require resolution. The focus of analysis is invariably the human person. It will of course be explained that people are embedded in social systems that affect them in profound ways and that everyone comes to therapy with the impact of their social settings and not just childhood influences. A serious omission nevertheless is how the social scripts come into the various conceptual models themselves.

For the most part, the emphasis on what is going on at the level of an individual psychology is not being brought together with what has shaped an individual *biography*. Social factors are crucial.

Marx made class-structure the driving force in his conceptualization. Freud took a different route. It was not correct, he argued, to see class and property relations as the engine of conflict.[203] It assumed that there was no innate destructiveness within humanity, once class relations were resolved. One of Freud's most significant contributions to the understanding of how modern societies operate lies in his insight into the way that cultural heritage operates for the most part unconsciously in people yet affects their connections with society.[204] Both social and personal dynamics have to be seen with reference to the invisibility of forces. Hidden psychological forces are of a piece with hidden external forces that constrain people at the level of social systems. Uncovering the mysteries is the task of the psychotherapist to root out the archaeology of mental forces and emotional chains as it is the task of sociological imagination to discern the invisible external and through reflection, raise consciousness and emancipate. Invariably, there are two sets of reasons that can be given for the dramas being played out in people's lives. One are explanations that can be framed in terms of the culture; the system-level explanation if you will. The other set is to do with unconscious or vaguely repressed thoughts and feelings that undergird mental events.[205]

One way of framing such issues is in terms of "the unconscious"; the unnamed and untamed unconscious releasing its unbidden fury and emerging from the shadows of invisibility into the full glare of social scrutiny. But systems of social life in which the subject is embedded constrain subjectivity just as much if not more. Inequality arises from both directions that cripples and assigns scales of importance. Subjectivity is thus inextricable linked with value-in-oneself or its deficit.

Consider, for example, the issue of furious husbands killing their wives for sleeping around. In many cultures, such a "crime of honor" was not even typically punished by the courts in the past. The reason the husband behaves this way is not just insane jealousy. It is because he believes his honor has been irretrievably damaged. It is, therefore, a social question, not just an internal mental event.

Between the waves above and the stormy seas beneath, human subjects attempt to garner value in their world, all the time convinced they are in control. The illusion of free-wheeling autonomy is maintained, until the next time we are overwhelmed. Baffled as to the source, social or psycho-dynamic forces do mighty battle on the surface of the unsuspecting.

Above us are systems of social life in which we lie unbidden; systems to do with the economy and culture. These are often perceived as impersonal forces beyond the level of the individual that bear down on the human subject. Underneath us are psycho-dynamic forces arising from frozen relics of previous experience and from relationships. How to relate the social world with inner world has been the quest of sociologists and psychologists for 200 years. It is not unlike the quest in science for ways of describing the interaction of the very small (quantum mechanics) and the physical universe (the sphere of relativity).

Conceptual analysis tends to regard the social world as a realm that stops at the front door. That is the realm of sociology. When you cross the front door and come to the interior halls and rooms, you enter psychology. Different forms of analysis apply. This cannot of course be the case. In one department of the academy, the importance of unconscious bias will be stressed as shaping perceptions about people that need to be brought to the surface. In another, the psychological life of humans would not normally include social factors within a line-up of unconscious mental forces.

A novelist understands this well. To take one contemporary example, the winner of the 2019 Booker Prize, *Girl, Woman, Other*,[206] traces twelve very different characters on their journey of discovery through modern Britain. Their lives are completely inseparable from all the factors that shape them. Constantly, the imperatives of class, race and gender press upon them. Where in our psychotherapeutic models do such imperatives feature, except as bit players?

Given the layers of disadvantage many people experience, it is presumptive that you can fully understand the lived experience of someone else. However, what you can do is to listen to and respect people when they share their lives with you.

What is needed is to integrate at some level the sociological with the psychological. Social scripts from which, for example, many may be trying to escape, *should be part of the model*, not exterior to it. A psychology that is not incorporating social pressures into itself is seeing these as a separate world. Social analysis belongs to the exterior world only if it is assumed that when the line is crossed into the interior world, something else is going on. The gap between the social actor and the system, however controlled by institutions such as family or education can hardly be maintained. An individual is not just embedded in social set up; the person is part of the system and the system of the person. Imperatives of class, race and gender shape very different people. Capacity for agency and means by which freedom and responsibility are exercised is in active flux with social systems. The idea of society did not make an appearance until long after a body of reflection on the working of an individual soul had taken shape through the centuries by religious writers and philosophers.

A more unified social theory should then fully recognize the weight and presence of such factors as gender, class and race within an individual biography. This is what has made someone who they are. Disability is not something that is added on to the balance of pressures within the human person. According to the ways this is experienced, the disability could validly be seen as part of the person.

Where in counseling models do we find the impact and implications of the sweeping changes to gender identity in the past generation? Where do we find the impact of considerable conflict about race as constituting a very different kind of person? Maybe counseling needs its "me too" moment.

The proposals here offer a framework by which the impact of social systems can be incorporated into how we see a client in distress. Conceptually, what is needed is a bridge of some sort, be it a common language or an integrating theme such as identity. What might supply a means of bringing the social within the human person can be an understanding of value as a psycho-social dynamic.

It is common in sociological analysis that "social divisions are sewn into the fabric of society and oppression and discrimination become institutionalised.[207] Yet the point to make here is that they are also sewn *into our inner psychology*. The dichotomy between individualism and "the social self" has a long running in Western political and psychological thought. Inner processes are shaped and re-shaped amid cultural imperatives, family systems, violence and social suffering. It is an interconnected network of power relations that generates and sustains human devaluation.

Social and intercultural factors and our response to them are woven into our very identity. The self does not exist in isolation. It is always entangled with culture.

Psychology's urgent need, argues the American Psychology Association, is to dismantle racism. A psychological science that is anti-racist is more adaptable to the reality of people's lives.[208] There are numerous calls to de-colonise the curriculum such that education generally (including therapy) is more relevant. Changing the level of analysis is fundamental away from racism being interpersonal.

It is widely recognized that there are multiple forms of disadvantage. If we focus on race, it will be stressed by others that gender is vitally important as a social factor. Focusing on class analysis as primary left out both race and gender but also disability, ageism, sexual orientation and religion as the basis for discrimination. Though championed by identity groups, the reason why it is permissible to group these various avenues of devaluation together is that they impinge upon an inner core.[209]

It is awareness that black people will often have a very different experience, especially when combined with other forms of disadvantage that has led to the idea of intersectionality, developed by law Professor Kimberley Crenshaw. It is important to hear the voices of those experiencing overlapping erosion of their value in order to understand the depths of the inequalities and the relationships among them in any given context. People's overlapping identities—including race, class, ethnicity, religion and sexual orientation—impact the way they experience oppression and discrimination. A white woman might well be disadvantaged by her gender but has the advantage of race. By contrast, a black woman is at a disadvantage by her gender *and* her race. A black lesbian experiences multiple discrimination because of her ethnicity, her gender and her sexual orientation. "Gender justice is racial justice is economic justice." This shapes perceptions profoundly.[210]

It is related to the analytical framework supplied by Critical Race Theory that is sharply divisive. US States have sought to keep it out of schools as implying that racism is built into the system. Overturning oppression is accompanied by engendering a sense of guilt amongst white people. In the ancient world and right up to early modern slavery, race was not an issue as the basis for systematic erosion of people due to the color of their skin. It is not only history that has been whitewashed history. Since the 1970s, another Law Professor, Derek Bell, and others focused on legal jurisprudence that devalued the testimony of black people.

There are sharp divides in many fields about critical race theory, with its call for white people to recognize their privilege and to examine the ways in which that privilege can make other women invisible within the feminist movement. Turbocharged by the death of George Floyd in 2020, these represented movements towards teaching principles of anti-racism and emphasizing the on-going effects of white superiority.

It is beyond the scope of this book to examine these claims or to be critical about critical race theory. History is a proxy for battles in the present day. Arguably, a more far-reaching category is that of *human devaluation* as that encompasses all forms of oppression—whether from social factors or inequality in emotional history such as arises from abuse or domestic violence. But it is impossible to avoid the impact of such powerful social explosions as the "Me Too" movement or "Black Lives Matter" that raised consciousness so strongly. What should be taken on board though is that enormous issues of race and gender have profoundly affected social experience and need to be taken seriously in our counseling models. The latter are not independent categories floating freely as self-contained psychological entities of human persons.

Heated discussion of the ideology of gender is going on in parallel within universities and mainstream culture. On the one side is the view that gender identity, the feeling that one is a man or a woman, is as important as biological sex. Those who claim to be transgender should be regarded as the gender with which they identify. This has allowed transwomen into spaces that were once reserved for females—school toilets, sports teams, prisons and shelters from domestic violence. On the other side is the view that as biological sex is unchangeable, surgery or other treatments in the conviction that one has been born in the wrong body should not be undertaken. Such "gender-critical" advocates argue that biological differences between sexes make the need for female only spaces to be ongoing and vitally important. This matters for universities: should gender-critical views be allowed to be expressed? This is not a divide about faith-based positions. Many advocates of gender-critical stances are feminist, atheistic and left-leaning academics. These matters are being played out in the courts as well as intense debate around fear of using the wrong language.[211]

The biography of a miner's daughter from north-east England illustrates the tension between an inner sense of worth and the weight of social realities. Fiona Hill went on to become a White House insider and Russia expert in the Trump Administration. But she came from a forgotten place in north east England, Bishop Auckland amidst a background of poverty, closure of mines and other local industries. An attempt to go to Oxford University failed as she felt completely out of place. ("Where are you from, what does your father do, what school do you go to?") Moreover, having to battle with social attitudes towards women added another disadvantage. Despite these obstacles, Fiona Hill pursued a university education in a journey from disadvantaged origins to success. Believing in herself allowed barriers to opportunity to be removed and overcome the initial drawbacks.[212]

What Is This Tapping Into?

Shame may be an effective response to the threat to one's social self, defined as a self-conscious emotion, experienced when a core aspect of the self is judged as defective, inferior, or inadequate.[213] Freud saw the impact on relationships of abuse as those caught in the law of guilt and self-punishments in the unconscious by the attempt to make us feel valued and loved for having participated in the act.[214] Survivors of CSA experience a variety of interpersonal effects, primarily characterized by feelings of isolation and detachment, distrust, stigmatization and being different from others. For example, a common response amongst survivors of Childhood Sexual Abuse is that "no man could value me without a sexual relationship."[215] A sense of unworthiness creates low self-esteem, being needy and clingy.[216] It highlights pernicious effects of feeling devalued and trashed.

At least three propositions articulate how pursuing a high value for the psyche plays a key role in intrapersonal and interpersonal processes.

i. Every biography is a complex mix of varied ways people pursue a high value for themselves against the many factors that devalue the human.
ii. The motivation to be of high value and worth is a key driver within the personality.
iii. Experiences of devaluation can trigger a range of demoralizing psycho-social effects.

We looked at the first two of these in chapter 5. Here we focus on the last statement.

Experiences of Devaluation Can Trigger a Range of Demoralizing Psycho-Social Effects

Demoralization

A good deal of depression is caused by feeling worthless, or demoralised. Here is a middle-aged woman describing how she has often felt unloved and unwanted. Experiences now seem to reinforce beliefs that she is not "worth anything." A familiar enough report conceals a curiosity. Why does the notion of "worth" come into her narrative, without which she feels hemmed in with wistfulness? A young woman greets me across the consulting room, eyes lighting up with sad indignation. "I am tired of a whole string of relationships where I feel used," she complains. "All I end up doing is feeling crap after." As she tells her story, what stands out is that being taken advantage of again and again results in a burden of worth that is steadily diminishing. It is at its most profound, an experience of devaluation though a series of such experiences, of being written off little by little.

A key question for analysis is why people can't see the chains that bind them. Why do they participate in their own oppression? Freud never forgot that his father had submitted without protest to anti-semitic insults.

Steve Biko, the black South African leader and founder of Black Consciousness in South Africa, who died under Apartheid-era police brutality diagnosed a submissive state of mind and lack of self-respect as illness. We collude with the definition of ourselves that others impose upon us. He defined its ideology: "Evil-doers have succeeded in producing at the output end of their machine black man who is man only in form. This is the extent to which the process of de-humanisation has advanced. . . . All in all the black man has become a shell, a shadow of a man, completely defeated, drowning in his own misery, a slave, an ox bearing a yoke of oppression with sheepish timidity."[217]

The sorry litany of people who give up must include those with a history of abuse or maltreatment during childhood who are over twice as likely to have recurrent episodes of depression in adult life. Data from more than 26,000 people was pooled in a 2011 study which used various markers of maltreatment—rejection from a mother, harsh discipline, unstable caregiving and self-reports of harsh physical or sexual abuse. Those who had experiences one or more of such markers were 2.27 times as likely to develop recurring depression than those who had not been maltreated.[218] Arguably, previous erosion of their worth has left them with a tendency towards life demoralization.

A client is keenly aware that he is operating in a social environment where many customers and acquaintances are on a higher plane. It is in the background behind many of the statements and practices about how he sees himself in relation to others. This is languaged as "they are above me" or "they won't want to mix with me." Identity surfaces as being a working man. Yet behind this narrative, another story is playing, one arising from personal worlds. This person suffers from a strong sense of inferiority. His father systematically put him down and belittled him. The point is, how do you separate the inequality apparently resulting from class from personal factors? Either they collide or collude, thus reinforcing each other.

Resignation

Resignation is a different response than demoralization. Those who accept their lot in life in a passive sense seem capable of making life-affirming responses that negate miserable circumstances. This too is an affirmation of value-in-oneself. For millions, social life is heavily constrained by systemic patterns that assign a place in the social structure from which little escape seems possible. Reflecting on the few options available to him in his life as an agricultural labourer in nineteenth century Kent, someone pointed out, "People say why did you put up with it? Because you bloody well had to, that's why!"[219] The experience of millions surely is that they greet their lot in life with resignation. They cannot see any way out of their situation and it rarely occurs to change the conditions of life. The subject accepts the version of life in which it is formed. The inspiration behind the Indian Independence movement, Gandhi believed India's shackles were self-made. He tried to instil new consciousness in the people. "Prisoner, tell me who it was who wrought this unbreakable chain? It was I, said the prisoner, who forged this chain very carefully."[220]

Where the borders are between resignation and Protest are contested. Martin Luther King referred to "the ominous clouds of inferiority" in the mental sky of black people

Steve Biko's narrative shows the extent to which there is unintended collusion between devalued and devaluers. It shows how human identity is created attitudinally, in dialogue and in symbolic interaction with others. The Protest is emancipation of the mind, the freedom to be who you are.

The Protest

The Protest is a capacity to subvert being devalued. In response to social groups claiming power as being higher value people, it sounds its trumpet call as, "we will not be edited out of the picture!" In response to depersonalizing encounters, organizational activity devoid of either name or face, the Protest cries out "I am not an it!" This reflex underlies much of the contemporary search for dignity and respect from organizations. Finally, reacting to de-humanizing or demonizing forces that strip away human dignity and desecrate the sanctity of life, indignant Protest of the victim (or those that mobilise on their behalf) is "you shouldn't treat us like this. . . . We won't put up with this anymore."

The pursuit of value is rooted in ineradicable traits, part of the human operating system. This should be factored in more widely than it has into psychological theory, and not just under the heading of inferiority. It is a reaction that at its heart is about the value of persons and what social factors tap into. In his autobiography, Freud gave prominent place to the irritant of anti-Semitism. Rather than meekly accepting it as his father had before him, Sigmund Freud responded with defiance. Rejecting the invitation to humility, he embraced the stance of an outsider.

This impulse seeps through many actions and interactions. Like the sun in eclipse, it can be observed against its shadow; the impulse to be of high value is detected especially against the backcloth of its opposite, devaluation. It is not enough that we are of worth; we must be of high value.

The quest for high value, for endorsement, is written into the human unconscious. It is there that the pursuit plays out against the backcloth both of interpersonal transactions and social realities.

But what happens when this quest becomes blocked? It is here that we enter the troubled zone. Demoralization and resignation are both strategies of the soul. So too is the Protest, the trembling indignation that asserts one's inner defiance—"I'm worth more than that!"

But violence and psychopathology are also responses to human devaluation, to be being trashed.

Chapter Nine

Widening the Unconscious

Violence and Psychopathology and the Roots of Dysfunction

"It's not about drugs anymore; all anyone wants is respect—that's what it' all about."

—GANG MEMBER[221]

How Deep Does It Go?

EVEN BEFORE THE PANDEMIC stuck, there were deaths of despair.

"Deaths of despair" are the deaths from suicide, drug overdoses and alcoholic liver disease ravaging swaths numerous lives. The victims are less-educated Americans whose loss of life was preceded by a loss of jobs, community and dignity, and whose deaths are inextricable from the policies and politics transforming the US economy into an engine of inequality and suffering. The big issue explored by Case and Deaton is what middle-aged white Americans are dying from. Three key players are drug overdoses, suicides, and alcoholic liver disease and cirrhosis. The US has seen a rapid rise in these deaths in almost all states since 1999. The three causes of deaths are related but they share one common feature—they reflect great unhappiness with life.[222]

"When we add up those numbers from 1999, the critical point where the turnaround began, to 2017," the authors report, "we get a very large total: 600,000 deaths of midlife Americans who would be alive if progress had gone on as expected." Case and Deaton liken that number to "what we might see during the ravages of an infectious disease, like the Great Influenza Pandemic of 1918." They also compare it to the roughly 675,000 deaths of HIV/AIDS in the United States since the early 1980s. The big spike was in the deaths of white working-class Americans. Blacks were not suffering the epidemic of overdoses, suicide, and alcoholism. What is needed though is an analytical framework that can show how the impact of feeling left behind or less than can translate into deaths of despair. The mediating influence is very likely to be the sense of worth that has been dented.

There is in human affairs an impulse which runs deep. It is the impetus to be valued, to be of worth. Like the wind, no one can say where it comes from. Through many avenues and multiples openings, we pursue this. In wider society, it is a social driver. The significance of significance is a key motivator in personal life. "I am a being of value" and thrive where this is unlocked. Where this is locked and blocked, I wither. Requiring significance, five years before assassination of President John Kennedy, Lee Harvey Oswald told American journalist Priscilla Macmillan "I want to give the people of the United States something to think about." In November 1963, Oswald claimed his place in history.[223]

In this chapter, we explore the question of psychopathology, or what happens when forms of distress become as malignant as cancerous cells that may invade someone's body.

Our concerns here are theological as well as pathological, remembering different languages and different disciplinary fields. The topic brings together many of the issues raised in this book so far. Theologically, our reading of human sinfulness and radical evil comes into play. Christian tradition is rooted in taking the Bible seriously about the messiness and the mire that people form and are formed by. It is not an unnecessarily dismal account of human life but an unvarnished realism. Jesus was very clear about the source of destruction and defilement:

> What comes out of a person is what defiles them. For it is from within, out of a person's heart that evil thoughts come—sexual immorality, theft, murder, adultery, greed, malice, deceit, lewdness, envy, slander, arrogance and folly. All these evils come from inside and defile a person. (Mark 7:20–23)

This is sobering diagnosis. Paul's catalogue in Romans 1 of the potential for sinful speech-acts seems to reflect this with its disturbing detail of "envy, murder, strife, deceit and malice" (Rom 1:29). This is not a rosy picture of the human condition. The fountain is polluted.

> No human being can tame the tongue. It is restless evil, full of deadly poison. . . . Can both fresh water and salt water spring from the same source? (James 3:11)

Biblically, the roots of human sinfulness lie deep underground. Versions of spirituality and holiness that seem to locate our misdeeds as conscious thoughts and actions can only be superficial and are doomed to failure. They will be betrayed by unsuspected forces and factors from within. Debate has raged about the extent and language of our depravity; whether that is total (as in Calvinism) and should we speak in these terms (as more modern theology would assert). But few would dispute with the lamentable protest in Jeremiah that the heart is tricky and with it comes our capacity for self-deceit. "The heart is deceitful above all things and beyond cure. Who can understand it?" (Jer 17:9).

There is a sharp challenge to the theory base for psychotherapy as it is a very different language and outlook. Can deep-seated malignancy in psychotherapeutic terms be mapped on to biblical language. The challenge goes both ways as it is worth asking whether our reading of biblically grounded reflection on the human condition (what is termed theological anthropology) is altered by the findings of properly validated psychology in such areas as neuroscience and human functioning generally. A clearer and more effective alignment may be needed—and to do that work often.

Psychopathology and violence—whether directed towards us or others—takes many forms and has many sources in internal dynamics. Tensions within ourselves are part of being human. Yet there is an interpretive approach to do with endeavouring to decode the meaning of violence, an attempt to read its ugly texts. What is playing under the surface when people are verbally or physically violent is laden with meaning. Psychopathology is rarely random; context and subtext is everything. Not all projects to build meaning in life is good meaning. There are numerous examples of malign meaning. Hitler ardently believed in his own significance and taught millions to find meaning in fascism.

Psychopathology refers to either the study of mental illness or mental distress or the manifestation of behaviors and experiences which may be show psychological impairment. Freud's second major work, *The Psychopathology of Everyday Life*, was about such things as jokes or mistakes in speech—Freudian slips—rather than the troubled soul.[224] It is beyond the scope of this book to outline a comprehensive theory of psychopathology. Two issues can, however, be noted briefly.

Reading the Texts of Violence

Issues of value and worth lie at the heart of psychopathology, literally, "the speech of the suffering soul." In human action that causes harm—pathological because malignant—there is much at play:

- Unconscious conflicts in which people are acting out dysfunction
- Patterns of relating that are part-objects of ourselves such as the paranoid state
- The impact of trauma that becomes unresolved
- Interpretations and enactments of experience

We propose that the essence of violence is "violentia"—a violation. Violence is an act of violation, a desecration of what is sacred, the citadel of the soul. A spiral is set up, a human tornado that feeds off desecration and in turn engenders further violation. *"I feel crap"* is part of the inner psychological environment that sets people up to doing things to compensate for the deficit, to relieve the pain.

"Violence as violation" is helpful for three reasons. It underlines how violence is an unwelcome invasion of the sacred space of an individual or group. In achieving this, the act of violence can either be physical or verbal. Thirdly, emphasizing violence as violation of sacred space shows there must be an intentionality to human violence. A "violation" or desecration carries with it the idea of violence being unwelcome and intrusive. The assumption is that humans have a sacred space, a value, a dignity, which is being forcibly invaded and infiltrated.

Violence forcibly labels victims but need not always constrain them. "Victims need to be treated like human beings first and a piece of evidence after."[225] The effect of violence or aggression, verbal or physical, is that it forcibly shapes our identity. Such labels, either adopted or projected are generated when violence occurs. Violence marks out labels and identities, bullies and bullied, criminals and victims, winners and losers.

Those who experience violence or participate in it are shown as someone to whom violence happens, someone who inflicts violence (a macho type of persona), or someone who lives in a violence—prone part of the world. Human identity is shaped by the felt interior experience of the person that positions someone in a force field of relationship power.[226] For so many, the process of forming their identity is inseparable from their experience of violence, as the abuser or the abused, dominant or the weak

An aggressor takes spray paint and paints a label on someone else marking them out as victim. It becomes part of their story. "I am a raped woman. I am a victim of violence." The terrifying use of rape as a weapon of war in Democratic Republic of Congo creates new identities: "My family refuse to eat from the same plate as me" says a 16-year old girl, rejected by rape.[227] The world is rudely divided into victims and perpetrators with far greater social taboo assigned to the former.

The notion that violence can be understood as a bid for respect is argued by James Gilligan.[228] He suggests that the mechanism by which unemployment and economic inequality stimulate violence is because both trigger feelings of shame, of inferiority. Some violent acts may be a reaction against perceived humiliation or loss of status. In acts of violence, its actors feel lack of respect—"he disrespected me." Forms of disrespect might lie in a perceived look, a verbal insult or a territorial claim. Violence is an assertion of self-respect. Violence is a forcible exchange of value, recovering someone's value through dehumanizing another. This also stands out in honor killings.

The traumatic roots of violence lie in harm visited upon us resulting in an injured psyche that looks for redress. A terrifying reality then confronts us. These strategies to re-value ourselves are transactions at the expense of another. It is a competitive market place in which my sense of worth can only be gained if yours is denied. The violent thus engage in a form of monetary calculation in which they assume there is only so much to go round. When it comes to intimate love, land and scarce resources, they may be right. Some sort of exchange is going on whereby we are driven to seek compensation somewhere and from someone. Retribution will ensure that my depleted bank account of value is filled again at your expense. The impetus to make up the deficit is then relieved.

Much violence is about an exchange, compensating for being trashed or made to feel rubbished by extracting it forcibly from someone else. Those who have a healthy sense of themselves rarely are the bullies. One young lady reported how she needed to re-create the experience of pain through rubbing soap hard into herself to blot out her overwhelming feelings of abuse. "I'm worthless. If he had just been my step-father, it might mean I had some value. But I was flesh and blood and he trashed me. He hurt me. So all I have memories is pain in my body's openings."[229]

By way of an example of this, a meta-study showed that narcissism is associated with aggression. Researchers examined 437 studies from around the world with a total of 123,043 participants. They noted that those higher in narcissism show a 21% increase in aggression overall and an 18% increase in violent aggression.[230] Risk for aggression was higher when those with narcissism felt ignored or insulted. These findings held true across different types of aggression and gender, age, and country.

Client history is replete with such raw and ragged history as domestic violence, abuse and the legacy of criminality as victims or with family members. Violence is turned on the body in self-harming and directly on the self when suicide seems the only escape from desperation.

Violence is often reproduced by those who are bereft of any sense of worth through abusive experiences, then try to scrape it off the face of victims as compensation to recover their value or to protect their own value (honor). The victims of violence have experienced jagged reality that is all around, pervasive in militancy. With searing abrasiveness, they have encountered power: the power that is at the heart of the darkness and the dark powers. In its lashing, they come up against the wanton essence of sin; the primordial power that stands over against God. Gratuitous scraping the value off the face of another as a China plate can be marked—this is what violence achieves. As the assassin of John Lennon, Mark Chapman, confessed in an interview. "I thought if I killed him, I would become him, I would acquire his fame."

Much violence in the world is driven by the motor of devaluation. Perpetrators will often have had experiences of being denigrated and depersonalized, becoming an It in the eyes of someone who is more powerful. We subject the other to the violence of devaluation because of a projection of hatred and devaluation of ourselves. We reject the stranger because we seek to expel strangeness from ourselves. Or we turn on the scapegoat as the repository of our sins and weakness because we must maintain the illusion of purity and strength.[231]

The American psychologist Rollo May saw violence as a bid for significance by the powerless: "An explosion into violence may be the only way individuals or groups can get release from unbearable tension and achieve a sense of significance."[232] It is the essence of violence that it engenders statements of an intrinsic worth being assaulted. In narratives of violence, victims report feeling stripped of their worth and dignity. Progress comes when a client can say, "this is part of me; it is not all of me!"[233] Identities need to be de-constructed, the alien element removed.

Childhood Sexual Abuse

Often, destructive behaviors become patterned into the psyche as people act out their dysfunctional experiences and move in the only world they know. Their lack of worth becomes manifested in ways to fill up the deficit and compensate through putting others down and bullying. The warp drive to claw back a sense of worth or esteem is played out in many interpersonal dramas.

Psychopathology emerges in from a nexus of worth and human value becoming defiled and trashed. It is in evidence in tragic narratives of traumatised women identifying with their own violent mothers and projecting dark feelings on to their child. It is also much in evidence in situations of abuse.

Sadly, the long-term effects of child sexual abuse are well-documented. The symptomatology includes low esteem, anxiety, shame, phobias, interpersonal issues and self-destructive behaviors.[234] An abuser is often one who internalizes both perpetrator and victim. Then he or she acts it out, maybe having witnessed domestic violence. They are trying to get their value back through the kind of people in their world that are highly prized and to whom they are apprenticed. "It's payback time!"

Childhood sexual abuse bequeaths a strong legacy of defilement.[235] The abused self is mired in shame and self-disgust. A working definition of shame is "an inner sense of being completely diminished or insufficient as a person . . . the self judging the self."[236] As Mandy Madden correctly notes, one of the problems facing both clinicians and theologians as they address shame is the failure to differentiates this from guilt.[237] There are various metaphors for shame but it is perhaps best situated in a nexus of metaphorical ecology that includes defilement, pollution and stain. People feel dirty.[238] Shame is an emotion that is felt in response to an external event that leaves someone feeling inferior, embarrassed, humiliated or with self-disgust. It refers also to a character type when shame becomes embedded and self-generated. A shame-based identity evokes feeling defective, worthless and defiled.[239] The self becomes alienated: deficient, worthless, and disowned.

Shame is a mediator of the long-term consequences of childhood sexual abuse. It is linked to mental contamination, a sense of internal uncleanness. The perpetrator contaminates. Someone feels dirty. The defiled self is infused with a sense of mental contamination, self-blame, and self-disgust—where the self serves as an object of disgust.[240] Products of the body arise from childhood sexual abuse and elicit disgust in the victim. Poor hygiene and body odors of the perpetrator will contribute to this. Abuse is commonly thought to be morally offensive. There is a question about the development of disgust in children.[241] It is in addition, not clear how disgust becomes directed towards the self.

Shame and self-disgust are clearly entwined. Does shame arise from disgust or self-disgust from shame? It part depends how these complex schemas are conceptualized. What does seem clear is that a lasting appraisal of the self is involved. The defiled self is a dirty self, to be rejected. A perceived lower status or rank is evoked with a reduction in self-directed esteem.[242] Non-offending mothers of children involved may show reactions of disgust which can then be internalized by the child. In addition to disgust and shame, childhood sexual abuse leaves ugly scars of trauma for life.

Here is a witness on record speaking of his childhood. "There is not one memory of childhood that is not clouded with humiliation or pain. He was very abusive. . . . [H]e seemed to get great pleasure from hurting me. A good abuser makes people around him protect him. My Dad told me I was worthless but Mum told me I was precious. I had to make own mind up about myself and my life."[243]

That does of course presuppose that the cognitive areas of the conscious brain can handle it!

Chapter Ten

A Theory of Emotional Cognition

"It is a remarkable thing that the unconscious of one human being can react upon that of another, without passing through the consciousness."

—SIGMUND FREUD[244]

We noted in chapter 1 the value and need of working in the here and now as well as deeper levels. The purpose of this chapter is to look at the connection between the analytical, conscious left mind and the deepest recesses of the human mind. It is clear that mind and emotion are woven together.

Neuroscience shows us that there is far more going on than we are aware of consciously. Our consciousness is more dispersed than being simply in our heads. Brain imaging has opened new pathways for how neural networks map on to what we call ego, our sense of self. "Neurological evidence supports what is called the primacy of affect (emotion) and the primacy of unconscious over conscious will."[245] The structure of mind and brain is shaped by emotional experiences and is not just a question of cognitive control.

Findings in neuroscience have sharply challenged simplistic assumptions about executive function. On the basis of old models of intelligence and cognitive reasoning, generations of children were told they will never amount to anything. Intelligence tests have largely fallen out of favour. It is not just the pre-frontal cortex that distinguishes us from other primates. Information from emotions, body and social relationships is vital for humans to navigate life. These doubts have engendered a growing interest in emotional literacy. Antonio Damasio demonstrated that judgement and decision making relies on input from areas of the brain that process emotional information and embodied awareness.[246]

Interest in solution-focused Brief Therapies is part of the trend in health provision towards something that can help people to get on with their lives in a better way. One form of this is Gestalt Therapy that can be described as "a universal or umbrella psychology, which requires the therapist to introduce whatever, in the field of the particular moment created with the particular person, enters her awareness as likely to tend towards effective therapy."[247]

It is not just a question of mind. It is hard to think of anything we call mental or emotional without bringing the body into it. Emotion may be thoughts that are experienced in the body. This relates to the importance of Cognitive Behavioral Therapies, the intervention of choice in health provision.

Since its inception in the 1960s, cognitive theory has been widely developed and researched. Protocols for addressing most psychological problems have been formulated. Dr. Aaaron Beck's 1979 book, *Cognitive Therapy of Depression*, was widely regarded as a classic text on the subject.[248] Beck focused originally on depression as benefitting from a cognitive approach.

It is closely allied in its approach with the work of another US psychiatrist, Albert Ellis, who developed a cognitive model that came to be labelled "Rational Emotional Behavioral Therapy."[249] This is still widely used as an alternative

The key idea is that of working with conscious thought processes. It is *present day* thinking rather than *past* experiences that hold the key to transformative change. Conscious thought processes shape how you feel. Faulty thought patterns arise because of core beliefs and incorrect processing. This is not to deny that experiences in early life do not have a large part to play in psychological disturbance. Rather the focus should not lie in dredging past history but concentrating on current problems people face.

CBT is a technique focused on what is going on right now. Never mind the inner drives that emanate from a realm that is notoriously difficult to pin down; focus instead on unhelpful thought patterns that cause negative emotions. Try to identify the self-critical "automatic thoughts" that occur through setbacks such as being criticized at work or rejected in a relationship. It is irrational beliefs that are causing problems but through homework, "take hold of those beliefs and change them"!

Compared with psychodynamic theories which are intended to promote insight through long term work, CBT is a short term, solution-focused therapy. It is at heart an educative model. Psychoeducation might very well be helping in recovery outcomes because results are quick and effective. It seems to make sense. Engaging in solution-focused work equips many clients with skills they can fall back on to revisit the homework they have been set that is so central to learning formats.

A session of therapy with a cognitive approach will conclude with deciding the skills to be practiced in time for the next one. Based on the topics covered, homework will help cement the techniques learnt so they can become part of the client's life. A simple set of standardised steps will be a catalyst for far more effective change. The superiority claimed for CBT is that it is based on evidence.

This is not clear cut. A raft of studies seemed to confirm this. But more recently the evidence for CBT has been questioned that seemed to show CBT getting less and less effective, as a treatment for depression, over time. A meta-analysis of CBT published in 2015 pointed to declining efficacy since 1977.[250] The UK Tavistock clinic concluded that the most severely depressed would benefit from 18 months of analysis and with much longer-lasting effects than a CBT-based form of treatment.[251] Two years after the various treatments ended, 44% of patients having psychodynamic treatment no longer met the criteria for major depression, compared to one-tenth of the others.

There are criticisms of this type of cognitive approach. Can Cognitive approaches such as CBT and CAT (Cognitive Analytical Therapy) deal adequately with the hate and rage that so often lurk deep down? By definition, these approaches are solution-focused and seek to challenge core beliefs through unwavering positivity in new learning formats. Will deep seated woundings not raise their head above conscious thought processes precisely and thus prevent lasting change?

DeYoung notes that "left brain explicit analytical reasoning . . . will only contain and manage, not solve, emotional and interpersonal problems."[252] Greenberger and Padetsky, while outlining useful strategies for cognitive change, did come to the conclusion that it is not extensive enough for abuse survivors.[253]

CBT can reinforce reliance on what is often termed left-hand brain reasoning and deepen the deficit in right-brain responses of emotional affect. This is to use the notion of brain laterality in a metaphorical way but the divide between emotion and thought seems to be valid. Or does it?

A theory of emotional cognition is long overdue. Politically, in the hands of liberal, centrist politicians, rational argument looks weak. Attachment to whatever conjures up powerful images is far more visceral than carefully calibrated argument that appeals to the head only. Feelings behind the thoughts were far more authentic. Emotional experiences were completely different. Educationally, it is what a child comes to like and indeed love that will determine subject interests and indeed career choices.

One strong move in twentieth century philosophy has been to analyze what statements are linguistically significant. Language is not a neutral activity—it is performed. Terms reflect power and affect perception. How language is constructed profoundly shapes meaning making.[254] Hidden in the healthcare model are numerous assumptions, relating not only to professional status but philosophical wrestling over previous centuries about mind and body. Famously, Descartes regarded mind and body as separate realms. The body pertains to matter and substances that have physical form and therefore spatial and open to direct investigation. Mental events were relegated to the realm of the intangible and spiritual. Such mind-body dualism was the foundation of Enlightenment thought. The big gap and mystery lay in how body and consciousness can be linked such that your thoughts as you read this can generate physical activity. If such dualism is valid, questions and practice that focus on the body are in a different realm to counseling that emphasize the mind. Our sense of the mind separate from the body might be illusory.

The pioneers of psychology and indeed psychotherapy were working in the dark regarding how the brain is organized. They were aware of neurological disorders and some, including Freud, were specialists in this area. Psychology is essentially the physiology of the brain. However, brain science as obtainable through scans were yet to be invented. The technology was not there.

The basis of neurophysiological phenomena underlying a particular psychic process observed was unknown. Moreover, there emerged a scepticism about phrenology which sought to localise areas of functioning in particular parts of brain structure. This was popular at one time. People went round comparing the size and shape of their heads: assuming it was different areas of the brain that were responsible for behavior. In theory you could cut out a bit of the brain that caused problems.

As classic forms of psychotherapy lost ground, pharmacology gained. Drugs and the whole idea of medicating symptoms came to the fore on the basis that mental problems were issues of brain chemistry. A chemical imbalance probably explained depression.

Much has changed. We now have the means of showing neural imaging networks in the brain. We can see far more clearly the mind-brain patterns of functioning as a whole unit. Cognitive neuroscience has allowed utilization of neuroimaging techniques, such as Positron Emission Tomography (PET) and functional Magnetic Resonance Imaging (fMRI). These are tools in order to investigate structures and functions of the brain both physiologically but also pathologically when disturbances and dysfunction become apparent. When developmental processes have not proceeded in a healthy way, these show up in brain scans.

Neuroscience has much to say about the structural organization of the brain and how it functions over the course of early and lifelong development. It throws much light on social interactions that sculpts individuals' becoming who they are.

It is clearer what happens when different activities are undertaken and which areas of the brain light up as it were. It is also clear what is the brain response to stress and the neurophysiology of trauma. With these powerful tools, the new landscape has acquired a new vocabulary. We speak now of:

Neural pathways: the routes in the brain through different aspects of experience are activated. Visual experience involves paths in the brain which are well-trodden. Learning a new task involves the creation of new pathways. A sequence of neurons is fired which are essentially electrical impulses passed through synapses. Sensory neurons, motor neurons and connector neurons are generally regarded as forming the complement of neurons. The terminally debilitating motor neuron disease is when instructions from the brain fail to result in action by muscles. By sending electrical signals from nerve cell to nerve cell in a vast network of connections, the brain creates thoughts as mundane as "What is for lunch?" Or "Who am I?" Or "Does God exist?"

Neural transmitters: the chemicals involved in synaptic transmission. Some are well known and have entered the popular imagination such as acetylcholine, dopamine, endorphin, and serotonin. Neural transmitters are vital in shaping subjective experience and mood as well as brain functions.

Neural plasticity: how nerve cells and brain tissue recovers from trauma or injury. Children can do this as damaged brain cells can recover through remaining brain tissue taking over. Adults can also do this but motivation and effort involved with repair and re-direction of neural pathways is high.

Synapses connect brain neurons to neurons in the rest of the body. Inspired by the work of Donald Hebb (1949) and Pavlov's "associative learning rule," it emerged that as connections between two neurons fire together, sending off impulses—the synapses—grow stronger. Learning takes place.

Neuroscience shows us that there is far more going on than we are aware of consciously. Our consciousness is more dispersed than being simply in our heads. Brain imaging has opened up new pathways for how neural networks map on to what we call ego, our sense of self. This work has challenged the primacy of the executive function of cognitive control. The therapeutic alliance, for instance, is grounded non-verbally and physiologically "outside conscious awareness and volition."[255]

What neuroscience has revealed is that it is the connections between the numbingly numerous cells that make the brain so amazing. The infant is an interactive entity replete with connected systems that communicate with each other through chemical and electrical messages. The growth of the brain represents a seething, dynamic system of responding to environment and whether the parents are responsive to the needs of the baby. Clinical psychology and clinical neuropsychology confirm this picture. To those who have worked with early relational right brain attachment trauma such as Allan Schore, deeper realms of human emotion and motivation operate at the unconscious level.[256]

These deep-seated influences were thought to be processed in the right and not the left brain. Schore argued for the centrality of the right side of the brain in development not only of the self but in how loving relationships but also psychopathology could arise. Neuroscience has much to say about the structural organization of the brain and how it functions over the course of early and lifelong development. It has uncovered the intricate and vast social interactions that sculpts an individual to become who they are. What it has *not* done is confirm the idea of two different hemispheres operating on very different terms. This idea of brain structure has been debunked.

The brain is not a muscle like other organs in the body. It has feelings and subjective experience. But are these located in say the right-hand side of the brain as the centre of creativity, intuition and emotion? The myth is that everyone has a dominant hemisphere (or side) of the brain. Left-brained people are thought to be logical and good with math and language, while right-brained people are thought to be more creative and artistic.[257] The areas of the brain work together in complex ways, and we are not, generally, left- or right-brain dominated. A team of neuroscientists at the University of Utah in 2013 had more than 1,000 people undergo brain scans while they were either lying still or reading. While the scientists did find that certain brain functions are more lateralized, they found no evidence of individuals having stronger left- or right-brain networks. Therefore, the left-brain/right-brain idea is considered a "neuromyth." "It is absolutely true that some brain functions occur in one or the other side of the brain," Anderson says. "Language tends to be on the left, attention more on the right. But people don't tend to have a stronger left- or right-sided brain network."[258]

It should be noted also that another way of understanding the brain that again cut through to popular culture is the three-brain. The idea was that different layers of the brain were built on:

i. **Survival**: The reptilian flight or fight instinctive response and autonomic reactions
ii. **Emotional**: The mammalian, emotional layer usually dubbed, "the limbic system"
iii. **Executive**: The human "cerebral cortex"

Especially important for counseling has been thought to be the limbic system, anatomically a subcortical structure that consists of structures and nerve fibres locate deep within the cerebrum. This term was introduced in 1952 by Paul MacLean to denote interconnected brain structures responsible for much of our emotional experience. It was often described as a set of evolutionarily basic or primitive brain structures located on top of the brainstem and buried under the cortex.[259]

The *Triune Brain Theory* is a poetic picture of how the brain has evolved and works in humans. It reflected one of the most persistent myths in science. Both Plato and Aristotle believed in a theory of human nature that inspired the triune brain concept. For Plato (around 400 BCE), the psyche (mind and soul) consists of three parts:

i. Rational thoughts
ii. Passions (emotions)
iii. Appetites and drives like hunger and sex

Rational thought was in charge, controlling the passions and appetites. Plato saw this as a charioteer in charge of two winged horses. Plato placed emotions in the heart, appetites in the liver and possibly other parts of the gut, and rationality in the head. But our brains are not fundamentally different from those of reptiles. All vertebrates from lizards through mammals and humans have the same general brain layout. Complexity does not mean different types of brain. There are clearly deeper layers of the brain but our brains did not develop according to an evolutionary scheme.

In psychotherapy as in everyday life, the influence of emotion on thought is considerable. It is deeper and also more influential. Can thought change emotion though and affect core beliefs?

But can we think ourselves into well-being? The problem is that we do not know our own minds. According to much modern therapy, painful emotions are something to be eliminated. Psychodynamics argue that things are much more complicated. Internal pain needs not to be eliminated so much as to be understood. We stand in awed ignorance about how little we can ever grasp about the workings of our minds. The mind is far more complex than we can grasp. Happiness is the objective of contemporary society but it is far more complex than we can suppose. We want contradictory things; and change can be painstakingly slow. We rarely realize what we invest in keeping the status quo. Life is viewed through the prism of our first set of relationships early in life of which, however, we are largely ignorant. We know so little of our own minds or of how society has programmed us and we have powerful motives for keeping things that way.[260]

Unconscious Influence

Is neuroscience uncovering evidence for deeper layers in the sense that Freud described? His mental map depicted the topography of the brain in terms of the conscious mind, the pre-conscious and the unconscious. Most mental processes are unconscious. The core functioning (brain stem and limbic system) could be said to correspond to the "id." Ventral frontal regions of the brain equate to the conscious activity of ego and superego. Neuroscientists show how cognitive processes involve both explicit memory systems at the conscious level but also implicit memory at an unconscious level.

There are many who dispute that Freud's ideas have any real relevance to the way that emotional difficulties map on to a theory of how the mind/brain works. Such things as dream states might be because of "normal" changes in brain states/chemistry rather than disguise and censorship at play.

Considerable progress has been made over the past 20 years in relating specific circuits of the brain to emotional functions. Joseph LeDoux, pioneered the study of emotions as biological phenomena, using rats to trace routes of fear. Psychologists and writers have described the churn of rage, lust, envy and shame in the human psyche. Understanding the origin and architecture of human emotions in the brain is another matter altogether though. There is evidence of a neuronal pathway that connects perception with a fear response that bypasses conscious cognitive processes. Seeing something or someone that reminds someone of a past incident triggers a response below the level of consciousness. Studies of fear conditioning show that the amygdala plays a critical role in linking external stimuli to defence responses.[261] Emotion and cognition are separate but interacting mental functions mediated by separate but interacting brain systems. This pathway does not allow for cortical processing and may be responsible for emotional responses that pass understanding.[262]

Neuroscience has also demonstrated that our earliest experiences occur before major brain structures affecting memory are formed. We cannot call them to conscious mind but they still affect us. This parallels the idea of the unconscious. The notion though that we are driven by unconscious thoughts does not itself imply that the Freudian concept is valid of a dynamic zone characterized by repression. However, following remarkable study of patients who denied paralysis of limbs, Ramachandran suggested a new conceptual framework that may help link several psychological and neurological phenomena such as Freudian defence mechanisms.[263]

Research points to four "systems" in our brain regulating motivational drives. These "mammalian" instinctual circuits overlap. They are:

i. Desire: The seeking/reward system (dopamine) governing the pursuit of pleasure.

ii. Hope: The anger-rage system that makes us want to lash out.[264]

iii. Significance: The fear-anxiety system, associated with a threat to a sense of significance.

iv. Connection: The panic system implicated in social bonding, linked perhaps to connection.

Through a biological lens, frontal regions implicated in the regulation of emotion, orbital, medial and ventrolateral frontal cortex, have been associated with the anger response. There is increased activity in these regions such that normal regulatory regions have been overwhelmed[265]

There seems to be a two-systems approach underlying two classes of responses elicited by threats: (1) behavioral responses with accompanying physiological changes in brain and body and (2) conscious feeling states associated with emotions such as fear and anxiety. One set of circuits does not seem to suffice conceptually: while the latter reflects more conscious feelings, the former operates unconsciously. A more nuanced approach is almost certainly needed when it comes to such impulses as hope, worthiness and spirituality. What areas of the brain light up when these human strivings are activated? Maybe we must wait until the deeper puzzle of what gives rise to consciousness is solved.

Relational Neurobiology

As we have seen, human beings are born into the world and form connections with attachment figures. It is the first experience of how differentiated individuals are linked with others. A template is set up which establish patterns of future relationships.

Important for counseling and psychotherapy rather than psychology as an academic study is the growing field of relational neurobiology. It is interwoven with these deeper parts of ourselves. Neuroscience throws light on how a baby's interaction with its mother shapes if and how the brain grows in the way that it should. This references the important work of Allan Schore showing that development of brain cells is a consequence of an infant's interaction with the main caregiver [usually the mother]. The growth of the baby's brain literally requires positive interaction between mother and infant. The development of cerebral circuits depends on it. If a baby is not given proper love and care in the first two years of life, the genes for various aspects of brain function cannot operate and may not even come into existence. Nature and nurture cannot be disentangled. The genes a baby has will be profoundly affected by the way it is treated and whether in time the adult has a fully functioning brain.

If it is true that 80% of brain cells that a person will ever have are manufactured during the first two years after birth, this has major implications for how the brain works but also social policy. It is well documented that chronic disadvantage reproduces itself across generations of the same families. Parents who were neglected as children so often neglect their own children. Deprivation has a malign circuit, a cycle that results in lack of educational attainment, addiction, criminality which reproduces across the generation and is so often impervious to interventions. Attempts aimed at rehabilitation so as to interrupt the persistence of early offending rarely work. Recent research indicates that a large majority—perhaps more than three quarters—of persistent young offenders have suffered from neglect in the first two years of life. If this prevented their brains from growing, they may be incapable of responding to the same incentives and punishments that will direct them towards more pro-social behavior.[266] Schore's *Affect Regulation and the Origin of the Self*[267] proposed the integration of developmental psychology and developmental biology in order to create a psycho-neurobiological model of emotional development. This is an inter-disciplinary project amongst different fields that are studying the problem of socio-affective development—neurobiology, behavioral neurology, behavioral biology, sociobiology, social psychology, developmental psychology, developmental psychoanalysis, and infant psychiatry.

There has been much interest in brain scans of orphans, neglected in virtual absence of care and loving interaction in State-run institutions in Romania during the communist regime of Nicolae Ceausescu. This was a particularly severe but time-limited form of institutional deprivation in early life experienced by children who were subsequently adopted into nurturing families. What stood out in a long-term study of 165 Romanian orphans was the lower total brain especially in prefrontal, inferior frontal, and inferior temporal areas. They grew up with brains 8.6% smaller than other adoptees. The time spent in institutions before adoption into families in the UK varied between 3 and 41 months with each additional month of deprivation associated with a 0.27% reduction in total brain volume. *Their "white matter"—the part of the brain which helps neurons communicate—was significantly damaged by their ordeal leading to poor language skills and decreased mental ability.* Early childhood deprivation affected adult brain structure, despite environmental enrichment in intervening years.[268] Despite being brought up by caring new families, emotional and social problems were commonplace. Yet one in five remains unaffected by neglect they experienced. Remarkably, *a 12-year study by Harvard University and Boston Children's Hospital in the US found those children who found loving foster homes were able to regrow missing connections and restore lost function.*

Love surely matters. Maybe love is there all along, written into that of which we are not conscious.

What is missing so far is a consistent and comprehensive theory of Mind arising from this work. What is worth stressing is that just because nothing happens without a brain does not mean that this is all that is going on. This is perhaps why there is fresh interest and indeed a conversation between cognitive neurosciences and psychoanalysis. There is now a fruitful dialogue between brain science and psychoanalysis. For example, the International Neuropsychoanalysis Society is an academic group dedicated to exploring the connections between brain science and the map of mind that the psychoanalytic theorists articulated a century ago. Its project is the neurobiological underpinnings of how we act, think, and feel. The suggestion is that as we begin to link brain activity with a psychoanalytic model of the mind at the deepest levels, a truly dynamic understanding can emerge.

Brain research supports the assertions of such developmental theorists as Winnicott, Bowlby, and Stern who studied the early origins of the unconscious: early experience is imprinted at non-conscious, nonverbal, bodily based levels, and before the conscious verbal mind operates. As Shore argues, to grasp human, overt conscious behavior, we must first understand the brain systems that operate beneath conscious awareness. An interdisciplinary perspective has shed light on what had previously been off limits. The study of circuitry regulating emotions has now become well established in all scientific and clinical disciplines, including clinical psychology. Neuroplasticity is known and justly celebrated as a healing force.[269] Knowledge of how early attachments are patterned into the brain can inform the way in which therapists work with their patients.[270]

There is a both a caution and a question here. It is to do with the relationship of biology and culture.[271] Can you reduce adult interaction to neurobiology; do mental events translate into images of the brain? Brain circuitry cannot be understood surely without reference to one's environment and the forces that shape our lives. Just because nothing happens without a brain does not mean our psychology is fixed by early events.[272]

The dynamic flux of connection with our world shapes, for example, the way self-esteem becomes influenced by gender in a growing female. We are an island chain, not separate from other islands. A sense of value must be successfully internalized for it to grow within personal life. This is vital for social connection and indeed provides its template.

Mind and Body

Brain science has underlined a recurrent debate in Western psychology and philosophy about how mind and body can possibly relate. In the Greek philosophy of Plato, mind and body were considered to be made of two different entities. Mind or soul was an immaterial substance; body was material and physical in which the soul was imprisoned. The soul existed in the world of pure forms and outlived the body. Augustine continued this approach, arguing for an immortal soul that is the real essence of someone and which survives the body. Twelve hundred years later, Rene Descartes made a strong distinction between mind and body, which was like a machine and explained by the law of nature. The soul was the ghost in that machine: it made humans different from animals.

The challenge to dualism is how a non-physical entity like mind can operate a physical body such as lifting your arm to reach for a coffee while you are reading this. There are alternatives to dualism:

i. Monism: The view that there is only one kind of entity which is physical. Mind equals brain: it is but the brain in action. Many philosophers of mind take this view, for example, Paul Churchland and Daniel Dennett.

ii. Epiphenomemon: The idea that the mind doesn't exist in its own right but goes with the body much like a shadow follows a body.

iii. The idea that no particular brain state can be mapped with a state of mind. New mental properties of mind can emerge from the brain.

Under the spotlight of neuroscience, the same area of the brain is active with visual perception as when we "see" an object in imagination.[273] There are similar close connections between activity in a brain and mental operations such as memory, decision making and even judgments like forgiveness.

Since the brain is highly complex—with the human brain having 100 billion neurons and each neuron having some 10,000 synaptic connections—it is hardly surprising that the relationship between mind and brain is complex. What has been termed the hard problem of how consciousness arises from the brain. In *Galileo's Error*, Philip Goff has pondered how science could encompass consciousness in its field of study without resorting to dualism—that there are two different kinds of substance (mind and matter). Echoing a stream of philosophic thought over the centuries, Goff's solution is panpsychism—the idea that everything is conscious.[274] This is not, he shows, a minority opinion as notable philosophers and scientists held that view. In a materialist science, matter is everything: the riddle of consciousness is solvable because Mind is a spasm of the brain. Mind really does matter![275]

CHAPTER ELEVEN

Relational Depth

Dialogue, Defences, and Disguises

"The personal emotional relation between doctor and patient was after all stronger than the whole cathartic process."

—SIGMUND FREUD[276]

THE ONE QUESTION NOBODY can ever answer is: "Of what are you unconscious?"

Approaches to access the unconscious mind have been developed since the birth of psychoanalysis. Freud's contribution was to endeavour to articulate the workings of the unconscious and devise a means by which conflicts and disturbance could be uncovered.

This goes beyond the deepest layers of psychosexual development described by psychoanalysis. Our theory of the potent force that is the human unconscious at the heart of things is the self who is a being of value, a being to whom value and purpose are the lifeblood of existence. The impetus to realize valuable personhood is crucial at the very centre of our being. Striving to be of worth is pursued against all the factors in life—both social and interpersonal—that erodes our sense of self.

It is because the pursuit of value and worth is so much part of our inner self that, especially when there has been an impaired capacity in the way we relate to others, that the role of the therapist becomes vital. The equivalent of this in times past was perhaps the wise mentor or parish priest who could become a soul friend and walk with you for a while in spiritual accompaniment. A healing alliance between therapist and hurting soul is perhaps an updated version of this for a professional age but nevertheless has the same essence of a person-to-person communication. If we think of a relationship that we have found "healing" and ask what was it about the relationship that made it beneficial, what would we say?

The focus of the therapy espoused in these pages is to bring to the surface that which lies underneath the surface that is agitating people. This includes:

- Examining relational patterns for clues to the deeper layers of the mind
- Free association (bringing statements that betray immediate reactions)
- Interpreting dreams
- Working with sand trays that many claim to be a fast route to the unconscious
- Analyzing transference and countertransference between client and therapist ("Who do I remind you of?")

Dialogue is a key concept. Encounters between internal voices and the multiplicity of selves are played out in the therapeutic relationship. A person is generally unable to change themselves though some forms of meditation and self-awareness might be able to provide some transformation. Usually, an outside person is needed to contain and hold the different forms of the internal self, different parts of oneself, that might emerge in therapy and which contain the key to healing. Dialogue prevents the change process from being self-referential. External input is needed. Internal and external dialogues are played out in therapeutic interaction.

Following William James, the psychology of the self was a turning point in centuries of reflection about the soul. The "dialogical self" brings two concepts together, self and dialogue in fruitful participation. The self is multi-voiced because the multiplicity of voices is also in the self and their mutual relationship characterize the self as "a society of the mind."[277]

A therapist actually wants to have a relationship with you. Most contemporary forms of therapy stress that the relationship that develops between the client and therapist is vital for healing work. It provides a model for how other relationships in our life can be positive and healthy.

Our theoretical formulation behind how we approach the therapeutic task matters immensely. It will be to us both resource and reference. It will give us a framework we can use numerous times. But at best, our theoretical base is an approximation, a model of how the inner world can be accessed and a human being helped. What seems to matter much more is the presence of a compassionate, dedicated therapist, and a client committed to change.

This is clearly true of person-centered therapy with its emphasis on "conditions of worth." But it is also a feature of most forms of therapy such as psychodynamic approaches. The effectiveness of therapy based on object relations is rooted in the ability to form healthy relationships through the therapeutic process. This can be transferred other relationships. Without a secure, trusting therapeutic relationship, those in therapy are unlikely to risk letting go of their internal objects of love and attachments, even if they are unhealthy.

The unconscious realm is replete with feelings locked inside a cupboard. They can still escape when there are events that triggers the original feeling. The counsellor seeks to help unlock the cupboard to let the client see what's inside. Once the client becomes aware what had caused those strong feelings, then he or she can control inappropriate behavior. Understanding that an overwhelming anger was not all caused by a trigger event would prevent blaming someone close. Not every client is suitable to receive this type of intervention as it requires them to be willing to face their painful past. Empathy and other basic counseling skills are needed for building a trusting relationship with the client for this to happen. The more painful the experience the longer it takes a client to open up.

The fact that it is in the unconscious means one does not know and has no access to what is locked up. It is in the manifestation of one's behavior, often masquerading as a defence mechanism which others find it hard to understand that can result in dysfunctional relationships.

There is an assumption built in here. It is the therapeutic relationship that heals when it becomes a way of relating between two people that is dedicated to healing. Counsellor and client participate together as a vital dyad. Something happens. Something else is going on in that open encounter.

> The therapist hopes to enable his patient to cease being a slave to old and unconscious stereotypes and to feel, to think, and to act in new ways.[278]

What, however, are the ingredients of a style of relating with healing intent? There have to be some special qualities that make that a human encounter therapeutic for clients load—bearing inner pain?

Michael Kahn explores what is perhaps the most important aspect of therapy—the therapist-client relationship. As he traces the history of the clinical relationship from Freud to the present, Kahn argued that the enmity between the humanists and the psychoanalysts limited their therapeutic effectiveness—and how their recent reconciliation has opened up exciting new possibilities for the way therapists relate to clients. This points to a new stage in the history of psychotherapy.[279]

The means of treatment has shifted. Instead of the Freudian emphasis on interpretation and free association, we have the importance of creating a lively, genuine relationship with the patient.[280]

One who gave special emphasis to this question in his counseling was Carl Rogers and his "Person-Centered" approach. In pondering the qualities that are necessary for an in-depth meeting to take place, Carl Rogers was influenced by Otto Rank, a Freudian "heretic" who had postulated that the relationship with therapist is vital. This did not sit easily with psychoanalytic neutrality. The whole conceptual frame-work of what Rogers advocated was based on his profound experience that human beings become increasingly trusting and trustworthy once they feel at a deep level that their subjective experience is both respected and progressively understood. In client-centered therapy, the person being counselled is regarded as having the capacity for self-direction towards healing, if given a safe context to explore feelings. In his seminal 1957 text, Client-centered Therapy,[281] Rogers developed conditions of the therapeutic encounter:

- Congruence
- The therapist is fully present to himself/herself, and aware of his/her feelings in the relationship
- Empathy
- The therapist is able to trace and respond to the feelings underlying the client's words and presentation—tracking the client's perception of their world
- Unconditional positive regard
- Conditions of worth

- The therapist feels an outgoing positive warmth for the client, extending to the full range of the client's feelings and attitudes and what is going on in the room.

Rogers was criticized by the ethical philosopher of "I-Thou," Martin Buber for being too individualistic and ignoring power imbalance in social interaction. Psychodynamic therapists critiqued him on different grounds; that this was an ignoring of the unconscious. Nevertheless, an empathic approach replete with warm, kind curiosity has now become an emphasis across the psychotherapy schools, even the psychoanalytic.

Relational psychoanalysis is a school of psychoanalysis in the United States that emphasizes the role of real and imagined relationships with others in mental disorder and psychotherapy. It is a relatively new and evolving school of psychoanalytic thought viewed by its founders as a "paradigm shift" in psychoanalysis.[282] Relational psychoanalysis began in the 1980s as an attempt to integrate psychotherapeutic emphasis on interpersonal interactions with the emphasis of British object relations theory on the psychological importance of internalized relationships with other people.[283] Personality emerges from the matrix of our early formative relationships with parents and other figures. Philosophically, a relational emphasis in psychoanalysis is linked to social constructionism.[284]

Because a primary motivation of our psyche is to be in relationship with others, early relationships, usually with primary caregivers, mould expectations about the way in which needs are met.[285] Desires and urges are inseparable from the relational contexts where they emanate. Motivational drivers stem from systemic interaction people have with their relational world. They may strive to re-create the pattern of early learned relationships in ongoing situations that may have little or nothing to do with those early relationships. Attempting to re-create relational patterns is a bid to meet someone's needs in a way that resonates with what they learned as infants. This re-creation represents an enactment.[286]

To treat clients, many relational psychoanalysts stress a mix of waiting and authentic spontaneity. For others, it is important to underline Winnicott's concept of "holding." Restraint is important, from which will emerge well formulated interpretations made at the proper time. Common to all relational analysts is the strong belief that psychotherapy works best when the therapist focuses on establishing a healing relationship with the client. Through facilitating insight, clients can be helped to break from repetitive patterns of relating to others that sustain psychopathology. Relational psychoanalysis places emphasis on mutual construction of meaning in the analytic relationship.[287]

Heinz Kohut was a twentieth-century psychoanalyst born in Vienna. Rejecting Freud's theory of the self as a structure, Kohut believed that a parent's failure to empathize with the child was at the heart of nearly every psychological problem.[288] Kohut's self-psychology is based on the idea that psychological problems arise from unmet developmental needs.[289] The self has four pillars:

i. The *nuclear* self, a biological construct that infants are born with.
ii. The *virtual* self is an image of the baby retained by her parents. This combination leads to . . .
iii. The *cohesive* self, though trauma, abuse, and developmental can get in the way of this.
iv. The *grandiose* self as the centre of the universe during early infancy.

The needs of the self, as Kohut suggested, are for Mirroring ("I'm just great! . . ."), Idealizing ("He's wonderful! . . .") or for Twinship needs ("I'm like her! . . ."). It is by simply sitting with the client as they experience their "void" that these needs are met in the therapeutic relationship. According to Kohut, it is empathy that can help undo some of the damage caused by unmet developmental needs.[290]

Clinical experience and empirical research demonstrate that when the therapist really cares about a client and shows a warm, caring attitude towards them, there will be improvement from therapy. It seems, however, that the converse is also true. If a client is detached and disinterested, the therapeutic process will be an uphill task. It is influenced by who the therapist is as a person as much as who the client is as a person. Each client-therapist dyad is as unique as each relationship.

Factors Contributing to Therapeutic Change

Research has identified a set of factors that contribute to positive therapeutic change independent of the particular form of therapy being practiced. What stands out is the importance of building a warm, supportive therapeutic alliance. But the therapist must also believe, along with the client that the therapy will work. Expectations bind both parties together. Effective therapy includes:

- The therapeutic relationship—how the client views the therapist and how the therapist feels but also sees the client and the transference—countertransference dynamic between them
- Who the therapist is as a person and his or her capacity to sit with and contain intense emotional experiences
- Use of specific techniques, deployed skillfully
- Empathy

Given the stress on relationality as the fundamental inner orientation, it is not surprising to learn that a therapeutic relationship characterized by empathic listening and acceptance is vital to the practice of object relations psychodynamic relief. Practitioners first try to develop an empathic, trusting relationship with a person in therapy. A context in which an individual feels safe and understood is fundamental to the practice because it follows from the theoretical base.[291]

A major contrast between how an Object Relations therapist might approach the healing task as distinct from a psychoanalyst trained in the classic Freudian approach is what happens in the working alliance.[292] The therapeutic exchange will generate much transference and countertransference but how we think about this is vital. Do resistances and projections give us important information about unconscious conflicts that need to be resolved? Or are they valuable clues as to the object relations a client formulated having carry strong resonance in the inner world? Defences might therefore be the root of the problem rather than barriers to problems in unconscious mind.

From both historical and psychoanalytic perspectives Henry Lothane dissented from some of the central ideas of relational psychoanalysis. Lothane maintains that, though Freud's theory of disorder was focused more or less exclusively on the individual, "monadic," Freud's psychoanalytic method and theory of clinical practice is consistently dyadic or relational.[293] Lothane has critiqued the term "relational" in favour of Harry Stack Sullivan's term "interpersonal."

The idea of a deeper layer of mental life underneath the radar of what is conscious has played a major role in the dramatis personae of psychological theory. Whether it stars as an unruly aspect of ourselves or as a fundamentally good and sophisticated force in touch even with a higher power and collective meme was a focus of sharp debate between two leading thinkers of the twentieth century.

Given that there is a submerged dimension of ourselves, what is the content of the unconscious? What sort of material lies down there in the great deep, waiting to be stirred like a fierce creature? And should the focus of therapy be instinctual conflicts, wish fulfilment that had been frustrated or aggressive drives within a personality—or uncovering emotional, affective experiences long buried?

The realization of the unconscious domain had been known about and discussed long before Freud. This did not mean it was accepted that unconscious mental life existed. Mental forces were thought to equate to that which was conscious. Freud's contribution was to demonstrate it was a dynamic force in human life and that accessing it offered therapeutic potential. Mental life was unconscious at least to start with. Conflicts could be cured if a reliable method could be found to access this core.

> Everything that had been forgotten had in some way or other been painful; it had been either alarming or disagreeable or shameful by the standards of the subject's personality.[294]

Of necessity, the therapy was interpretive. It was to draw out what was going on at a deep level and interpret it within the interaction of analyst and analysand, enabling re-interpretation and healing. But there was a problem. The very reason why something had been pushed down and forgotten was because it was painful to deal with and very likely shame-inducing. Even with techniques that seemed to light up a path to the inner life of human beings, for the most part they did not welcome it but fought hard against something coming to the light of day. Recognizing both the effort someone was making to keep things well and truly hidden and the corresponding effort the therapist had to make to overcome that resistance led to the psychoanalytic theory of repression.

The ego had to put in a great deal of work to prevent something coming out. Such mental disassociation was the outcome of dynamic factors in which the ego was heavily invested.

Defence Mechanisms

> The ego makes use of various procedures for fulfilling its task which, to put it in general terms, is to avoid danger, anxiety and unpleasure. We call these procedures "mechanisms of defence."[295]

Are defence mechanisms negative or positive? Slochower suggests it is important not to dismantle defences against vulnerability which help to facilitate the client's experience of their own agency, "creating a buffer against . . . humiliating exposure . . . of acute shame states." There should be a sense of respect for the client's autonomy to "access and sustain a non-humiliated self-state that would paradoxically allow both therapist and client to face the shame together which would have been elusive outside the holding experience."[296]

The concept of defence mechanisms is an example, along with the idea of the unconscious, of where psychoanalytic thought has entered popular culture. So is the linked idea of repression. "Repression" refers to the internal life: it is what we do to ourselves rather than such concepts as projective identification or splitting which are to do with what happens at an interpersonal level.

Defences arise from conflict that lies at the heart of our inner world. External reality constantly generates inner tension. Different agencies or departments of mind regulate our mental state so as to minimise anxiety. The primary defence system according to classic psychoanalysis involves repression. Because unconscious material always pursues "the return of the repressed," the purpose of the defence barrier is to ensure that anxiety will not rise up to disturb equilibrium.

By contrast, other psychodynamic perspectives see defence mechanisms through different eyes. Defences perform a service; they have formed a protective ring around the inner world. Relational models such as the Object Relations school ask what purpose the defence barrier performs. Rather than be a negative force, repressing things in order to keep them out of sight, it has been helpful to the person. Winnicot took this line[297] as did Kohut in his provocatively entitled *How Does Analysis Cure?*[298] when it comes to interpersonal transactions, Alvarez argues that defences are all part of development. A small boy projects himself through boastful claims in order to wade off inferiority. Defences are designed to overcome fear rather than the conflicted state proposed by Freud.[299]

Some have argued that such strategies are both conscious and that they are geared to handle the demands of the external world. The problem with this approach is that emotional reactions to what is going on in our environment invariably have a background in our unconscious mind which is shaping responses. Can we distinguish between internal and external aspects of coping strategies which function at the level of automatic reflex rather than being a conscious desire to suppress?

Anna Freud's stance on defence mechanisms was that they are indeed adaptive. Defences can be deployed to protect against external threats and the press of culture.[300]

In short, defence mechanisms can be normal and healthy rather than pathological; coping strategies to help the individual adjust to life. But they can also produce symptoms and lead to pathology.

In her theoretical work, Melanie Klein discusses a range of defences such as projective identification.[301] Those who followed showed how defences can solidify into "systems" such as narcissistic organization, defence organizations and pathological organizations. Rosenfeld describes a narcissistic strategy in terms of a "mafia gang" that demands emotional protection money from the good parts of the personality. The mafia gang idealizes destructiveness; the good parts are obliged to go along with it! This clearly links defence systems with the aggressive aspects of narcissism.[302]

In the hands of such theorists as Bion, structuralizing defence mechanisms can be applied to the connection between an individual psychology and social systems.[303] Groups in society might well seem to be held by destructive interactions, for example, collective narratives and memories.

Also, such mechanisms as sublimation and humour that can deflect in a socially acceptable way. Defensiveness in everyday life.

Repression has been a key concept in psychoanalysis. Freud noted that his patients had forgotten many of their experiences, especially if they were painful, alarming or shameful. He concluded that the reason for this was because the ego of the patient drew back from the constant threat. The repressed impulse was obliged to find ways of emerging, notwithstanding such resistance, which it did through neurotic symptoms.[304]

When repression fails, mental illness in the form of severe neurotic forms will arise. In this model, the ego acts as a sort of executive, closely regulating what is or what is not allowable. Repression is necessary for civilization. Without repression, unconscious impulses will burst out unconstrained.

The aim of therapy therefore is to bring these hidden dynamics into the light of day for mature, conscious judgement to sort out what is allowable and what form that can take.

Transference and Counter-Transference

In psychodynamics, notions of transference and counter-transference became hugely important. Material from the infantile unconscious seemed to be in dynamic flux with the relationship the patient is experiencing with the therapist. Analyzing transference came to be a requirement for cure. It was a route to the unconscious.[305]

There are different ideas on what these are and the role they play (according to the school of thought). Is transference the expression of instinctual wishes?

In the period of his association with Breuer, Freud initially saw transference as something that got in the way, as contamination generated by the influence of the therapist on the patient. He came to view transference as being therapeutically useful. He grasped that "he was the recipient of affections that belonged to an important figure in the patient's life."[306] Kleinian work sees transference in terms of how unconscious phantasy is being represented.

What though is being transferred? Is analyzing transference material a strong guide to the unconscious and therefore of great help when it comes to therapeutic intervention?

Counter-transference represents emotional responses of the therapist to what is emerging. Perfectly aware of love's manifestation in the analytical situation. Freud has described transference love as both resistance and as an extreme variant of normal falling in love.[307] The view since is that interplay between patient and analyst allows for exchange of meanings. Caution is needed. "Any interpretation that is based upon interactive communication needs to be linked to some identifiable cues from the patient, that he or she can recognize when made aware of them."[308]

This underscores how imperative the therapeutic relationship is. Cozolino argues that psychotherapy is an interpersonal learning experience, in which someone is likely to learn more when supported by a nurturing, empathetic counsellor.[309] When a client trusts their therapist, they are likely to share the more vulnerable parts of themselves, allowing space for deeper exploration.[310]

What happens when and how a therapist meets a client at relational depth is similar to what it is like to relate deeply to another person in another context.[311] Internally, people talk about feeling energized and experience an emotional intensity that feels like an electric spark. Between people there are often powerful feelings of connection, closeness and intimacy (a heart to heart encounter). The meeting is described in terms of mutuality and equality. These moments of connection are experienced notwithstanding different theoretical orientations, especially when the therapy is long-term. They are somewhat gendered: a male therapist will tend to experience less connection with a male client. Evidence shows that the more relational depth is a reality, there will be greater improvement and potential for change. An increased connection with their own selves will result. Beyond a professional duty, the key is a genuine very real commitment and sense of care.

One extraordinary finding of neuroscience is to use tools such as EEG, MEG, fMRI, and NIRS to scan what is happening in social interaction involving reciprocal exchanges in depth.[312] Emotional transmission and co-regulation of brain dynamics lie at the heart of the therapeutic relationship. Inspired by work on mother-baby transactions, it has been shown that adult, interpersonal exchanges share attention and cues of all sorts in which both parties are modifying their actions. This is paralleled with what has been going on in the clinical literature in the direction of as two-person interpersonal psychology. The old one-brain neuroscience has much less validity.

The emerging field of interpersonal neurobiology (IPNB) suggests complex interrelationship between the mind, the body, the brain (including genetics), the environment, and especially the role of close relationships.[313] IPNB strongly emphasizes the role of attachment relationships across the whole spectrum of caregiving—ranging from parent-child to teacher-student to professional-therapeutic—in shaping both the brain and the mind.[314] Recent findings in neuroplasticity, memory, and brain differentiation have helped shape an integrative paradigm for psychotherapy. Psychotherapy is thus becoming understood not simply as a transfer of factual information but as interpersonal learning that occurs implicitly and explicitly. "Theories of psychotherapy must take seriously the role of the therapist as an image-bearer of God who provides clients with opportunities to learn new ways of understanding their behaviour and relating to themselves, others, and God."[315]

Such an approach points to careful integration of Christian theology with sophisticated psychology.

What matters most may not in fact be the theoretical stance but an interpersonal relationship characterized by warmth and trust. Irrespective of the type of therapy, a client must believe that the therapist will at least try to understand and is concerned about the challenges faced.[316]

That stance is likely to win the trust of a client. In turn, such empathic warmth will generate confidence of success. As Brian Thorne notes, the client can be trusted to find his own way forward if only the counsellor can be the kind of companion who is capable of encouraging a relationship where the client can be trusted to find his way forward.[317]

PART TWO

Domains of Disturbance

REMA Questions

Chapter Twelve

Relationality and Object Relations

"In providing his patient with a secure base from which to explore and express his thoughts and feelings, the therapist's role is analogous to that of a mother who provides her child with a secure base from which to explore the world."[318]

First Domain—What is happening in patterns of relating? "Who do I remind you of?"

When people in distress come for counseling, they are living out their story. This is deeply intriguing. Here is a client aged 35. As Jung observed, this is now an age when they are in search of their souls. But what about the anger that the child carried from an experience when they were ten? Something really significant happened to them clearly which is affecting their story hugely.

Here is someone who lost a twin in the womb.[319] All their lives, they have been unconsciously re-enacting the connection they yearn for from deeply imprinted bonding. This will be a theme that presents itself through attachment styles and it requires meaning to be created as it is drawn out.

Grasping the immense complexity of how human beings function needs to be based on an understanding of their development. We are all the outcome of our story—a story still being written.

The first domain in which we explore counseling and psychotherapy is to say that human beings are deeply relational. For the most part this would not be seen as ground-breaking. It will be commonly understood that relationships are key to the human story; that humans are profoundly social beings and do not thrive if we are isolated. However we understand the term, we were made for community, for association. We have a social brain that at some level is networked with others.

The interpersonal dimension of psychotherapy is strongly emphasized at this time. Guides such as "Interpersonal Psychotherapy" can be used to provide scripts for treating depression, bipolar disorder, anxiety and eating disorders and post-traumatic stress.[320]

Our lives can be depicted as a series of concentric circles in which we relate.

i. Self to itself—different parts of us if we are conflicted
ii. Self to immediate network of significant others
iii. Self to local community and town
iv. Self to those with whom we are grouped in a national identity
v. Self to the wider world

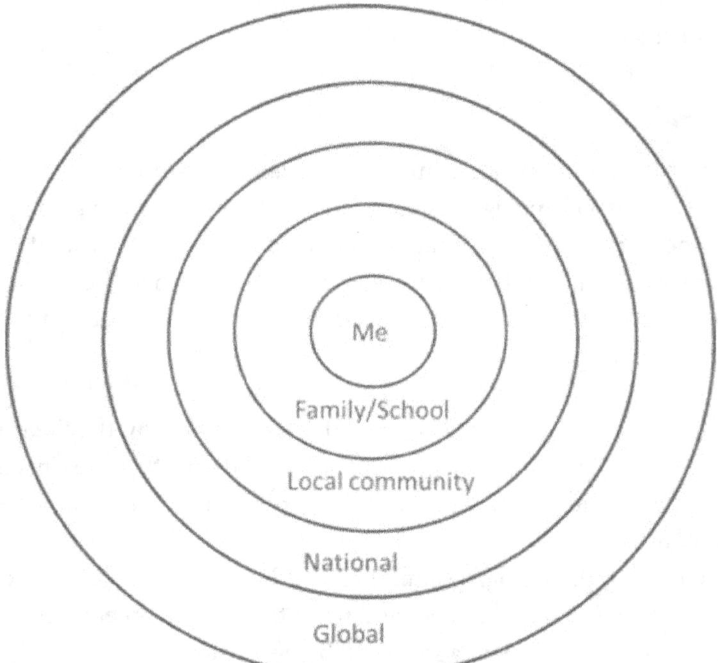

The question for Christian theology is whether there is a further sphere of relating which is to God or at least some sense of the ultimate, the transcendent horizon of what lies beyond ourselves?

This is similar to the model of human development proposed by Urie Bronfenbrenner whose ecological systems theory suggested that people play out their lives in different social environments at the same time. The analogy used is that of Russian dolls where each is inside the other. Multiple layers of our social ecology represent contexts in which we live, move and have our being simultaneously. Child development is a complex system of relationships affected by multiple levels of the surrounding environment. Human development cannot be studied in isolation but must look at the interaction of the larger environment as well as the child and the immediate environment.[321]

Bronfenbrenner maps the social world of interaction with the child through four different systems:

i. The *microsystem* of immediate interaction that the child is experiencing immediately.

ii. The *mesosystem* such as school and friends that the child participates in simultaneously.

iii. The *exosystem* of social networks the child is affected by but not directly involved with.

iv. The *macrosystem* shaping the culture and ethnicity, political system and institution.

The person cannot then be isolated from the field which constitutes their setting. This multiplexity of system analysis might be acceptable in theory as a broader view and conceptualization. How it can be studied in social research is a question how it can be used as a basis for interpretation? Client experience is enmeshed in multiple systems at the same time. Each environment affects the other.

Bronfenbrenner's theory is one of a number of models of human development. From Rousseau onwards, social theorists have been interested in the inner child. Developmental theorists have been inclined towards Stage Theories that set out defined stages of the growth of a person. Leading theories of human development are usually Stage theories. There are clear phases that children go through and will move beyond to the next level with its own set of characteristics.

Transitions

Today my history is being lived out. Psycho-social development is about what happens to people at different stages of their lives.

But is this at clearly defined stages? Stage theories emphasize age-related periods. You don't skip a stage. Will people at similar stages will act the same? Or will it be more of a continuous stream of change and gradual development? There are various models of human development. A model is a means by which people try to make sense of their world. Most models will incorporate nature and nurture. Every psychologist agrees that both heredity and environmental factors interact. Some theories emphasize a biological viewpoint and some a sociobiological stance in which external factors are most important in shaping personality and how we respond to the world.[322]

According to the stage theory of *cognitive development* suggested by Jean Piaget (1896–1980), who presented children with problems to solve, knowledge is not a set of facts but action-children are acting on something either physically or mentally.[323] They sort their knowledge so it can be useful (organization). Everyone must adapt to its environment in order to survive (adaptation).[324]

We could cite the pre-set plan (epigenetic principle) suggested by Eric Erikson and his *eight stage of model of psycho-social development.* If children develop trust, they can grow to the next level for exploring their world: Unlike Freud's theory of psychosexual stages, Erikson was interested in how social interaction and relationships played a role in the development and growth of human beings.

- i. Trust vs. mistrust (a sense of trust)
- ii. Autonomy vs. shame or doubt (a positive sense of autonomy)
- iii. Initiative vs. guilt (implementing their own ideas)
- iv. Industry vs. inferiority (learning skills both academic and social)
- v. Identity vs. role confusion (adolescence and a sense of who they are)
- vi. Early adulthood (attainment of intimacy)
- vii. Middle age (must find a way to stay productive and be of help)
- viii. Old age (developing a sense of pride about their achievements)

Fail to successfully complete a stage can limit your ability to progress further stages leading to a more unhealthy personality and sense of self. The good news is that the individual can play catch up and resolve these successfully at a later time. Each stage constitutes a psycho-social crisis. For example during the ages of 5–12 the test comes along the lines of Industry (competence) vs. Inferiority, the child can gain approval by showing skills that are valued by society. If the child cannot develop the specific skill that is highly prized, for instance being sociable or sporty, a sense of Inferiority might ensue. Though this theory stresses psycho-social development through the life course, can we test it experimentally? It is very general statement of personality development.[325]

> The adolescent mind is essentially a mind or moratorium, a psychosocial stage between childhood and adulthood, and the morality learned by the child, and ethics to be developed by the adult.[326]

The behavioral approach is widely seen as a very mechanical approach to human development. It is the social environment that shapes behavior. Change environment: then behavior changes. Behavioral approaches involve the process of learning using classical and operant conditioning (reinforcing behavior-rewards or penalties).[327]

Vygotsky argued that the basic unit of study is not the individual but the child in a social context. This is the social learning approach: learning by observing and imitating others. Within the dominant culture, subcultures exist teaching the kind of skills needed for that context. Working with a competent partner (an adult) in zone of proximal development, children can learn more effectively. Vygotsky argued for the four stages of cognitive development, which include the sensorimotor stage, the preoperational stage, the concrete operational stage, and the formal operation stage. For Vygotsky, childrens' development must necessarily precede their learning: "Learning is a necessary and universal aspect of the process of developing culturally organized, specifically human psychological function."[328] Vygotsky states the importance of cultural and social context for learning. Cognitive development stems from social interactions from guided learning within the zone of proximal development as children and their partner's co-construct knowledge.[329]

Freud's psychoanalytic theory proposed psychosexual stages, entailing an unfolding of sensuality and pleasure. The first five years of life are crucial to the formation of adult personality.[330] The unconscious must be controlled in order to satisfy social demands; this sets up a conflict between frustrated wishes and social norms. Sexual tension (defined broadly) is released through the oral, anal, phallic, latency, and genital stages. During each stage libido is expressed in different ways and through different parts of the body. A particular conflict must be resolved before the individual can successfully advance to the next stage. It might be that tension was not resolved, which leads to frustration. Or it might be that a particular stage (such as the oral) was so pleasurable that the child in the adult is fixated, for example, on deriving pleasure from kissing rather than sexual intercourse.

Theorists have distinguished between forms of pleasure that babies experience. There is delight when a new skill has been achieved or a discovery made (meaning-finding). There is pleasure in social interactions, especially in synchrony with the mother. There is a homeostatic pleasure when physical satisfaction has been achieved and relieved—what Winnicott saw as orgasmic.[331] And there is the more overtly auto-erotic, for example movement such as tickling or thumbsucking.

Me or Not Me

In this book, we cannot possibly do justice to the milestones that mark the path of who we are. Here are the main features of that story up the age of five.

It is clear that family traits and heredity can affect someone's temperament. Genes from father and mother can combine to form new traits. Heritability (the proportion of differences due to genetic factors) varies but siblings, for example, share 50% of their genes in common.

In early childhood, there is little sense of what is me or not me. Life is experienced life through the body. A key concept was that of "narcissism." In a key 1914 paper, Freud defines it as infatuation with one's own person, the adoration someone accords themselves as an object of sexual desire. He views auto-eroticism and narcissism as some sort of neurosis. Yet everyone has a level of narcissism throughout their developmental course. In his paper, Freud differentiates between two types of narcissism, primary and secondary narcissism. Primary narcissism is latent in all human beings by which narcissism stirs the affection of individuals towards an object. It is the same type of energy evident in young children who believe themselves to be super beings worthy of adulation. Then comes love for others. As Freud observes, whoever loves becomes humble. Those who love have yielded a part of their narcissism. Freud suggested that secondary narcissism develops when individuals turn this object affection back on themselves. As a result, an individual is cut off from society, pre-occupied with itself and disinterested in others. The inability to express love to others and have it reciprocated causes an individual to seek self-preservation. Paradoxically, narcissists given to self-adoration often have low self-esteem, are full of shame, guilt and very defensive.[332]

Narcissism means that love of oneself merges with everything else. Nothing else exists apart from oneself as if we are the only person in that reality. Gradually we realize there are two. A sense of self-value unfolds through life. It is linked to developmental stages as value is instilled. In a healthy process of maturation and emotional regulation, the young child moves from:

i. **Me**: There is one single entity (His Majesty the Baby as Freud noted in his 1914 paper on narcissism).[333] The ego forms during the oral stage of psychosexual development. During this time, the child is highly egocentric and the centre of the world. Needs and desires are being fulfilled by his mother.
ii. **Two**: A diad of mother and baby as attachment security correlates with sensitivity to a child's needs
iii. **Three**: Other caregivers become important to teach ego-strength in response to an external world
iv. **Four:** The world of people and communities as a child might start to learn love for others.

In the second half of the first year, self and the external world are differentiated and begin to be structured. The external world can be differentiated and manipulated. Separating what is internal to us and what is external is crucial to human development. Self-differentiation enables the growth of the self. As we will see with regard to attachment theory, there is awareness of loss though the hope also of return. The baby is unable to control external reality. This leads to rage. The sense of self is born amidst aggressiveness as Winnicot observes. Frustration and enjoyment coexist. The differentiation of self develops as the infant gets to know itself. Switching occurs with great rapidity as the bad mother is denied when the infant is once again picked up and cuddled. She has become the good mother once again. The child wants to keep the image of mother as benign.[334]

In this brief resume of human development and how emotional blockages might begin to form, it is worth noting also the formation of guilt and shame between one and two years of age. A child might feel coy or bashful. A sense of self is easily damaged. Shame comes as the child wants to run and hide if an adult laughs as a result of something that has been done. To avoid the embarrassment, defence mechanisms such as splitting which results in projection or denial which saves the young child from confusion.[335] The British Object Relations School observe that the child up to about three relates to part objects—a loved one or a hated one. Resolving the ambiguity leads to whole object formation. Often this never happens.

Anna Freud noted that the symbolic play of children bears resemblance to dreaming by way of working through the experiences of the day. A good game satisfactorily resolves leaves a child calm as if waking from a good night's sleep.[336] Psychoanalysts have, however, discussed ruthless play (not just mutual play) where there is little concern for another and there is mocking cruelty. A boy is smacked by his mother and responds by being cruel to his little brother. Such fantasies emerge in adulthood, regardless of whether there is conscious awareness of aggression. They were repressed. Unconscious play has a big part in neurotic symptoms, being "compulsively caught in highly charged ruthless games locked within the mind."[337] It is at the three to five year stage of life that the Oedipus Complex was hypothesized by Freud, focusing on the genital stage. There is no resolution of an impossible conflict and the child learns to accept reality. This is a controversial formulation!

The Relational Turn

Psychological theory needs to take into account an insatiable thirst to be recognized, to be noticed.

We are gripped by an unaccountable sense that we matter, that we have dignity. The status of a sense of valuable self is difficult to assign. Is it an impetus adhering to the conscious, experiencing mind, a drive emanating from the hidden, unconscious realms? Does it work on distinctly separable brain circuits and chemistries? Where, however, do we acquire such knowledge?

The basis of the relational psychodynamic therapy advocated here is that we need to have good relationships with others. Its roots are in depth psychology (particularly contemporary relational psychoanalysis), interpersonal neurobiology, the dialogical philosophy of Martin Buber, the theological idea of the sacredness of the person and the working alliance between client and therapist. Unlike some forms of therapy, this approach looks at how social realities like culture, race, class and gender might be affecting the power dynamics between a client and other people.

The value of people is repositioned here *as a psychosocial dynamic driver*, not just an ethical imperative. High value is a powerful motivation. Where not forthcoming in our social or interpersonal world, something happens inside. Theological reflection and psychology underpinning the study of human beings can talk to each other. It is a two-way street. Where they can meet is around human worth—both a deeply theological idea *and* a social science construct that does heavy lifting.

The movement towards relation and not looking at an individual entity only has a distinguished history in thinking about how people and societies function. We briefly note this in fields such as:

- **Philosophy**: Things exist and function only in relation to other things. This is "relationalism," a philosophical mode of thought that takes relations among people and events as primary, over and above conceptions of simple particularity or abstraction. In branches of physics such as special relativity, reality is understood only by looking at the positions of objects in relation to other objects in its field. A strong emphasis in the Western imagination has been the primacy of an individual or the experiencing subject. Descartes famously proclaimed "I think therefore I am" as the basis for the undeniability of the thinker and the distinction between subject-object. What relationalism does is to assert the primacy of relationship as constituting identity and subjectivity. The legacy of Descartes is reductionism to an individualism that disavows what we most truly are. We are what we are in connection with something else and that includes someone else. Ideas such as Hegel's "mutual recognition" or Heidegger's "being-in-the-world" have offered alternatives to subject-object dualism.[338]
- **Theology**: Consensus amongst theologians is that the relational model of personhood has prevailed and derives from a relational understanding of the Trinity.[339] This offers considerable explanatory potential for conceptualizations of the self in psycho-social contexts.[340] However, the focus of this relatedness tends to be that of "the self's conversation with itself"[341] or the inter-relatedness of male and female.[342] The focus is on interpersonal transactions;

less about social imperatives and wider realities of different cultures where we are embedded. Genesis 1:26—made in the image of God—is but the starting point for the notion that humans have immense value. The "imago dei" is used very sparingly in the Bible. Yet since the strong implication is that a divine person is inherently relational, the implication for human personhood is that this too is inherently relational, bearing in mind the next verse "Male and female he created them" (v. 27). As Barth recognized, in his pioneering work on a relational view of the divine Trinity, human sexuality is a fundamental feature of our existence.[343] Many scholars followed him in this idea.[344]

- **Ethics**: As inherently relational beings we are co-implicated in each others' lives, and drawn into responsibility for those with whom we stand in relation. We stand in intricate and intimate webs of connection with all those with whom we come into contact—be they human or animal, animate or inanimate. Emmanuel Levinas wrote of psychology as being about recognition, not cognition only. What is it that enables us to stand in relation to another whereby intersubjective recognition brings a sense of ethical responsibility?
- **Social theory**: Relationality as the ontological foundation of the social world, primarily constituted by relations among social "actors" not actors themselves. How do we think of the social world? Static or as unfolding of dynamic patterns? This relational perspective was introduced by some of the founding fathers of sociology, such as Karl Marx and Georg Simmel, but during the last few decades has become the predominant approach within the study of social networks and systems. The idea of the "trans-action" highlights the "relational" approach in sociology, where entities are not conceived as something ontologically independent of, or logically antecedent to, the relations they establish; substances acquire their ontological status within their relations.[345]
- **Psychology**: The relational perspective comes out in the early object relations theories of Fairbairn, Guntrip, and Winnicott that quickly emerged to challenge Freud's original drive theory with its implicit focus on the individual ego. Developmental theory is more relational.

Our relations to others play a part in mediating our knowledge of self. Our sense of self is evoked through interaction with other selves; other humanities that calls to our own humanity. As has been argued here, psychology needs to take on board where we are in relation to others but also our social context into which we are "thrown," to use the terminology of Heidegger.[346] We are always socially situated. This is true also of our theological anthropology which is informed and illuminated by the "turn to relationality." It is this relation to relationality that characterizes the approach here.

Paradoxically, it is in relationship that value in oneself is born and made secure. Human life is characterized by a longing for a secure link to another; the desire for connection noted already. This has clear theological underpinning. Christian theological anthropology would be unthinkable without doctrines such as incarnation, Trinity, sin and the very nature of our humanity. These ideas are inherently relational.

Philosophical history discloses a major strand in which the relation of entities to each other and not just the essence of things in themselves comes under scrutiny. From Aristotle onwards, the emphasis has tended to be on "substances"; what things are in themselves. The substance stayed the same no matter what happened to it (the "accidents" of circumstances and relations). The philosopher G. W. F. Hegel argued that the basic separation of substance and accident was misplaced. "Substance" should include the totality of the whole. Subjectivity is a higher category than substance; being is subsumed into becoming.[347] Despite his critique of Hegel, for Kierkegaard, relationality was also a key concept.

Gestalt Therapy and Relationality

Relationality is increasingly important for psychotherapy. An important principle of Gestalt therapy is that the human being is "dialogical," i.e., formed in connection with others. "Otherness" and connection are experienced at the "boundary" between persons. The "between" is thus the focus of therapeutic work. The ethical philosopher Martin Buber is a key influence on this work with his articulation of the radical difference between "I–Thou" and "I–It" relations. The human being strives for moments of deep I–Thou connection.

The shape of a human life is defined by a reaching for secure, loving relationships. Relational Development—especially early years—is of the greatest significance for laying healthy foundations for adult life. This in turn has enormous significance for therapeutic work. What though is a relationship? Broadly defined, a relationship is contact between animate beings which involves each taking notice of the other. Recognition or noticing, is fundamental. Whether it involves fleeting connections, functional connections, relationships of emotional exposure, or relationships of manifest commitment, relating to others constitutes the human story.

As Hycinth and Jacobs argue, the human heart yearns for contact—above all it yearns for genuine dialogue. Dialogue is at the heart of the human. Without it, we are not fully formed—there is a yawning abyss inside. With it, we have the possibility of our uniqueness, and our most human qualities emerging. Each of us secretly and desperately yearns to be "met"—to be recognized in our uniqueness, our fullness, and our vulnerability. We yearn to be genuinely valued by others as who we are, even that we are. The being of each of us needs to be revered—by ourselves and by others. Without it we are not fulfilled—we are not fully ourselves.[348] We are in a loop of reciprocal relations.

What we are, we are in relationship. This might be our relationships with family, colleagues, partners. We have a strong imperative to have balanced, trusting relationships with others that are emotionally satisfying. Relationships are a screen on which we project our inner world and act out our psychodramas. It is in relationship that we can be healed and new ways of relating found.[349]

Depression or anxiety often can be located in difficulty and breakdown in relationships, or an inability to connect. We need to be connected yet often have a tendency to push people away or we may have difficulty finding and forming connection and romance. We may be using strategies of disconnection that disrupt close bonds and leave upset people in their slipstream.

Many of life's problems are relational: that is, they are disturbances formed in relation to others. Note the prevalence of relationships to the "personality disorders" (styles) according to the DSM-5.

i. Paranoid: people/the world are against me
ii. Schizoid: the world is unsafe, dangerous
iii. Schizotypal: relationships are deeply threatening
iv. Antisocial: other people don't figure, don't matter
v. Borderline: the world is crazy and I don't know who I am in it

vi. Histrionic: I'm okay if I am loud and make myself seen (often seductively)

vii. Narcissistic: I'm not allowed to be weak, I have to be great

viii. Avoidant: I can't cope with relationships, I'm inadequate, my failures prove it

ix. Dependent: I can't exist without someone to take care of me

x. Obsessive-compulsive: I have to keep a tight control so I don't go wrong

Therapies place different emphasis on impairment of capacity for healthy interaction with others. Cognitive behavior therapy will address the beliefs that a client has that shape mental working models about the behavior of others and how past experiences are making us relate to others in ways that leave us unhappy. Past relationships shape assumptions we make about how present and future relationships should work. Freud's focus was on psychological conflicts per se: probing the role of resistances to change in the difficult endeavour of understanding oneself. This might well cause us to engage in regular sabotage of connection with others. The British Object Relations school of thought examined the internalized impact arising from splitting the objects of our love and desire.

We can draw though, not only on psychodynamic traditions but on a fast-developing interpersonal neuroscience to show that relationships build our brains. It is central to the human situation that we live in constant relationship to others. Interaction is vital to regulating our emotional and social behavior. We are social creatures with inter-dependent, interwoven brains and biologies. Our brains exist in relationship to other brains; indeed our brains are a social organ built through experience. The focus of advances in interpersonal neurobiology (IPNB) is from individual brain structures to functional neural systems. The brain is activated when we are thinking about others and ourselves. How do we come to know others and whether the notion of an "individual self" is anything more than an evolutionary strategy to support our interconnection is an issue.[350]

From an IPNB perspective, humans are psychosocial beings comprised of two interdependent facets in the form of mind and brain but also mind-brain and relationships as irreducible aspects of interaction.[351] Siegal proposes a triangle of human experience conceptualized as mind, brain (including the flow of information throughout the body) and relationships in the form of connection with others. The latter could be extended to include communication with God.

Gerson suggests the relational unconscious is the fundamental structuring property of each interpersonal relation. There are modes of engagement specific to a dyad and influences subjective experience. The field between two parties constitutes "thirdness" aligned with unconscious processes and intersubjective resistances—clinical manifestations of the relational unconscious.[352]

Object Relations

A departure from classic psychoanalytic theory that humans are motivated by sexual and aggressive drives is Object Relations Theory. Humans are primarily motivated by the need for connection with others, to form relationships.[353] What happens if we internalize love objects that are incompatible? They can't both be loved at the same time. Two different kinds of identification live alongside each other. Object relations theorists stress the importance of early family interactions, especially the mother-infant relation. Confusion arises because the term "objects" seems to refer to inanimate entities and is impersonal. This is a misrepresentation. It refers to the objects of love, attachment and desire for those to whom an individual relates, be it mother, father, or primary caregiver. However, the term "object" can also refer to a part of a person, such as a mother's breast, or might signify mental representations of significant others.

The term "object relations" can speak of the dynamic internalized relationships between the self and objects in the form of significant others. An object relation involves mental representations of:

- The self in relation to the object
- The relationship between self and object
- The relationship itself

A young child might think:

- "My mother is good feeds me when I am hungry" (The object as perceived by the self).
- "She takes care of me so I must be good" (representation of self in relation to the object).
- "I love my mother" (the representation of the relationship).

The focus of object relations is the mother-infant relationship. Infants form mental representations of themselves in relation to others. Such internal images significantly shape subsequent interpersonal relationships. Given healthy development, such mental representations evolve over time. Where there is unhealthy development, the images remain at an immature level. Whether healthy or unhealthy, these internal images endure to serve as templates for future relationship patterns. Initially, the neonate infant might form two contrasting mental representations. One image is that the caregiver is deemed to be good if its needs are met. By contrast the image is "bad" if the needs of the infant are not satisfied. The process of separating objects into "good" and "bad" parts is known as "splitting." Infants first experience splitting with regard to the primary caregiver: both aspects of the object (the caregiver) are separate. If the mother is able to satisfactorily meet the needs of the infant, the mother is "good enough.

The three early theorists about object relations brought different approaches.

Melanie Klein was a key figure in developing the object relations approach. She engaged in direct observation of infants and young children but the conclusion she drew differed from the classic positions of Freud: they were more concerned about relationships with those who care for them than the need to control sexual impulses secreted from the body. Whereas Freud had emphasized the first few years of a child's life, Melanie Klein was interested in the first few months.

The Kleinian school considers the role of the life and death instincts (libido and thanatos), the depressive position and relationships, developmental and anti-developmental relationships. The Freudian landscape looked different. With its fantasies of the death of the same-sex parent so as to usurp, the Oedipus complex was still central. Phantasies about the maternal body were now associated with new understandings of both the male and female complexity. For Klein, the Oedipus complex and the depressive position are closely linked. Given increasing awareness of whole and not just part objects that previously had been seen ambivalently, reality leads to the imperative to relinquish oedipal desires and to repair the internal parents, allowing them to come together.[354]

She took psychoanalytic thinking in a new direction by recognizing the importance of our earliest childhood experiences in the formation of our adult emotional world. Klein drew on her analysis of children's play to formulate new concepts such as the paranoid-schizoid position and the depressive position. What do these signify? The "paranoid-schizoid position" is a range of anxieties, defences and internal and external object relations characteristic of the earliest months of an infant's life. These mental states are thought to play an important part throughout life. The paranoid-schizoid position involves the splitting of both self and object of desire into good and bad. A developing child splits both ego and object. That leads to projection of life and death instincts (loving and hating) into separate parts of the mother (or breast). A maternal object is separated into a "bad" breast (felt to be frustrating) and a "good" breast (felt to be loving and gratifying). The former leads to rage and aggression. Both "good" and the "bad" objects are then introjected into the unconscious. A cycle of re-projection and re-introjection thus ensues, with at first little or no integration between them.[355]

This "binary splitting" is essential for healthy development as it enables the infant to take in and hold on to sufficient good experience to provide a central core around which to begin to integrate the contrasting aspects of the self. Extreme paranoid anxieties and schizoid defences are largely given up during the early infantile paranoid-schizoid position and during the working through of the depressive position. Central to the latter is that hateful feelings and phantasies about the loved object had been perceived as two separate part-objects: ideal and loved; persecuting and hated. But in the depressive position, the infant feels anxiety is also felt for the object. This is the birth of love. However, Klein holds that schizoid ways of relating are never given up completely and her writing gives the impression that the positions can be conceptualized as transient states of mind.[356] It can stay with someone. The depressive position also refers to the experience, at any stage of life, of guilt and grief over hateful attacks and how external and internal objects are damaged. The impact can range from normal mourning for loss to severe depression. This can stay with you.

The Scottish psychiatrist Ronald Fairbairn retained a theological interest as well as psychoanalyst.[357] He is associated with a theory of mind in which the libido is not primarily pleasure-seeking (as in Freud's delineation based on the desire to gratify instincts.). Rather what is fundamental and more urgent in us all is our search for relationships.[358] The libido does not seek simply to discharge energy through using an object but it seeks the object for itself. Influenced by Melanie Klein, Fairbairn underlined her suggestion humans are object-seeking, not pleasure-seeking. In their development, individuals move gradually from infantile dependence on the caregiver toward a state of interdependency when they can also be relied upon.[359] Fairbairn's pioneering thinking about borderline states is still used today in treatment.[360] He described a "splitting" process which was a defence against the pain of being rejected when parents were insufficiently attentive. The child splits off the emotionally responsive experience of parents from the unresponsive aspects. The ego splits off into "good"-"bad." Thus "good" and "bad" objects are created and leading to borderline states.[361]

A third leading figure in the British Object Relations school was Donald Winnicott who underlined the need to raise children in a context when they are encouraged to develop inter-dependence and indeed independence. They also know that their caregiver will protect them from harm. If the caregiver is not attentive to the needs and potential of the child, a false self is waiting in the wings to form. Winnicot said it must be communicated that your baby is worth getting to know as a person; for gradually, the baby is becoming a person. It seems that to be worthwhile and be able to cultivate self-respect, we have to be worth something to someone—if not parents then grandparents or carer. If one does not feel worth very much, it is because uncertain messages have been downloaded from when your inner computer was switched on. The mysterious, daring feeling that we are worth something is the foundation of accepting yourself. As young children, we start to pick up messages that tell us we cannot be ourselves because we are not good enough. When we come to construct the awareness of a self, these messages have a strong influence on foundations of who we are. We can address these aspects of themselves so as to live more authentically.

Winnicot proposed the concept of the "good enough mother," who looks her baby in the eye and by mirroring the child's face shows the child that he or she is known, safe and seen. The most essential parenting psychological function, Winnicot suggested, is "eye-love."[362] "The good-enough mother . . . starts off with an almost complete adaptation to her infant's needs, and as time proceeds she adapts less and less completely, gradually, according to the infant's growing ability to deal with her failure."

Each of their theories place great emphasis on the mother-infant bond as a key factor in the development of a child's psychic structure during the first three years of life. The focus of therapy focused on object relations is helping people identify deficits in their interpersonal functioning and how childhood object relations impact current emotions and relationships and shape problems.

There is a theory of self in object relations theory: a composite of multiple self-images and representation of object images internally. Those aspects of the self that became split and repressed begin to surface during therapy, and individuals. A client can be helped to explore ways to integrate "good" and "bad" aspects of internal object representations as to see others more realistically.

This chapter might be summarized as follows: as Louis Conzolino argued, brains only exist within networks of other brains.[363] Flows between brains are bound by neither skull nor skin. "Neural integration seems to underlie the capacity for compassionate communication and the mindsight ability to see the mind—the subjective experience—of another with respect and kindness."[364]

Chapter Thirteen

Working in the Second Domain

Embodied Emotions

"We now have the means to exert an unprecedented degree of control over bodies, yet we are also living in an age which has thrown into radical doubt our knowledge of what bodies are and how we should control them."[365]

"My blind friend didn't give a toss how she looked. She cared about people's character, what they said and did as Jesus would do. We are distracted by the visual and physical, of which she knew nothing. So her blindness was a blessing to her but not the way this world views things."[366]

What Is Going on in Your Body?

How we inhabit our bodies speaks loudly of how we are in the world. It is as bodies that we enter the world, dwell and finally exit. Our sense of being "living bodies"—with attendant joys and frustrations—is vital to human existence. From being within the body of its mother, a baby is primed to seek bodily contact with others. Expressions and movements of caregivers are tracked and imitated within 42 minutes of birth.[367] Little children are skilled at creating embodied relationship.

"Body" refers to the overall human form of a person. Embodiment is something further: a vehicle for embodied subjectivity and embodied emotions. It is also a major area of concern for those who aspire to practice an integrated therapy that is holistic. Embodied personhood is essentially about a person and their community: the varied ways in which a person relates to those around them. It is when we are disconnected from our bodily being that we do immense harm, identifying with our body and emotions seemed unmanly in a time when it was supposedly weaker females who did that.

Embodiment is a big theme in contemporary theology as well as sociology. Contemporary theologians have a strong interest in the body, repudiating centuries of dualism where our corporeal existence was inferior to the mental and spiritual powers of the soul. Experiences of disembodiment depends on the prior sense of embodiment. As therapists, we encounter counter-transference which is a hugely embodied experience.

The "consumerist body" is the body that many of us are very aware of though it has been women who have borne the brunt of society's demands.

The body has moved to the forefront of how we understand the human being in society. Trends such as body modification, body image, virtual reality, reproductive technologies and religious dress have joined the claims of neuroscience as underlining our bodily identities. Issues such as self-harm and anxiety due to social media play out in the body. Our bodies are contested building sites. They have become the focus of self-identity, far more than the cognitive emphasis in the western philosophical tradition that equated our humanity with our minds. This was a bias towards living life in the mind rather than through the body, which was considered unreliable.[368]

Much is changing. A limited conception of our physicality is no longer viable. The body is far more than flesh and bones but enables a wide range of capacities—social, moral and intellectual.[369] It is central to our identity as well as the most obvious aspect of how we encounter each other. Far more too than a blank canvas on which social life is inscribed (as post-structuralists suggest), our human capacities occur within and from our embodied experience. Damasio, an academic researcher of consciousness, stresses that the body does not exist in isolation from cognitive thought but rather is "a foundation of the conscious mind."[370]

Our sense of our body is a construct, not just skin and shape. Social relations and our environmental context sculpt the way we come across and encounter each other physically. This is not to say that our clients sense of their physicality is not purely a matter of the forms and structures of society. The givens of nature and biology clearly play a major role. Our physical capacities generate social relations. Disability, for example, cannot be "read off" cultural attitudes such that it is society that disables. Biological foundations are more than about cultural preferences. The physical elements of our being are central to embodied identity and emotions.

In a society defined by the market, ideals of sporting prowess and an athletic body vie with the beauty industry in defining the health and shape of contemporary bodies. More traditional societies still maintain cultural markers of identity that are often religious. Body improvement projects are more a feature of a desacralized society in which traditional religious beliefs have declined and with it, a loss of meaning and value which has to be defined in individual terms. Options and choices to do with the body bewilder contemporary people. What is "natural" about the body is under scrutiny when fertility treatments, reproductive technologies and the means of gender change are prevalent.

It is not just social theorists who have interest in the body. So too do medical-cultural practitioners who promote a vast industry of dieting, healthy bodies and plastic surgery to makes us feel good about ourselves. Advocates of virtual reality and providers of internet platforms such as Zoom (where disembodied images make us refugees from our own existence) forge new ways of encountering each other. Psychologically, our capacities for language and consciousness are constrained by bodies. Embodied dispositions propel us towards social emotions and relationships with others.[371] The body conveys meaning. A sense of agency depends on reflexive potentiality that our embodiment facilitates.[372]

Visible Markers of Identity

Embodiment is not just about our sense of our own physicality and how that is constructed in contemporary society. It is also about our social location; indeed inseparable from it. Race and skin denote visible aspects of ourselves that create different identities for how people see us.

The human person is a being in the world with Others through the body. Our worldly life is neither isolated nor disembodied. As we have seen in chapter 3, how we see and create the world is shaped by your experience. Culture defines what is good and what is important; our values and norms. But race differentiates people physically. Skin color has been a marker to not only the way someone looks externally but also who is inferior and who is superior. Groups of people were treated in a certain way because of their bodies. Dramas agitating our contemporary world such as race, gender and disability are played out on the body.

The human person is not an isolated entity or disengaged in nature. It is through the body that my existence is connected with you but also with others in the world. A human body and human subjectivity are inseparable. What is body if not an embodied subjectivity and consciousness? Embodied subjectivity includes sexuality as well. To be human is about subjectivity; that we have a unique source and core full of meaning. Language does not create reality but helps bestow meaning on reality. Yet an embodied subjectivity is not limited to rationality and language. To be human means to have that subjectivity play out through the body as well as language for this is how we communicate. The body is not just defined by external signs and mirrors of social experience. It mirrors our subjective experience the contents of which are only known to us through introspection.

Mind Incarnate

Damasio argued that Descartes imagined thinking as an activity separate from the body. Efforts to understand the mind in general biological terms was retarded as a consequence of Descartes' dualism. Descartes' error was that his sentence "'Cogito ergo sum' (I think therefore I am) created an 'abyssal separation of body and mind . . . the separation of the most refined operations of the mind from the structure and operation of a biological organism. . . . I had grown up accustomed to thinking that the mechanisms of reason existed in a separate province of the mind, where emotion should not be allowed to intrude, and when I thought of the brain behind that mind, I envisioned separate neural systems for reason and emotion. This was the widely held view of the relation between reason and emotion, in mental and neural terms.'"[373]

From case studies of persons with specific forms of brain damage, Damasio asserts that this widely held concept is completely wrong. Feelings, memory and perceptual images play an important role for our reasoning. Since the body and the mind are so entwined, feelings and reasoning interact. Emotions play an important role for our minds and for our ability to act in society. Far from being a luxury, feelings and emotions are as "cognitive as other percepts" and they guide our decision making and reasoning in important ways.[374]

More than just "the body" with its flesh and bones, our sense of embodiment expresses our mind and emotions. Our very self and personhood is contained and expressed in a body. To be a human being requires a functioning human brain, in a living human body, interacting with complex physical, social, and cultural environments, in an ongoing flow of experience. Traditional Western religious and philosophical traditions routinely assume the transcendence of mind over body. They assume that our inmost essence is mental and spiritual, which they regard as distinct from the bodily. Our bodily substance exhibits and supports a set of actions such as digestion, perception, body movement, locomotion which seems different from mental and emotional activity. But this differentiation is hard to justify. The terms "embodied mind" and "embodied cognition" point to a new understanding of the relation between mind, body and emotions for all of this is inherently embodied, formulated through bodily sensation.

Embodiment theory—that we use our own bodily experience and processes to understand our own emotional experience, and the experiences of others—helps to understand emotional processing. The link between emotions and the body is quite obvious. Every culture seems to have bodily expressions for talking about emotional states, from broken hearts in our own culture to bad intestines in Tahiti.[375] Bodily change is indeed necessary for emotion, but cognitive interpretation is needed to determine what emotion a bodily change amounts to. Embodied processes are responsible for the anticipation of emotional events and for the feeling of emotions. Though socially conditioned, different experiences of embodiment are a guide to the countertransference that goes in psychotherapy. There is no form of therapy that is body-neutral.

Current embodiment theories of the mind challenge the former idea that body and mind are separate and independent forces that can act upon one another in an emotional episode. Rather the body helps to constitute the mind in shaping an emotional response.[376]

Yet what are emotions? Are emotions feelings or words? Emotions are not always consciously felt but even when they are, is this in the moment of realization only? If so, where do they go?[377] Perhaps emotions are embodied thoughts, dispersed around the body rather than being in the head.

Intersubjectivity—the capacity to infer the mental state or the emotional status of other individuals—is a basis for thriving in a social environment. Much of this happens through the body. Facial expressions convey important information regarding internal states. A comprehensive account of emotion requires a concept of embodiment. Feelings may be the bodily expression of thoughts. Psychosomatic illnesses reflect the variety of ways that emotional conflicts show up in the body.

Certainly, emotional dynamics are hugely important to well-being. There has not been, it is true, consensus as to what emotions actually are? Are these tricky feelings a straightforward reaction of the autonomic nervous system—an arousal state as a precursor for action—or mental appreciation of certain events? Theoretical debates aside, there are many grounds for believing that emotions are vital contributors to positive development. Because the deficit-model has reigned supreme, there have been far fewer studies of the role of positive emotions than negative emotions. Emotions are vital ingredients of secure those attachments necessary to bond with givers of care.[378] Emotions are vital to the development of empathy[379] but also creativity.[380] The ability to regulate emotional responses so they are less intense and not so overwhelming is an important part of healthy development. A child's ability to regulate emotions is crucial in building resilience, coping and social competence. The idea that early attachments shape a working model of subsequent relationships has been a vital component in attachment theory. The literature seems to confirm that experiencing positive affect or emotions from significant care givers helps to forge strong secure base from which to explore life. These states seem to be patterned into the brain to become embodied experience.

Intact Bodies, Intact Minds

As with counseling generally, the credibility of any contemporary theology of disability rests in large part on its capacity to engage both the broad spectrum of the humanities—and the various social, cultural, economic, political and philosophical discourses and the wide range of medical and, biogenetic, sciences, all of which continue to mould our understandings of disability.[381]

Attuning to such voices and reflecting on the life experiences of people with disabilities, it hopes to re-think and recalibrate aspects of theology and counseling practice that serve to exclude or to misrepresent the human experience of disability.

Counseling is always an embodied and interpretative enterprise; we inevitably use our bodies and our minds (and our implicit and explicit assumptions about both) to make sense of the world. Such bodies inhabit cultures and contexts which profoundly impact and shape what we see, how we see and importantly how we should respond to what we see.[382]

In *Illness as Metaphor*, Susan Sontag showed how psychological theories of illness can serve as powerful means of placing blame on the ill.[383] Disability lies within a normal human variation rather than an abnormality to be discarded.[384] Therapy can often be a part of the problem, not the solution.

As a snapshot in time, in 2020 in the UK, there are 14.1 million people who have a disability:

- 8% of children have a disability.
- 19% of working age adults have a disability.
- 46% of pension age adults have a disability.
- Approximately 13.9 million people in the UK have an impairment.
- It is likely that one in five clients has an impairment.[385]
- More than 4.4 million disabled people are in work.[386]
- Those with disability are almost twice as likely to be unemployed as non-disabled people.
- Life costs you £583 more on average a month if you're disabled.
- Families of disabled children on average, face extra costs of £581 a month.
- For almost a quarter (24%) of families with disabled children, extra costs amount to over £1,000 a month.[387]

There are different lenses for understanding disability.

- **Tragedy**: Sees the individual as a victim of circumstance, helpless and dependent on care from others (perhaps the hardest to understand because it is masked with kindness for example, charities).
- **Medical**: Sees the impairment or adjustment to it as problematical, where the solution is to fix/help and make "normal."
- **Moral**: Based on beliefs that impairment is a punishment for bad deeds perpetrated by the individual or their ancestors. Within therapy the task might be to explore offering clients a different experience: one that promotes inclusion and overcomes segregation.
- **Social**: Focuses on the disadvantages or barriers experienced in the physical and social environment—how society is structured, services organized and delivered; institutions, language, culture, and attitudes.

Another area where sociopolitical intersections might impact what is going on in therapy is to do with disability which affects a significant proportion of society. Reflecting the systems within which people live, disability studies sought to re-imagine human disability by focusing attention on the fact that disability is as much a social construct as a biological or psychological one. Disability is a social construct, the product of negative beliefs, values, assumptions, policies and practices. Rather than a focus on the notion that disability resides within the mind or the body of an individual (the medical or rehabilitation models) the social model of disability noted that the experience of people with disabilities was one of exclusion and injustice. Exclusion and injustice do not match directly on impairments people were encountering; it was society's responses to impairments that was disabling.[388] Being deaf is only disabling if the people around you have not learnt sign language. Being blind is disabling if the environment around you is assumes everyone can see. The impairments themselves do not produce disability.[389]

Social attitudes are often introjected at the social and psychological level.[390] Disability can be a focus for a sense of self-identity and value. "Whenever someone treats us as if we smell bad, we suffer a profound decrease in self-esteem . . . those that accept this label . . . will live with chronic shame that becomes a part of the very structure of their personalities."[391] When a disabled client or supervisee needs to be assisted into the practice room, each session begins with inequality.

Based on the reframed idea that disability is not a personal tragedy; it stems from social conditions, the Union of the Physically Impaired Against Segregation sums up this understanding of disability: "In our view, it is society which disables physically impaired people. Disability is something imposed on top of our impairments, by the way we are unnecessarily isolated and excluded from full participation in society. Disabled people are therefore an oppressed group in society."[392]

Addressing physical barriers to therapy is the first step towards inclusive practice. Therapy can also be shaped by third parties in clients' lives, such as family members, personal assistants, care home staff and service dogs. This runs counter to most therapy training that instills the principle of autonomy and client privacy such that third parties are not involved. For some clients though, third parties might be necessary. The problem is that third-party relationships might be controlling or abusive. It is important to discuss with a client that this is their therapy and you will be working with them on their agenda, not those of the third party.[393]

Questions arise for someone with disability about how to live; knowing they may continually be relinquishing power, control and independence. Choices are limited, and there are frequent invasions of privacy conveying reduced dignity, assigned to a minority, stigmatized in society.[394] "We need therapists . . . who are used to confronting the depth of despair with their clients, whilst keeping their eyes on the possibilities ahead. We can never fake authenticity or existential courage. We can only help people to go as far as we have gone ourselves in our own lives."[395]

How does it impact one's wellbeing when someone acts/speaks/gestures in an invalidating way, or when access to a venue is through the back entrance where the rubbish is kept?[396]

Those not fitting the "normal" category are more likely to be treated differently or marginalized.[397] "Impairment" and "disability" are used interchangeably in everyday. "Impairment" is a "medically classified bio physiological condition"[398] and "disability/disabled" seen as "the disadvantage or restriction caused by a contemporary social organisation which takes no or little account of people who have . . . impairments and thus excludes them from the mainstream of social activities."

Most influential writers on psychotherapy have been able-bodied and have thus assumed an able-bodied hermeneutic as the norm for deciphering human experience. The ways in which we construct our understandings of beauty, normality, strength, intellect and reason have a direct implication for the ways in which we interpret and respond to disability. Our "normal" constructions mean that disability can only be perceived as an abnormality.

Dependency, a universal human trait, means we are all dependent to some extent on the help and support of others but becomes unconsciously denied to keep the myth of independence alive and well.[399] Particularly in the western world, we see ourselves as independent, using power, choice and control to express identity, helping us feel safe and secure.[400]

By contrast, disability theology is the attempt by disabled and non-disabled Christians to understand and interpret the gospel of Jesus Christ, God, and humanity against the backdrop of the historical and contemporary experiences of people with disabilities. It has come to refer to a variety of perspectives and methods designed to give voice to the rich and diverse theological meanings of the human experience of disability.[401]

The most influential text within the field is Nancy Eiesland's book The Disabled God. Eiesland, a sociologist and a person who had a severe physical disability, set out to construct a contextual Christology specifically for people with physical disabilities.[402] There are limits to our power; there are no limits to God's power. If we can do some things, God is able to do anything. Thus, human "ableness" provides us with the image to think about God's power. In this context, the image of a disabled God disrupts that idea. Theology and practice has served to exclude people with disabilities. Unhelpful associations of disability with sin, concepts of virtuous suffering, negative and segregationalist views on disability and charity, and oppressive readings of the healing miracles all contribute.[403]

The theological community must learn about the philosophy that drives the disability movement and, then, be willing to critique the Christian tradition in the light of that philosophy. In like fashion, the disability community must be willing to search the Christian tradition for ways that can give meaning to the experience of being disabled. Jesus' scars are marks of redemption and hope, not of oppression or disability. What if we are weak, dependent, vulnerable and helpless? How could we participate in such a process or find a place in such a model of disability?

This is a vital conversation that seeks to reframe the perceived limits that disability places on people and to enable a fresh perception of limits as neutral, natural and universal to human beings. In order for creation to have form it requires limits indicates that limits are built into the order of the universe and need not be pathologized. However, the vulnerability of people with disabilities is a revelation of the vulnerability of all human beings. There is, in the end, no hard-and-fast dualism between ability and disability, but rather reciprocity rooted in our vulnerable humanity. All of life comes to us as a gift, an endowment received in countless ways from others in our lifetime. When we acknowledge this, the line between giving and receiving, ability and disability, begins to blur.[404]

To be a person means that one must be able to live one's life, develop one's potential and live out a purposeful life-course without any necessary reference to others. Such things as independence, autonomy, and intellectual skill have become primary social goods and fundamental markers with regard to what a good life might look like. The lives of people with profound disabilities bring this sharply to the fore. Such lives may share few of these culturally valued norms for humanness.[405]

Some forms of disability can also be considered a form of trauma. Rather than impairment, trauma is often at the root of client distress. Common in the lives of disabled people, it can take many forms. There may be grief and loss if impairment arose from an accident or injury. The likelihood of abuse is increased for disabled people. Coercive abuse is common. And disabled children and young people may be targets for sexual exploitation. This can constitute an extra layer of difficulty.

Trauma

Trauma is everywhere. It runs through our individual lives and through our world. No one is untouched by trauma. Trauma always involves the body. Even when the trauma is "just" emotional or circumstantial, there will be a bodily impact and bodily ("somatic") memories. Human experience is replete with different types of trauma—single-incident, repeated, or complex forms of "Post-traumatic Stress," "Post-traumatic Stress Disorder" (PTSD), or other episode—that may repeat reactivation of the original traumatic response. "Dissociation" is a significant response—which in cases of repeated trauma might lead to "DID" (Dissociative Identity Disorder) as people become detached and cope by switching to a different and safe place. Splitting and dissociating are common responses.

Trauma involves memories that differ from everyday experience. These memories are sharp, raw and ragged. Those who have them are tormented by flashbacks and nightmares. Intolerable sensations and feelings must be avoided or they will be overwhelmed. Bodies tighten and people brace against the fear. Traumatic memories and helplessness in the face of threat challenge key assumptions about life in the western consciousness such as free-will and autonomy.[406]

Psychological trauma can be defined as "the experience of extraordinarily stressful, disturbing, or violent events, over which the victim is helpless and overwhelmed."[407] Examples include:

- **Eating Disorders**: usually an attempt at regaining control.
- **Dissociative Disorders**: excessive threat interferes with the integration of our mind-body experiences resulting in various kinds of fragmentation.
- **Post Traumatic Stress Disorder (PTSD)**: tied to how our brain responded to the original threat.
- **Depression**: the kindling and stress on the nervous system contributes to mood disorders
- **Anxiety Disorders**: e.g., panic attacks, OCD, phobias

- **Physical Diseases**: unresolved trauma leads to chronic pain, autoimmune disorders and illnesses.
- **Addictions**: often used to numb the pain associated with trauma.

In some cases, trauma can be inherited as well as physical characteristics. Generational trauma (also known as intergenerational trauma or transgenerational trauma) is still a relatively new field of study.[408] This is trauma that is not just experienced by one person but extends from one generation to the next. Families become desensitized. In 1966, Canadian psychiatrist Vivian M. Rakoff and her colleagues recorded high rates of psychological distress among children of Holocaust survivors, and the concept of generational trauma was first recognized.[409] A 1988 study, published in *The Canadian Journal of Psychiatry*, found that grandchildren of Holocaust survivors were overrepresented by about 300% in psychiatric care referrals. Since then, Holocaust survivors and their progeny have been the most widely studied group, but in theory, any type of extreme, prolonged stress could have adverse psychological affects on children and/or grandchildren, resulting in clinical anxiety, depression, and post-traumatic stress disorder (PTSD).[410]

It is clear that being systematically exploited, enduring repeated and continual abuse, racism, and poverty are all traumatic enough to cause genetic changes.[411] Symptoms of generational trauma may include hypervigilance, a sense of a shortened future, mistrust, aloofness, high anxiety, depression, panic attacks, nightmares, insomnia, a sensitive fight or flight response, and issues with self-esteem and self-confidence.[412] This may lead to a dysfunctional immune system—either too active or not active enough. This can result in more autoimmune diseases or a greater propensity for illness.[413]

There is no specific diagnosis of generational trauma, according to the *Diagnostic and Statistical Manual of Mental Disorders, Fifth Edition* (DSM-5), the standard classification of mental disorders used by professionals. But the phenomena of intergenerational trauma is well accepted. Trauma can manifest itself through stress, anxiety, fight or flight, and other heightened alert systems in our brain and bodies, but intergenerational trauma can also mask itself through learned beliefs, behaviors, and patterns that become engrained. This kind of wiring impacts personalities, relationships, parenting, communication, and views of the world.

Traumatic events push the nervous system outside its ability to regulate itself. The system gets stuck in the "emergency" mode, and the person is overstimulated and unable to calm. Anxiety, anger, restlessness, panic, and hyperactivity can all result when you stay in this ready-to-react mode. The criteria for posttraumatic stress disorder PTSD have changed considerably with the newest edition of the American Psychiatric Association's (APA) *Diagnostic and Statistical Manual of Mental Disorders* (DSM-5).[414] Posttraumatic stress disorder (PTSD) has attracted controversy since being classified as a psychiatric disorder in the third edition of the American Psychiatric Association's (APA) *Diagnostic and Statistical Manual of Mental Disorders* (DSM-3) in 1980. Changes to the diagnostic criteria from the DSM-4 to DSM-5 include: "the relocation of PTSD from the anxiety disorders category to a new diagnostic category named 'Trauma and Stressor-related Disorders,' the elimination of the subjective component to the definition of trauma."[415] DSM-5 definition of trauma requires *actual or threatened death, serious injury, or sexual violence* rather than a subjective component. Exposure to a stressful or traumatic event was no longer vital to classification. PTSD was removed as a disorder from the anxiety disorders category. That was due to research demonstrating that PTSD entails multiple emotions such as guilt, shame, or anger outside of a fear/anxiety spectrum. Apart from a sudden catastrophe, medically based incidents are longer categorized as trauma.[416]

But a writer on rehabilitation and neurology, Robert Scaer, contends that the threat to the survival as a human being represented by trauma "is based more on its meaning to the individual based on prior traumatic experiences than its intrinsic severity."[417] Psychological meaning is important to the equation of stress response. Whiplash injuries are experience-based rather than injury—based.

Whiplash victims—the term comes from Mark Twain's Huckleberry Finn who used to catch snakes by the tail to use as a whip—have emotional effects. People commonly feel detached, experience anxiety, panic attacks when cars get too close. Whiplash might cause neurochemical impacts in the brain that are experience-based rather than injury related.

Scaer's research into whiplash injury raises interesting questions. Recovery seems to be decidedly uneven and it is far from clear what actually happens and what the effect is.[418] The back and forward movement of the head is less than had been thought. Some in the insurance and legal communities who have to assess medical injuries are not convinced about the validity of whiplash despite the emotional symptoms of anxiety about travel, nightmares and perhaps cold sweats.

Peter Levine, a contemporary psychologist specializing in trauma, argued that trauma results when our instinctual responses to a traumatic event are not allowed to cycle all the way through without a way to safely release the energy in our nervous system. The arousal stays in the body and leads to symptoms of PTSD. Trauma originates as a response in the nervous system, not in the event. Trauma is not what happens to us, but what we hold inside in the absence of an empathetic witness.

Response of the brain to trauma is well documented. Immediate affects of preparing for fight or flight mode of neuromuscular activity. The action of parasympathetic nervous system in the face of threat is the same as when about to attack. Prey or predator is common to most animals and people; there is only a thin line between based on the meaning of the event.[419] Memory mechanisms endow some events with enormous significance, such as the death of a loved one or bad news of diagnosis.

A relatively new form of trauma therapy is Eye Movement Desensitization and Reprocessing (EMDR). It is particularly relevant in treating PTSD arising from military combat, physical assault, rape, or car accidents. EMDR is an interactive psychotherapy with its particular form of treatment. EMDR does not rely on talking therapy or medication. Instead, it utilizes a patient's own rapid, rhythmic eye movements in order to unfreeze the intense emotions around traumatic episodes. The idea is that the rapid eye movements impact on the memory centres of the brain as the EMDR therapist will have you recall a disturbing event. The experience include emotions and body sensations that go along with it with the intention that their intensity is reduced.[420] Whether effectiveness of treatment utilizes basic principles used in prolonged exposure therapy (widely used psychotherapeutic treatment for PTSD), the counseling community is unclear how EMDR works. Significantly, the US Department of Veterans Affairs and the Department of Defence have jointly issued clinical practice guidelines. These guidelines "strongly recommended" EMDR for the treatment of PTSD in both military and non-military populations.[421]

Describing symptoms as being in search of meaning takes us into the third REMA question—to do with meaning-making. So far we have looked at two of the questions that REMA poses. Our first was "What is going on in the way you relate to others?" Our second question was "What is going on in your relationship with your body?" Now we come to "What are the meanings you wrap around events and people say about your inner needs?" For our metaphors and narratives are not entertainment to be avoided by rational thought but universal structures by which we understand and make sense of the world.

Chapter Fourteen

Compulsive Interpreters

Meaning-Making and Human Existence

"Contemporary culture often produces a kind of neuroses different from that described by Freud. Contemporary neuroses are characterised not so much by repression . . . not by lack of insight but lack of a sense of purpose, of meaning in life."

—NICHOLAS HOBBS[422]

"That I may know the meaning of the voice."

—1 CORINTHIANS 14:11

Working in the Third Domain—What Meanings Are Coming Up for You?

At Corinth, Paul addressed the situation faced when people seemed to be moved by the Spirit such that they were caught up in forms of utterance that others present did not understand. "Speaking in tongues" (glossolalia) might take the form of private utterance and worship (1 Cor 14:2). What is much better when it comes to a public arena such as a church community is that there is interpretation so that all can comprehend and participate. Discerning the correct meaning is vital.

The construction we put on what happens to us is what humans are particularly good at doing, less so at translating and decoding the meanings others place on their experience. Because of the sheer challenge posed by inter-subjectivity and knowing what is in someone else's mind, we can construe things and interpret in ways that have no relationship with what was in the mind of the speaker.

There is a distinction between singular or plural? It is the contrast between meaning (in general) or meanings that arise constantly in emotionally-laden situations. This is true also of cultural meanings that understood by different people in different ways. To discern the meanings that we give to all sorts of situations is the stuff of life.

The interpreter deals in the currency of meanings. The interpreter does not just take the words used and translate them into the language of another. Rather, the communication is one of taking the meanings that are inherent in things that are said and lodging them as accurately as possible within the heads of hearers.

This is important across human endeavours. The historian's art is one of discerning what actions and processes meant to the participants of the day, not to bring today's cultural meanings and wrap them around events that took place in the past. Rather than putting the people of the past in our shoes and judging them by contemporary standards, it is the other way round. What meanings were relevant at the time? Instead of endeavouring to classify the experiences of people who have lived before from the outside, the contemporary historian is much less of a curator or collector but an imaginary. Considerable imaginative effort goes in to re-creating how things seemed to the participants at the time. Respect for what they thought and felt sits alongside a new respect for the subjective experience of those who walked the world before.[423]

This change of register is noticeable too in the sociologist's art, which includes trying to discern what perspectives shape human action, in what way they reflect the markers of identity, how people would describe themselves and what is most important about them. Where you sit determines what you say. To be sure there are differing views of the world within the very idea of trying to describe social reality. Can what is going on be discovered by counting and qualitative methodology? Or do we use the interpretive model and seek to gain in-depth insights as a clearer window on the world?

The anthropologist's art, and indeed that of the linguist, is to understand meaning of the action and the voice and the culture that gives rise to them.

The art involved in leadership of faith communities is to hold the meanings of life and ultimate purpose for a while, especially in the landmarks of life.

The politician's art (if art it be) is to assess the scope for action within the web of power relationships and human interests that crowd the public square. Leaders of quality do not merely reiterate fixed positions but try to tease out jaundiced positions and get beyond the conflict politics that have shaped things.

The therapist's art is to try to understand what is important to distressed souls in front of them; what comes up for them in different circumstances, what existential meanings they bring to that distress and why.

The Interpreted World[424]

To enter the human life-world is to enter a messy zone where each consciousness constructs reality.

It is to embrace that which is and is not; to embrace the reality of a real world that is real to some but not others. In the relativity of perspective, things look different according to your vantage point, there are few hard and fast facts and where you stand is shaped by where you sit. It is to embrace a timeless zone where history and psychology blend and bleed into one another as we contemplate human actions and human actors. As we read the narratives of past lives or the history of nation and movements, we need to read the past not in terms of the cultural meanings we wrap around actions but to ask about the cultural meanings for those concerned at the time.

The human unconscious is of this order, of what is real and unreal. Conflicts and yearnings are shadows, subterranean forces that need to emerge into the light of conscious day to be interpreted. Even then, what rules would apply? The drive to find meaning for our lives is very powerful. "Meanings are made within contexts not only of private thought and event but within the contexts of dialogues with those significant others who teach us, confirm us, challenge us and contradict us."[425]

Therapists work with clients to discern meanings. The task in which both are engaged is the co-construction of meaning; that is, to arrive at a joint interpretation of that which is troubling. This may take the form of an interpretation of dreams or insight into unconscious processes. Or it could take the form of therapist hearing client distress and helping to make sense of it.

Our lives are understood through the stories we tell of them; of childhoods, of weddings and funerals, triumphs and disasters. Story looms large in this enterprise. We dream in stories or infuse the future with narratives of despair, devoid of a reason for optimistic living and empty with the absence of God. Storytellers all, humans seem driven by the compulsion to assemble what has happened to us into a narrative of meaning-making that can at least attempt to make sense of what is going on. Such disempowered communication adopts a narrative structure in the effort to explain.

Lack of a satisfactory ending complicates things. A cinematic story without resolution sends audiences crazy. Films have to have a good ending and preferably one where the good guys win. For some, this is where a monotheistic insistence on an Assize in a realm beyond this one fits into a narrative structure; the bad guys deserve to have their comeuppance and wrongs righted in a way that is emphatically not the case in this present life. Immanuel Kant certainly saw it that way in his moral argument for the existence of God. Injustice is bad for human beings and it is bad narrative.

With what tools shall we construct meaning narratives? Maybe this is where Jung's idea of archetypes might help us. To create narratives, we might use a mental representation of say, the heroic figure battling against the odds to survive and overcome. It might be the reluctant good guy coming out of retirement to fight injustice and overcome malign violence with lethal force employed for good. Or it might be the box we put something in is that of a journey. There is now less need for the journey to have a destination as cultural meanings have shifted hugely. It is sufficient to be on a journey: an illustration surely of the reality behind archetypes in the collective unconscious as being about meanings and myths in cultural rather than psychological forms directly.

Client and therapist together are engaged in meaning-making; that most common yet difficult of tasks. People mean very different things in their actions and speech. "Why did you place this or that construction on what happened?" is a relevant question as is to probe the statement—"I didn't mean *that*!" Acknowledging that someone may have taken something "the wrong way" shows how an interpretive perspective is central to the business of fraught human communication.

Emotive statements loom large in discerning meaning. Clients may well be affected by material they have not processed sufficiently. It may leer in the night but they are not yet ready to put it to permanent sleep, let alone answer the question, "Why are you thinking this way?"

The Languages of Love

A "fundamental illusion" of modernity is that it left us with the social isolation and the solitary self. Contemporary individuals do not just live on their island; they are the sole arbiter of truth and meaning. This is a dilemma of the voice and choice society that increasingly replaces honor/shame or sin and guilt as drivers of social mores.[426] Where does it leave us? For those who feel their isolation keenly, this is existential. It is profound because it can call into question life's meaning.

For those who are well connected, the question of meaning arises differently. To navigate family and couple relationships, partners and spouses learn that in order to flourish, they must learn to discern. Deciphering the meanings that one party to a relationship attaches to something that has been done or not done is vital to build bridges of understanding. This is a matter of meanings (plural).

The concept of "Love Languages" is widely used in couple relationships. It also applies to family and indeed interaction in organizations where teamwork is vital. If you try to express appreciation in ways that aren't meaningful to your coworkers, they may not feel valued at all. This is because you and your coworkers are speaking different languages.[427] The languages of love and appreciation are:

- Words of affirmation
- Quality time
- Physical touch
- Acts of service
- Receiving gifts

Psychologist Gary Chapman devised this list from patterns he observed in couple counseling where it became clear that the couples were misunderstanding one another and each other's needs. Couples can work to learn their partner's love language rather than trying to convince their partner to learn theirs. Ideally, both will want to express love in a way that is meaningful to the other. He has applied these principles to children and organizations with widespread appreciation as they relate to how human beings like to be valued. Once again, we are into the interpreted world. "There is not one space and time only, but as many spaces and times as there are subjects."[428]

The question is, though, what is shaping the different kinds of meanings we wrap around speech and actions of other people? Most obviously, the request for love to be communicated demonstratively will very likely be rooted in the emotional history of the client. Speech and actions that are seen and heard so as to cause misunderstanding at one level arise from speaking different languages. Yet what has caused the versions of interpreting speech-acts? Indubitably, meanings stem from history.

Nevertheless, the unique experiential world of the human being who comes for therapy is bigger than the sum of the various aspects of ourselves; the parts that might need attention. The meaning to ourselves of our own inner life is not something that is deduced readily from research findings. There is no standard tool with which to measure the things that really matter such as love, value, meaning and purpose.

The Shape of a Life

In a 2022 best-seller, Harvard Professor Arthur Brooks argues that the shape of a life after the age of 35 should be about finding joyful meaning.[429] Success, he suggests, is a dopamine hit that stops working after a certain stage and people become bored. 35 is the age that C. G. Jung said is a change point towards a more spiritual path. Brooks argues that faith is vital though that can include a philosophy that takes you into something bigger than yourself. The second factor is relationships while the third is friendship. It is after that work features. People of faith are reluctant to talk about their spirituality. Leaders de-emphasize the importance of family and love. Friendships become work-centered. What is needed, Brooks declares is a "pension plan for happiness" and not to be a work or success addict. As part of that we must confront and accept our death and plan accordingly.

The great exponent of existential counseling, Irving Yalom, proposed that "death is a primordial source of anxiety and, a such, is the primary fount of psychopathology."[430]

As the philosopher Hegel proposed, history is what humanity does with death. The terror of death, Yalom argues, is ubiquitous, universal. It is of such scale that a considerable amount of life's energies is devoted to its denial and transcendence. Freud argued that social life was formed out of the fear of death. People huddled together out of a fear of isolation and of what lurks in the dark.

Losing an immediate family member in the pandemic brought more severe mental health symptoms. It was exacerbated by not being able to have a funeral, sometimes resentment toward medical professionals who were keeping them away from loved ones, whom it was not hard to picture suffering and isolated. Family presence at the end of life is beneficial for patients and families.[431]

Prolonged grief is well documented historically. Famously, following the death of her beloved Albert, Queen Victoria went into extended period of deep mourning for the remainder of her reign. Though not a regular churchgoer, increasingly, she identified faith with a widow's search for consolation.[432]

A review of philosophical literature suggested that at its heart, the fear of death is about extinction.[433] It is the ultimate threat to our sense that we matter, of our valuable personhood.

Some look death in the face and experience personal growth as a result. This is often the experience of those who are terminally ill. They relate better to others and become gentler, humbler and less arrogant. In literature, there is no finer example than Tolstoy's *The Death of Ivan Ilyich*. Tolstoy's biographer calls this double story of the decomposing body and awakening soul "one of the most powerful works in the literature of the world" as successive stages passed through by a dying man's soul. The balance sheet of life reveals terror of what is coming and emptiness of what has been.[434]

It is here that Yalom's work on the role that death plays in psychotherapy is important. He argues:

i. The fear of death haunts us as nothing else does; rumbling under the surface and "a dark, unsettling presence at the rim of consciousness."[435]
ii. A child is pervasively occupied with death and the fear of obliteration.
iii. We erect defences against death anxiety. If defences are maladaptive, clinical syndromes arise. Psychopathology is the result of trying to transcend death.

Yalom's contention is that death "whirs continually beneath the membrane of life and exerts a vast influence upon experience and conduct." It is *the* primary fount of psychopathology.[436] Certainly, philosophers ranging from Seneca to Heidegger have emphasized that everything fades; that in order to die well we have to live well. Seneca asserted that "no man enjoys the true taste of life but he who is willing and ready to quit it."[437] Heidegger suggested that death makes a positive contribution to life: if we can move from forgetfulness of being in the world of ordinary things to mindfulness of being in the world, we embrace both possibility and limits (including death).[438]

The theologian St. Augustine addresses the same idea: "It is only in the face of death that man's self is born."[439] Christian theology has indeed addressed this very firmly, rooted in ancient texts that assert "deliverance for those who all their lifetime were subject to slavery because of the fear of death" (Heb 2:15). This is fundamental to salvation.

The terror and fear of death is so universal that much of life is spent in an anxious state of avoiding it. Humans joining together against threats to survival is what has produced civilization. Anxiety about ceasing to be is at the root of anxiety that is about something as it travels from a generalized state to a focus on something specific. The philosopher Kierkegaard wrote of this when he suggests that "the nothing which is the object of dread becomes, as it were, more and more a something."[440]

So it is that the developing child develops defences against primal anxiety as it is transmuted into something else. Existential threats become something that can be named rather than be formless.

It is therefore curious why death as an existential and personal concern has not featured more in the psychological lexicon—any more than the quest for high value. These are linked. Belief in one's specialness is a very strong instinct. Our response to our own mortality and periods of illness are cut from the same cloth as concern to have a legacy that will outlive us: the need to control death.

The Role of Meaning-Making in Psychological Theories

According to existential psychology, we are meaning-seeking creatures and what is really interesting about us is not some unconscious arena that we can only access in a glass darkly but the meanings we attach to things. Our lives are held together by stories, to which we attach profound meanings. Some notion of human meaning emerges in Sartre's discussion about what it means to live in bad faith. We could, he observed, simply stop worrying about what life means. Get a job, get a car, get a house and advance your social status! Don't think about the fundamental issues yourself. Simply do as you are told by your peers, society, advertising.

You could lead the unexamined life! But there are three problems with this approach he says. Ignoring the troubling facts of existence is to surrender your sense of self and we give it away if we refuse to examine the substance and meaning of that experience. Secondly, we will still not be happy. We will wake up at night and ponder. Even the most smug person realizes they will be dead one day without having done anything more in life beyond acquiring material possessions. But there is a third problem. Choosing not to think about the big issues of life is itself a choice. Live as you choose. You might as well create a life from the unpromising materials to hand around you. Create your own sense of value![441] Through doing what is right for us, we define ourselves and become human.

Existentialism in the hands of one of its forefathers was a recipe for pessimism. "Human existence for Schopenhauer is less grand tragedy than squalid farce, . . . a mistake which should have long ago have been called off, and that only some crazed idealism could possibly believe that the pleasures of existence outweigh its pains."[442]

A growing body of counseling theory embraces the quest for meaning-making. Humans are not instinct driven so much as personal beings who have value and purpose and who seek higher goals.

James Fowler's Stages of Faith theory has been used in pastoral counseling and spiritual care. Fowler suggests there are seven primary stages of faith (including Stage 0) in people's story:

- **Stage 0: Primal Undifferentiated Faith (Ages Birth–2).** This parallels both Erik Erikson's first stage of "trust versus mistrust" and also Piaget's sensori-motor stage of cognitive development, where thinking takes place in and through the body. An infant acquires experiences from the environment that either provide feelings of trust and assurance or mistrust and fear about the universe and the divine.
- **Stage 1: "Intuitive-Projective" Faith (Ages 3–7).** Through language, the child can work with symbols to express thoughts. A spiritual sense is experiential and develops through stories and a sense of right and wrong in how the world should work. This parallels Piaget's stage of pre-operational thinking marked by the absence of consistent logical-mental structures.
- **Stage 2: Mythic-Literal Faith (Ages 7–12).** The child has a sense of justice and fairness and also an anthropomorphic image of God This phase is close to Piaget's concrete operational stages of

cognitive development where logical thinking begins to develop in the child's mind.

- **Stage 3: "Synthetic-Conventional" Faith (Ages 12–Adult).** An identification of the adolescent/adult with a religious institution, belief system and developing one's own spiritual identity. Having a faith-based identity can result in rejecting challenges to it. This corresponds to Piaget's stage of formal operational thinking whereby the adolescent or adult sees the divine realm as an abstract or formless manifestation.
- **Stage 4: "Individuative-Reflective Faith" (Ages Mid-Twenties–Late Thirties).** The individual takes personal responsibility for beliefs or feelings even though there may be greater complexity. More open-mindedness can though result in internal and external conflicts when different beliefs are in collision.
- **Stage 5: "Conjunctive" Faith (Mid-Life Crisis).** Paradoxes and mysteries beyond ourselves are acknowledged as the person to move beyond what had been known previously. Often this will lead to a multi-verse of faith perspectives rather than any single belief system.
- **Stage 6: "Universalizing" Faith (or "Enlightenment") (Later Adulthood).** As Fowler saw it, this is rare as an individual is not constrained by differences in religious or spiritual beliefs. All are as worthy of compassion and deep understanding.[443]

This scheme is not prescriptive but descriptive. Fowler describes the six stages that emerge in working out the meaning of our lives. The making of a human life is progressively centered on a basic set of meanings and values that shape the faith people live by.

Symbol Making

Since Peter Berger's notion of the sacred canopy, it has become clear that human beings are poorly equipped to handle the social world they create. A yawning sense of spiritual homelessness became central to the Romantic movement that followed the rationality of the Enlightenment.

And so symbol-making becomes important in the contemporary quest for expressing our response to life. Creativity, art, fashion, music, sport become arenas where the medium is the meaning. People invest huge cultural and personal significance in play and storytelling, in the parables, legends and stories, in our deep-seated symbols and media-shaped narratives. Meaning may be focused anywhere and everywhere. The rise and rise of anxiety and depression seems to signify the loss of hope. Yalom suggests that the less a sense of meaning the greater the extent of pathology.[444]

> Tangled through the roots of mania and psychosis is this recurring dream of significance. It is as though I am newly born in the world, craving meaning and interaction as I once craved milk and contact. I will do nearly anything to satisfy that need, from terrorising myself to ranting in the street.[445]

In Buddhism, the concept of "dukkha" or "suffering," expresses the general unsatisfactory sense of ordinary empirical existence, that things are not as they should be. Bad things happen to good people. This is the universal problem of pain, of suffering that bites us to the core. According to Jung`, the question "Why has this happened to me?" haunts 30% of patients.[446]

We live in a world of fragmenting forces that disintegrate society. We witness the rise of religion but it is not the old time religion rather the rise of "no religion" and the emergence of a new cultural majority stressing de-industrialized forms of spirituality and post-institutional forms of religion. Spirituality is the buzz of our times. It's not "do you believe," like it used to be. It's "what do you believe!" Some sort of faith is everywhere.

How can the spirit keep intact in a place where everything is evaporated as the dew of morning? What is it about us that we even ask such questions? We are born with a gap. There's a hole. It needs explaining. Even more, it needs filling. Is there an anything out there that corresponds to what's in here? Does the cosmos give any personal meaning to our lives?

As the dimensions of the cosmos have exploded into unimaginative scale, human insignificance seems smaller and smaller. Yet there is a huge gap. Our personal lives protest hugely against being written off. The gap is between the objective laws of physics and the everyday subjective experience that yearns for significance. For believers, that takes us straight to the existence of God. What ultimate realities are suggested by the drive to feel we are significant, that we count? How does the universe generate human participants who not only are conscious and self-aware but have an imperative towards high worth? Or has an impersonal universe given rise to this fundamental way we are wired up? A personal God is the most satisfactory explanation of valuable personhood. We can object all we want but we only have to look within to know we need to be of value as people. What's that based on? I am a person, I hurt. But is there any echo? Does the universe respond to my cry to count, to be conscious, to be loved and valued? Or is all our humanity met with a cruel mocking laugh, like the laugh of an empty horizon? How does a being who needs meaning as one who is thirsty seeks water find it in a universe that is devoid of meaning? That is the question. Lacking the former sense of a grand cosmic design and plan, contemporary people will gravitate to deriving no guidance for living beyond what we create for ourselves. One word for this is "purpose"; another is "significance." The notion of "purpose" speaks of having an aim in life, a design for which one is being fitted and to which one is working. At one level it can seem functional: "what is the purpose of a lawn-mower?" constitutes intelligent design. But to have a life of purpose is a spiritual idea (with the assumption perhaps that the purpose is a benign one commanding positive loyalty). To feel that one is significant goes beyond having aims at an individual level. It speaks of fitting into the grander scheme of things at a cosmic level. A client may experience a crisis of meaning at both levels. Although it is hard to get a handle on, offering a guide to the perplexed should be part of the training of psychotherapists.

CHAPTER FIFTEEN

Agency

The Protest, Voice, and Freedom

"Therapy can bring about personality change only in so far as it leads a patient to adopt a new mode of behaviour. A real change occurring in the absence of action is a practical and theoretical impossibility."[447]

Working in the 4th Domain—Where Is Your Voice and Agency?

WORKING IN THE FOURTH domain is highly rewarding.

- "You have to make an effort" a client might have heard.
- "We can't help you if you won't help yourself!"

The therapist's position on this reflects much of inner assumptions. Clients often engage in the blame game: "Who do you blame?" They might assert behavior is controlled by the unconscious: a deterministic view of functioning. Does the process of uncovering inner drives and conflicts avoid responsibility and make it less likely someone will exercise freedom to act?

Person-centered counseling integrates especially well with counseling abused women who have been told what to do for most of their lives. Domestic violence and abuse entraps women in relationships where personal power and autonomy, as well as self-worth, are eroded.[448]

Reinforcing a sense of agency is where relational depth to engage clients in an equal partnership becomes important.

Arguably, the goal of psychotherapy is to bring the patient to the point where he or she can make a free choice. A client might assert that his or behavior is controlled by the unconscious, but whose unconscious is it? It pertains to no one else. Where is the agent who is choosing? Where is the seat of autonomy, the one who can take charge and exercise moral responsibility?

In his positive psychology, Seligman postulated that the various components of depression are outcomes of previous learning that rewards and punishments are out of our control.[449]

The concept of freedom has evoked a strong debate in human thought. It contrasts with philosophic determinism that has depicted our lives as on a given and probably pre-set trajectory, such as:

- Belief in divine providence
- Scientific causality
- Hegel seeing history as going somewhere
- Marxist or Freudian deterministic theories

Theologically, robust debate has ensued regarding whether free-will is a myth. Martin Luther observed "the bondage of the will,"[450] pointing out to Erasmus that this was the battleground of the new Reformation. Are we severely limited by sin?

A deterministic view of functioning leaves little space for the psychic agency to which an appeal for change and action can be made. Yet there is a tension here: Freud noted that the therapeutic task had to include "the patient's ego freedom to choose one way or another."[451]

Philosophically, the question arises in the context of the nature of freedom and whether everything is determined? Are we shaped such that our lives are pre-determined and predictably? What is the nature of our freedom?

Ethically, are we free to do the right thing? Can we take responsibility for our actions?

In the study of social science, a big theme is understanding the relationship between structure and agency. Structure refers to the complex and interconnected set of social forces, relationships, institutions, and elements of social forces that work together to shape the thought, behavior, experiences, choices and the lives of people generally. The social constrains' has been a dominant idea since Durkheim's day. We are constrained and hemmed in by social structures and systems. Can we ever get beyond the way we have been brought up or the social facts of our existence?

We do not have the same starting point. Our capacity and resilience varies hugely. In psychological theory, we are shaped internally by our upbringing or emotional experience (attachments).

Our approach here in this fourth domain takes account of the individual desire to create his or her own life. The freedom to change, to desire, to act, to choose is vital. The therapist may seem to be pursuing therapeutic goals such as insight, interpretation, self-actualization and so on but what we are really after is action, a definite change. Therapist and client in fruitful dialogue will seek to explore, understand and then act.

Cognitive Behavioral Therapy assumes that client can take charge. The Therapist can empower their client's agency by uncovering the connection between moods and thoughts, and challenging the negative thoughts and beliefs that underlie negative moods

Discussion of agency leads to the notion of responsibility. As Fritz Perls, Gestalt theoretician, noted: "If you take responsibility for what you are doing to yourself, how you produce your symptoms, how you produce your illness, how you produce your existence—the very moment you get in touch with yourself—growth begins, integration begins."[452]

Responsibility entails authorship, to be "the uncontested author of an event or a thing" as Sartre wrote.[453] Agency represents our ability to author our own experience.

A sense of agency and not being paralysed is about feeling of control over actions and their consequences. Rather than be passive, we can do something about our situation. This goes beyond autonomy. It is about freedom to act. Agency refers to the thoughts and actions taken by people that express their individual power. It is linked to ideas of responsibility, not being determined by the scripts handed out to you.

Recognizing use of the passive voice in interactions with others enabled us to understand where we become reliant on manipulations of communication, rather than empowering others through open communication.[454] Clients often deploy strategies so that the therapist will make decisions for them. What then is the role of *decision* in psychotherapy? Strategies for avoidance are common features:

- Not dealing with the paralysis of guilt

- Procrastination
- Following a rule book
- Being at a crossroads yet taking neither path because they cannot take both

Crossroads require the wisdom to make renunciations. To every "yes" there must be a "no"!

The Expression of Agency

The concept of agency assumes we are free to be free!

Agency is not a nebulous or theoretical concept. The exercise of such autonomy is expressed through voice, choice, empowerment, dignity and the Protest.

Agency entails finding one's voice. "Where is your voice in this situation?" a therapist might ask. This entails that there is something to be found.

- You have not been heard
- No one is listening

Voice is entwined with *choice*: allowing what the client wants to surface.

Empowerment. Why is it that feeling disempowered lowers a sense of worth? For many people, receiving power raises confidence levels and imparts value. Assertiveness seems to be expressing the real you. The assertiveness training emphasis of the 1980s and 90s recognized that instinctively. It brings career benefits. Psychiatrists at the Harvard Medical School in the US measured how the careers of 824 individuals had progressed in relation to their personality profiles and coping strategies. They found that those who could express their frustrations tactfully and constructively were less likely to complain they had hit a glass ceiling in the workplace.[455] Empowerment is usually understood in secular terms. Agency is the capacity of individuals to have the power and resources to fulfill their potential. A Christian perspective might see this differently. It is not a question of self-assertion only but in position to something higher, to God.

Recovery of dignity is vital. It is relevant to ask: "Can you recall when you experienced loss of dignity? What did that feel like?" "Value yourself—uphold your dignity" is a valid cry.

The assertion of agency finds its expression in **the Protest**: "I'm worth more than that!"

The Protest is a capacity, both a reaction and a consciousness; a reflex against the depressive effects of devaluation in the form of an indignation. The Protest is a flower or the grass that has been downtrodden and is now springing up in freedom. This reflex does not happen automatically in interpersonal life any more than it does in social or political life. People do not always and inevitably react with indignation against the erosion of their value. There is, however, that which can be mobilized, that which can be aroused slowly into a new birth of consciousness.

In the psychology of human resistance, "Excuse me! I'm a human being!" is the language of those who feel used, taken for granted or trodden upon. Behind this statement is concealed a statement of a healthy ego, a valuable self. This book is a proposal for how issues of value arise in the power lines of everyday life. The statement "I'm worth more than that!" goes to the heart of the Protest. It is an uprising of assertive value.

The latent capacity to affirm that "I am" or "we are worth more than you say" marks the reflex reaction that seems to be embedded within our psychic structure. The lady who re-gains self-respect by learning to say no is learning to value herself. Discovering that she can say no for the first time in fifty years and being prepared to risk relationship has given her a liberation that is palpable. She wants to run and leap! Paradoxically, saying no has increased the respect people have for her as well as finding a well of self-respect that had lain deep underground.

The Protest emerges in the affront to sacredness that often generates the outrage that makes us human. Anger is liable to being misinterpreted. There are forms of anger that involve lashing out. But anger can often be far more than someone losing their self-control. Some—though not all—anger people hold, stems from the inner Protest, a response to the put downs or an environment perhaps where emotions were not validated. It is curious that powering up the indignation in a situation such as this raises levels of self-respect rather than experiencing the depressing effect of inadvertent collusion by going along with it. It raises a question about a relationship between power and value.

In contrast, a client suffered from a long-term depression that barely concealed a life-time of being dumped upon. Suppressed anger raged under the waters of the deep. Anger is hugely illuminating about what is troubling someone deep down.[456] Reports of being downtrodden conceal a Protest; a Protest against going through life second or even third class. To throw off the chains is to move from a subject position of "being someone whom others do things to."

The lack of a person owning their agency has a tremendous impact on their worth and causes psychological distress. "I was fifteen years married, treated like dirt on the floor. No more!" says a woman with spirit that betokens a new sense of a valuable self. "I didn't mean anything to him. I can see that now!"[457] What is the connection between being treated "like dirt on the floor" and a subsequent statement of worth—"I'm not going to be treated like that!"?

Agency entails taking a position with regard to labels. What does it feel like for a client to be told they have a mental disorder? Many have been given multiple labels and can recite them like a shopping list. Bipolar, schizophrenia, treatment-resistant schizophrenia, psychosis, psychotic depression: these can be placed on people with diagnostic intent. Yet they can erode agency and militate against autonomy. Diagnoses can harm people by erecting barriers between the "sick" and the "well"? The language psychiatrists use can have a huge impact on a person's self-perception. Alternatives to the power of labels is available. In 2018, Lucy Johnstone and the psychologist Mary Boyle published a model they said could provide an alternative to diagnosis. "The Power Threat Meaning Framework." Instead of symptoms, the framework invites people to think of "threat responses"; instead of disorders, there are "general patterns" of behavior. "How is power operating in your life? What kind of threats does this pose?"

Shame is a powerful emotion and a potent social force. It can assert collective values, hold power to account, and uphold the social good. But shaming has also taken a dangerous new turn. Cathy O'Neil explores how shame is manufactured and mined by industries that grow big when we feel small.[458] What sustains the shame machine, and who profits from it? By understanding how this type of weaponized shame operates, she argues, we can dismantle its toxic effects on us and turn it into the power to fight back. Huge sectors of the economy are built to capitalise on our wishes to live up to certain ideals, targeting those—often the powerless and vulnerable—seen to be falling short. The shame associated with bodies, health, habits, money, and morals is a lucrative industry which is poised to amplify its efforts exponentially. The power of silencing and hiding is typical of shame. We might ask, "when has that been true for you?" Agency is the power of Speaking and Doing.

PART THREE

Transformative Repair

Chapter Sixteen

Sources of Healing

"He restores my soul."

—PSALM 23:4

"You shall be called a restorer of streets to dwell in"

—ISAIAH 58:12

Soul repair has to be one of the most rewarding but also skilful tasks given to human beings.

Repair of the body requires some years of specialist training. Knowing how to weave intricacies of skin, muscle and organ is immense work for surgeons and doctors. No less awesome is the labour undertaken by practitioners of soul repair. In pastoral work across the centuries, it is the labour of skilful shepherds. In recent times came the advent of healers of mind and emotions. Counsellors and therapists became part of the culture of modernity.

The good news is that centuries of theological reflection and Christian insight into pastoral practice have not been replaced. To be sure those insights and reflection were set in a particular frame; that of reference to God. The warp and woof of our lives here were thought to be inseparable from this bigger picture much as the details on a painting were set against a wider canvas. Within that picture frame, insights into the human condition and sources of healing are not redundant. The terrifying reality of the human heart is combined with deep compassion for the hurting. Biblical history no less than human life mirrored in centuries of the church is a record of people in pain and of the struggling soul. No less than a record is the biblical content a spiritual and moral reflection on our situation. Set in a cosmic sea; pinned between worlds, human beings wrestle with their conflicts, their ambiguity, their fraught emotions and often their inner demons. Centuries of pastoral practice and writing about the ups and downs of pilgrimage through life are both rich and highly pertinent for our times.

Sources of healing adorn the pages of Scripture and Christian writing. We speak of such things as:

- Confession and forgiveness
- Acknowledgement of our sins and faults
- Prayer and text
- Spiritual transformation
- Assurance and acceptance
- The change process via mental renewal and habits of thought and action

There is a very particular focus for a redemptive moment that becomes the basis for a redeemed life. Christians speak of the death and resurrection of Jesus as profoundly redemptive because it is atoning (according to what is no doubt the majority view about the significance of the cross). It is because of that every life can be redeemed in hopeful reconstruction. Putting the past right and embracing a new future because we have been cleansed: this is as powerful as it is profound. It may not be immediately obvious to people as they work through their problems that here is a highly relevant focal point for healing and restoration. Pushing a re-set on someone's moral standing with God may not seem to apply to human dilemmas or the change points in their lives when they are sick, anxious or depressed, bereaved or facing loss. Traditions of reflection and often penetrating writing how affirm though that this the answer because it aligns with the question—"how can I be rightly related to God?" "What does God think of me and how should I think of God?"

It is on that basis that another level of restoration comes into play; that of assurance. A sense of assurance and re-assurance about standing and position before God has been written about for centuries: rightly so for it is incomparable resource for the soul to believe that one is validated and endorsed by the highest of higher powers. Loved and assured that we are profoundly accepted and embraced as a child of God is of immense consequence.

Sources of redemptive repair are not, though, a question of believing certain things. Skilled hands, sharply attentive minds, attuned ears and empathic hearts are vital to those who aspire to reach across the aisle of human experience and bring a lonely soul to a deep sense of restoration and repair. It is through a fellow human being that relief will come to the troubled; mediating peace and connection with God. Opening ourselves to a spiritual dimension (however loosely defined) may help to take someone outside themselves and awaken studied awareness of someone or something there that bestows deeper meaning. But at a higher level than the beauty of a sunset or mindful attentiveness to life around us, establishing—or re-establishing—connection with God takes going beyond ourselves to a sense of personal encounter that is commonly described as highly liberating.

In a word, what this comes to is love. When someone is embodying a personal soul connection, it is in such dialogue in depth that authentic love creates a safe space to be authentic and vulnerable. It is in profound encounter that real love holds and heals the wounded. To restore the wounded ago from wounded history, to heal the trauma, pain and shame of the ego is the task of wounded angels.

We have considered a theoretical foundation for how disturbances and problems arise. On this basis, how do we approach the task of healing? Client and therapist constitute a dynamic yet relational force field; a trinitarian, personal system in which there are different entities present:

- The person in pain
- The therapist
- The interactional space between

So often, deeper issues are throbbing pains in the background. Short-term exploration of what agitates will sometimes "do the trick" but will rarely suffice. What has brought someone to embark on a therapeutic journey might indeed be an arena where a fresh perspective and way of thinking brings tangible relief. An exploration that takes a matter of weeks rather than months can be greatly beneficial, especially if a healing relationship is embraced as a temporary alliance and it is not just a quick fix. Having neither the time nor money; nor indeed inclination for deeper layer work by no means debars someone from seeking help. Clients may well not have resources or capability to probe root causes yet can find a good measure of relief through unburdening themselves or looking at thinking patterns so as to discover more effective ways of responding to their world.

Nevertheless, a therapist in the therapeutic approach we present here will want to be on the look out to explore what has given rise to the distress. If not, underlying distress will fight back as it were.

Constructing formulations is one of the best ways for mental health professionals to understand their clients and set treatment goals. As well as the ability to formulate clearly what is distressing about the client's story, it enables forces that are below the surface to be considered and what is going on in the process of transference. Arriving at an effective formulation draws on a model of:

- **Describe** the client's problems and patterns and what is being acted out in the client story
- **Review** the client's personal developmental history
- **Link** the problems and patterns to that history using organizing ideas from theoretical knowledge[459]

This is where questions about relationality, embodiment, meaning, and agency (REMA) are helpful ways of linking theory with practice. What is going on in the way someone is relating to others, in relating to their physicality, their quest to feel significant and of meaning, or difficulties in exercising agency are of great interest to the therapist as providing clues to what is troubling someone. The root causes of such disturbances lie deeper underground and need to be probed. We will notice such patterns by probing:

- What is going on in the way you relate to others and to me? Who am I reminding you of?
- What is happening in your body as we explore the impact of various events?
- What meanings come up for you as we explore issues of significance, purpose and hope?

- What prevents you from exercising agency? Where is your voice and value here?

Drawing out what is going on deep down therefore entails a view on the contents of the unconscious and discovering why someone is conflicted. We have looked at this through blockages arising from:

- Early emotional history (issues of attachments and splitting into part objects)
- Traumatic incidents in childhood which may have happened before conscious language
- Traumatic incidents since that have brought about an emotional "freezing"
- Social experiences that have either eroded our value or meant we never acquired it
- Our spiritual quest for value, purpose, and hope ,and especially our image of what is ultimate

The main point to make is that drawing out the deep-seated problems a client has comes out of therapy. It arises from a healing partnership. Relational depth provides a seedbed for tangled weeds to be examined and seeds of new growth to be planted.

These headlines signify means of healing arising from Christian, biblical reflection to foster renewal:

i. **Resonance**: Making sense of transference and client reports to practice empathic attunement. What are the conditions for identification and resonance such that two humanities are encountered and people relate to each other beyond difference?

ii. **Repentance**: Via dialogue, to acknowledge destructive aspects and need to change.

iii. **Re-membering**: Facing broken world and inner fragmentation to draw meaning in narratives that promote re-ordered thinking and allow different futures to emerge.

iv. **Recollection**: A condition of all truly wakeful and deep modes of living and fundamental to our transformation. A formal integration of our mind an integration of the entire person; a realization of its true self out of the depths of its being.

v. **Reconciling**: Looking at patterns of relating that have served as a screen on which to project our inner dysfunction thus seeking harmony between different parts of us and reorientation towards the transcendent being that is God.

vi. **Re-valuing**: Grasping how being diminished, facing indignity or indifference impacts clients so they can flourish: recover agency, dignity, and worth, and affirm their story.

We will look at these in turn in the context of redemptive repair. The key word here is redemption. "Redemption" has a number of meanings ranging from buying back so as to restore what has been lost, deliverance from a terrible situation or recovery of reputation. Less so now but in times past it has referred to exchange for something of value, such as *redemption* of empty soft drink bottles. Economically it might signify the exchange of paper notes or metal coins for purchase of an item or when a company purchases its own share stock. Theologically, it came to have a special meaning for deliverance from the guilt and power of sin, renewal and freedom in a new life.

Resonance (Who Am I Reminding You of? What Is Coming Up for You? Can I Enter Into That?)

The practice of therapy requires of us unconscious awareness and then conscious awareness. We do not "know" other minds and the subject of therapy much more than we can know our own subjectivity. Sometimes you have to let go of your own knowledge and assumptions about what is going on in the client so as to break down barriers and enter into someone else's life world. For that to happen, therapist and client need to come into attunement.

Attunement means that we do not meet at the surface necessarily but we go deeper. It is under the surface of things where deep calls to deep (Ps 42:7). This is two humanities meeting. As their concerns and pain comes near, the other becomes brother and sister. It is our humanness which Sanderson advocates is necessary to balance out dehumanizing abuse experience.[460]

Therapist and client may pursue peace of mind as a goal of healing. Pursuit of such harmony is not wrong—harmony with God, harmony with close relationships or workplace, harmony within oneself—but it cannot start there. Rather we learn to listen to discordant voices and cacophony of sounds that play within. We ought not to shrink back from such a task for the discordance needs to be faced. The angry, unsettling, blaring notes must be heard; deeper motivation and conflict exposed.

A therapist in this approach is learning to discern the themes emerging. Tuning into what lies within brings illumination and the potential for transformation but it also brings disturbance to a therapist. Such is countertransference that operates in a therapeutic relationship. The client unconsciously projects intolerable aspects of the self onto the therapist, and the therapist internalizes this discord. As a result, a therapist feels within emotions of the client, as though they had sprang from oneself. Using Winnicott's ideas, holding and containing provides "an optimally responsive environment that meets a need for affective attunement . . . [to] stabilize experience of self and safe connection."[461]

Taking on board such resonance can produce conflicted reactions for most have experienced deficits of attunement in our lives. As we have seen with attachment theory, it is loving eyes and kind voices of parents that assure a child that one is are seen and noticed. Lack of such attunement might arise from caregivers in early relationships or in later relationships. If an attuned caregiver is the building block of the secure hold to feel safe in the world and to engage in relationships, deficits that the client has experienced may well be felt within the therapist. It is vital that this is allowed to happen. Rather than a focus on counseling techniques, a practitioner learns to stay with moments of distress and pain as part of the therapeutic process.

Attunement and resonance requires the therapist to practice close discernment. Most of us are very poor listeners. The metaphor of music is a helpful way of developing emotional and therapeutic literacy. Tuning into the underlying themes is a listening skill. When we listen to music, we sub-consciously pick up or pick out the themes. There are maps of meaning around human action and distress that are there to be illuminated. Most people do not get beneath the top melody—or maybe the overall rhythm. To listen to serious music and get the most out of it, you must seek for more than the top line. In every therapy and dialogue; as in every demand and negotiation, there are underlying themes to be tuned into that if heard and recognized, will bring break-through in understanding. But first we hear the negative notes; the jangling of discord inside in the minor key.

What messages can we hear amidst noise within another human being? Instead of harmony, we have jarring notes. These must be listened to and given full attention. It will not suffice to be so relentlessly positive in pursuit of resolution that we hear only the good and hopeful major notes.

When something does not fit, disharmony can be resolved into harmony but not immediately. There will be disharmony, discord and conflict. Music without the tension of discord is like a story without a dilemma. Without a resolution, we end on a jarring note. Diversity is to be valued. Music would be without life if played on one note. Respecting the other and respect differences is vital for the therapeutic project. In playing a duet you learn to follow the other person's part as well as your own.

Therapy offers evocative power to stimulate reflection and discovery moments that break cycles and help facilitate new cycles and alternative cultures to those of devaluation. There is scope for transformative learning to occur. Such discord and disharmony occurs in the social field as well as the individual life. On the contemporary landscape, ideas about difference and diversity have splintered and splintered again and again. Can there be any resonance between therapist and client such that there is some possibility of identification beyond a trite statement of "I know what that is like!"

We have a fragmented field. But what we have left is resonance. A sound is evoked from an instrument, a crystal, a stone or a wine glass. It sets up a sympathetic echo in other entities. Good concert halls are resonant places whilst some recording has can have too much resonance. A metaphor for the way that association cortices of the brain process information is "sympathetic chords," internal resonances that are self-activating.[462] A good musician works with the resonance. In harmonic singing, singers must attune to other voices and wait for their emergence.[463] In social life, experiences that "strike a chord" have the potential to be transformative, to move from recognition of fellowship amongst difficult client experiences to a situation pregnant with new possibilities for transference identifications and healing.

Psychotherapy has its concept of identification. With classic projection, feelings and behavior are put upon the therapist. When a behavior is attributed to others in order to identify with it, this is projective identification. It represents a response to someone else's impulses as one's own. In the hands of Melanie Klein, projective identification is acting out an unconscious phantasy in which aspects of the self or an internal object are split off and attributed to an external object.[464] The wish to identify is a strong force through life. Appropriate identification with the therapist may be a crucial aspect of the emotional history of clients who have misidentified or who over-identify with others. Such transference may be part of the healing.[465]

Christian theology also has its source of identification. "Don't condemn a man" says the old Indian proverb, "until you have walked a mile in his moccasins." The empathy of God means that the Creator wears our moccasins and embraced what it means to be human. The life, death and resurrection of Jesus was a thirty-three-year period of constant identification with humanity. This brings a strong sense of comfort that comes from shared experiences. As the New Testament book of Hebrews puts it,

> For this reason, He had to be made like His brothers in every way, in order that He might become a merciful and faithful high priest. (Heb 2:17)

Politics used to be about economic interests that were competing for attention and resources. Late modernity attunes us to the voice; where is the voice situated and who is it speaking for? Modern forms of identity are about solidarity defined by people's pain and shared experiences. People feel themselves to be representatives of sections of society such as gender, black, ethnic minority, transgender, sexuality, disability, age, class or religion. The problem is that each of those categories of differences can be sub-divided further. We are left with a splintered social fabric and "the politics of recognition." I too am an under-privileged victim. My claim to recognition is greater than yours!

Who was this one who lives, who spoke as He did, lived, died and lived again? Can Jesus speak for the women of Africa or Afghanistan? Can Jesus act as the representative of humanity and does such an entity even exist? Christian theology affirms precisely that.

Anyone addressing the deeper issues of the human heart needs to be able to tune in to the spiritual and emotional needs playing in that person's life. Search for resonance. Be attuned to themes in the background of troubled souls and then learn to relate those themes to sources of healing. What is playing in this person's life? Is it guilt, loneliness, fear, insecurity, anxiety or a desperate longing to be loved? This only comes through attunement, or, to change the metaphor, dialogue in depth.

There is something about weakness and vulnerability that is instantly attractive. A relationship based on honesty and disclosure can, as long as it is mutual, become strong. One-sided vulnerability only reinforces the power that one party thinks they wield. When there is a degree of weakness and shared difficulty, then the common experience draws people together rather than polarizes them.

The inescapable reality of death pits us against an identity based on youthfulness and healthy bodies Theology as well as social criticism challenges this profoundly. As Stanley Hauerwas comments, "for the God we Christians must learn to worship is not a god of self-sufficient power, a god who in self-possession needs no one; rather ours is a God who needs a people, who needs a son. Absoluteness of being or power is not a work of the God we have come to know through the cross of Christ."[466]

In the Greek philosophy of Heraclitus, being and nothingness are engaged in the creation of the universe when they enter into dialogue. "That which is in opposition is in concert and from things that differ comes the most beautiful harmony."[467]

Repentance (Confession)

Our problems are a rope with two strands. We are profoundly affected by what people do to us—their injustice and their devaluation, the lies and the violence. But there is also what we do to other people and to ourselves to hurt people or make our problems worse. An inadequate concept of sin and responsibility will always focus on what others have done to us. A naive and unbiblical view of the human condition will downplay the reality of evil and blind people so they only see themselves purely as victims of circumstances. This is where concepts of sin and responsibility are important.

Repentance is a very strong word in Christian-based pastoral practice and one which can be heard in a harsh way. What it is not is judgmental; that is, taking a moral stance in a way that writes someone off and leaves them shrouded in condemnation. Neither is it an attitude of pointing out the faults and failings of others. Encouraging someone to come to repentance means more than feeling sorrowful. It entails the capacity to say "I have done wrong. . . . I was to blame." This is profoundly emancipatory. In *Whatever Became of Sin?*, the psychotherapist Karl Menninger drew attention to the need to take responsibility for what one has done wrong. He brings morality and the existence and consequences of sin today. Menninger believed in sin, that we have become lenient in holding people accountable for breaking the standards of God.[468]

Repentance in a counseling context entails something of the following:

i. Relating to God or the lack of it. Clearly this is problematic where someone has little sense of the divine or has vaguer sense of something beyond us rather than a personal God.

ii. Confession as therapist and client go to a dark place.

iii. The reality of human experience as a mixed cocktail that we are predators as well as prey, perpetrators and not victims only. Counseling can operate in the mode of victimhood but it is important to recognize that we may have been part of a problem and contributed to it.

iv. Exploring what sense of remorse is appropriate when there has been a pattern or act which has been destructive to others and/or is the exercise of harmful power or abuse.

v. In a humble way, encouraging a client to acknowledge that others got hurt through actions but awareness also that blame-shifting and evasiveness is all part of self-deceit.

vi. Providing the language of acknowledgement, which is a stronger word than mere "apology."

vii. Give a stimulant towards probing issues of guilt and shame while recognizing that guilt-laden personalities may have soaked up any guilt going spare or hating themselves.

viii. Not leaving it there but opening the client towards redemption and hope.

Going the other way and changing your mind is at the centre of repentance. Repentance does not mean that the therapist is evaluating the client according to his or her own standards. Jung, for instance, spoke of us having a shadow side which needs to be integrated, rather than disavowed.

Re-Membering

The Gospels record a man who was split apart so severely that his inner world was like six thousand pieces, each screaming out. In that encounter with a sorely troubled man, there is one thing Jesus wants to know. "Then he asked him, 'what is your name?' And he answered him, 'My name is Legion, for we are many'" (Mark 5:9). "What is your name?" shows an act of reaching into the residual humanity and seeing the individual. The man cannot yet name himself. And yet after the invasion of divine love, he is restored to his right mind, clothed and talking with Jesus (Mark 7:15).

Many feel a sense of their lives in fragments, broken into pieces. The broken world experience is all too familiar with those who come for counseling. Often anxiety is related to external factors but in depression especially we look inside. The pain is so overwhelming that they feel unable to hold themselves together and function. As therapists, we accompany our clients in encountering this overwhelming pain, and do not disintegrate when we do so. In this way, we become a sign of hope as we dwell in the possibility of integration.

"Remember me like this," Jesus said at the last supper (Luke 22:19). Think what such memory entails. To remember is to re-member, that is to bring together the fragments of memory as to stitch back together the members of a body. Jesus spoke of his broken body—"take, eat: this is my body which is broken for you; do this in remembrance of me" (1 Cor 11:24). Communion is an act of re-enacting the drama so the hearers are drawn in. Our broken world experience means that in the broken body of Jesus, the emotionally laden memories of experiences that can shatter the moral and mental state of people can be made whole. Re-integration becomes possible in a new unity. We are then "re-membered" even as we remember.

This underscores the importance of the one who acts as healer or in a healing relationship being empathically present so as "to hold . . . in an integrated state a core self that is at risk of disconnecting, dissociating, and disintegrating."[469]

Being open to the story of the cross takes us into the integration of fragmented experience. In Christian tradition, nothing can separate us from the love of God. Experiencing the depths of the human condition, Jesus has carried the love of God into rejection, into despair, into betrayal, into cruelty and into death. The cross is the greatest possible demonstration and witness that there are no holds barred against God's love; nothing too messy and unrefined. Death cannot keep it out, and neither life, angels, demons, present nor the future can extinguish its blaze. The love of God has already penetrated the highest or the lowest experience, from the heights of heaven to the depths of the grave and of hell. The love of God was embodied in the vicarious sin-bearer.

There is a sense in which all the human experiences of Jesus were vicarious, endured on behalf of others, arising from the conditions he imposed on himself. The innocent sufferer of Isaiah 53 is taking up our infirmities and carrying our sorrows. Through what is done to him, he is entering into what others have done to us; identifying with all the innocent sufferers that crowd history. We can make a profound connection with the trauma and tragedy that surfaces so often. The rejection that Jesus experienced, the way he climbed into mockery and humiliation, the way he was pierced by the betrayal that pierces us, his immersion into cruelty and descent into darkness—all this showed a deep identification with the human condition in a way that truly liberates us. It was our betrayal, our rejection, our cruelty and our mockery that he was drinking deeply into. Jesus was humbled with humiliation. "Surely he took up our infirmities and carried our sorrows" (Isa 53:4).

The good news not only addresses fundamental human concerns, it addresses fundamental human needs. But there is more in the package. The innocent sufferer is not only identifying with the sufferers, but he is also standing in the place of the guilty.

> But He was pierced for our transgressions, he was crushed for our iniquities; the punishment that brought us peace was upon him and by his wounds we are healed. We all like sheep have gone astray, each of us has turned to his own way; and the Lord has laid on him the iniquity of us all. (Isa 53:5–6).

Re-membering comes to special focus with disability. Communion represents solidarity and reconciliation with humankind: the temporarily able-bodied with those who have disabilities and we ourselves with our own bodies. In the Eucharist we encounter God who displayed signs of disability, not as a demonstration of failure and defects but in affirmation of connection and strength.[470]

Recollection

> Therefore gird up the loins of your mind, be sober and rest your hope fully upon the grace that is to be brought to you at the revelation of Jesus Christ; as obedient children, not conforming yourselves to your former desires. (1 Pet 1:13–14)

"Yet this I call to mind and therefore I have hope" (Lam 3:21). What do we mean by "calling to mind"? Recollection has a long and serious history in Christian spiritual practice. It is a formal integration of our mind and beyond that the means an integration of the entire person; a realization of its true self out of the depths of its being into the potential associated with openness to God.

> He shall be like a tree, planted by the rivers of water, that brings forth its fruit in its season, whose leaf also shall not wither, and whatever he does shall prosper. (Ps 1:3)

Mindfulness is a well-documented practice that has become part of re-approaching traditional psychotherapeutic practice. Much understanding of this combines eastern mindfulness practice with western relational psychotherapy such as Marjorie Schuman's emphasis on "inquiring deeply."[471]

Remaining in traditional modes is fully possible, however. Spiritual writers down the centuries have been clear that we must proceed to the depth in order to gain full and adequate awareness of things, hearing God's call in the depths of our being, and bringing our most intimate selves to full awareness. This is fundamentally an unpragmatic and non-functional attitude shaped ultimately by relationship to God. Usually accomplished through silent meditation and prayer, recollection brings deep awareness of truly wakeful and deep modes of living and is vital for our transformation. It is somewhat different to mindfulness with full alertness to all that is present in the present; recollection takes us to intuitive penetration of the essence of things and conscious dwelling of truths already established (knowing that and not just knowing about). In a state of anxious distraction, we do not attend fully to anything to penetrate to the heart of things but are dragged along from one object to another, never touching any of them but superficially.

> A person who exhausts himself in the moment's concern, who passes without a breathing space from one concentrated work to another, who always gives his unreserved attention to the task of the hour without ever pausing to recollect himself—such a person is as little recollected as one who dissipates his life in dreaming, playing, and empty chatter.[472]

Reconciling

What shall we do with the anger that lurks within? Can we hear it and turn it to something positive? A divided self results in being hard to live with yourself.

In psychotherapy, the "divided self" was given expression by psychiatrist R. D. Laing. Using case studies of patients he had worked with, Laing argued that psychosis is not a medical condition, but an outcome of the "divided self," or the tension between the two personas within us: one our authentic, private identity, and the other the false, "sane" self that we present to the world.[473]

Sometimes we might encounter failures within ourselves. What we criticize in other people is usually present within ourselves. When we enter into relationships, it may be we are found putting barriers up. Those who are strong are prevented from connecting with each other at a deep level. Like two positively charged particles, their very strength drives each other away. A relationship based on the need to prove strength and perfection often means that people miss one another and never build a bridge. All too easily, we can end up suppressing so much of ourselves. There are multiple layers and these can become conflicted and tangled like so many roots.

Repression operates so as to keep hidden what must not speak its name. Considerable ego energy is deployed in order to suppress or disguise unconscious influences. Invariably, we can feel the upheaval as internal worlds collide but may have very little understanding of why we are divided. It may be too that we have a sense of civil war with the classic statement of "part of me wants this, part of me wants that." In Christian theology, that is expressed in the New Testament as "I do not understand what I do. For what I want to do I do not do, but what I hate I do. . . . For I have the desire to do what is good, but I cannot carry it out" (Rom 7:15, 19)

Or the idea of "internal family systems therapy" could be cited where Schwartz realized he was echoing Jung and Assagioli who theorized that the mind is composed of numerous subpersonalities. Schwartz argued that the parts relate to one another dynamically through an overall entity which manifests a capacity for self-awareness and scrutiny. This he calls "the self"; an internal system.[474]

Reconciliation therefore has a meaning around integration, the bringing together of different aspect of ourselves that have been at odds. In a Christian context, it speaks of bringing peace between parties that have been tense or angry with each other through conflict. Beyond that, it speaks of reconciliation with God; a re-orientation to the personal transcendent with whom we are not close.

> The old has gone, the new is here! All this is from God, who reconciled us to himself through Christ and gave us the ministry of reconciliation: that God was reconciling the world to himself in Christ, not counting people's sins against them. And he has committed to us the message of reconciliation. We are therefore Christ's ambassadors, as though God were making his appeal through us. We implore you on Christ's behalf: Be reconciled to God. (2 Cor 5:17–20)

It is a worthy goal of personal therapy to integrate the disconnected parts of self.

This has to be the ultimate level of reconciliation; harmony with the ground of our being.

Re-Valuing

As we have explored, within interpersonal exchanges, not to be heard or listened to, to feel that one is belittled or diminished, or to feel a lack of dignity is to experience an erosion in worth. Within social experience, to feel that one is "less than" on account of the reduced value placed on you results in negative impacts that damage a sense of self. It might be a vicious hatred of self. It might be perceived failure as a person or limited sense that one is worthwhile. A low sense of worth can however, be countermanded. It is not the end of the story.

Psychoanalysis documented the idea of resistance, that the client is affected by unconscious mental processes that block integration. Freud had someone clinging on to their illness a central plank of his approach.

> The discovery of the unconscious and the introduction of it into consciousness is performed in the face of a continuous resistance on the part of the patient. Psychoanalytic treatment may in general be conceived of as such as a re-education in overcoming internal resistances.[475]

But we can look at the idea of resistance differently. A client growing up in the second half of the twentieth century laments how the way the world seems to be ordered is confounded by possession of secret knowledge. He knows things could be different, that acts of injustice militate against what should or shouldn't be. Such deep-down Protest will be a precarious foothold through much of life. A client dares to believe it. The Protest is a capacity for this daring belief. It felt like an entitlement suddenly received, as if a will had been opened and gracious discovery made. "I am valuable," proclaimed a client. "I am now not longer just useful!" "I AM VALUABLE!"[476]

Antidotes to indifference can be instilled through internalizing whispers of love. What an amazing sleight of hand is conveyed through vision! The act of seeing magically transforms people and situations. Self-worth feeds self-identity—the way we perceive ourselves. An individual seeks to break free from the all-encompassing way he or she is seen.[477] A social group demands to be seen differently, to have a greater stake in the politics of attention. Perspective means a different way of seeing which counteracts the asymmetry of vision. Positive experiences are vital for emotional regulation and the development of a healthy sense of a valuable self.

Relationships that have the time, that demonstrate the magic ingredient of a love that is expressed and combined with boundaries are creating a secure environment where someone feels valuable. That is vital in building competence in understanding the emotions and thoughts of others.[478] This is where working in relational depth with a skilled therapist can be profoundly healing. Structure with benign intent is not incidental to a journey of healing. It is profoundly therapeutic.

Theologians of different stripes have found much of interest in the work of Carl Rogers with its signposting an acceptance, which has its source beyond ourselves. Rogers communicates a message of acceptance is beyond the empirical world.[479] Thomas Odin suggested that the effective psychotherapist is one who, through dialogue, helps the client to achieve congruence, openness to experience, personal self-disclosure, and self-understanding. The basis for conditions of worth labours under the presupposition that the client is acceptable not only to the counsellor but as a human being, by the ground of being itself, that "the final reality that we confront in life is for us. This mediates an ontological assumption that is theological in that it is this assumption which the Christian proclamation of God's self-disclosure in Jesus Christ makes explicit. (Odin refers positively to Karl Barth's "analogia fidei," i.e., an analogy which reads not from therapeutic experience to theological categories, but the other way around). There is an analogy, similarity, between revelation and therapy. Just as the incarnation witnesses to the God who does not just diagnose or analyze man's needs but actively participates in them, so effective counseling is not just objective diagnosis of the individual's conflict but active empathetic involvement in the client's suffering.[480]

Rogers discovered towards the end of his life that he had greatly underestimated both the mystical quality of the therapeutic process and the power of the person-centered approach to give access to the spiritual dimension of experience. Brian Thorne sought to probe the implications of regarding person-centered therapy as an essentially spiritual discipline.[481] Rogers' later trust in instinct was spiritual, said Thorne. Within that very communication of empathic regard is an openness to God.

Willing to be vulnerable is important. A much-circulated TED talk was that of Brené Brown on this. Brown studied human connection—our ability to empathize, belong, love. Value—or its lack—is vital. Its absence has impact. The thought that we are not worthy leads to fear of connections. Her key findings were that vulnerability is the core of shame and fear and our struggle for worthiness, but it is also a site of ambiguity, the birthplace of joy, of creativity, of belonging, of love.[482]

Formats of healing

According to Winarick, there are five primary mechanisms of change in therapy are:[483]

i. Transference-countertransference matrix in what is going on between client and therapist
ii. Emotional experiencing/affect expression and tolerance
iii. Internalization/learning of adaptive coping strategies and skills
iv. Holding environment/new relational experience is corrective
v. Insight

Internalization and learning of adaptive coping strategies are vital for being able to embrace a journey of transformation whereby clients can start to believe in their valuable personhood. Beliefs about the self are hard to shift, as the challenges of Cognitive Behavioral Therapy will attest. The old material and conflicts within will fight back and be highly resistant to new experiences. But new neural pathways can be developed that give effect to a powerful passage in the New Testament: "We have known and believed the love that God has for us" (1 John 4:16).

Our model of formulation is a psychodynamic one aimed at deep-seated problems. It seeks to:

i. **Describe** the client's problems and patterns
ii. **Review** the client's personal developmental history
iii. **Link** the problems and patterns to that history using organizing ideas from theoretical knowledge[484]

Such exploration and insight can draw on the means available through the REMA questions such as "What is going on in your patterns of relating in the past and now (who do I remind you of?)" "What is going on in your body as we explore certain emotions and wounded history?" "What comes up for you in meanings you place on certain experiences?" "What do you want here?" "Where is your voice?"

When it comes to linking patterns to client history, using organizing ideas from theoretical knowledge can most certainly embrace knowledge about the basis for our valuable personhood; namely that one is profoundly loved by God and of immense worth and infinite value. As Jesus said, "So don't be afraid; you are more valuable to God than a whole flock of sparrows" (Matt 10:31).

Revaluing will result in:

- A new sense that we are loved and listened to, heard by God and others
- A new sense that we are included in the conversations of life, not excluded
- A new sense that we have dignity and that we value ourselves

A strong case can be made that therapists should not collude with the language of the self in itself. It is in relation to God and others that our sense of value can most safely be fostered.

However, one of the staunch resistances (and often the last bastion to fall in being revaluing) is overcoming a profound lack of self-acceptance and guilt. It is to this that we now turn.

Chapter Seventeen

Acceptance and Forgiveness

(Shame and Guilt)

"Moral injury is usually characterised by shame and guilt, often leading to loss of identity and meaning. It is a deeper, spiritual condition—a soul-wound."[485]

"All our sins and failings, our inadequacies, were somehow dealt with there, so that we—the apostles and all who are called to be 'ministers of reconciliation'—could embody in our own lives the faithfulness of God. At the cross, God made the sinless Messiah to be sin on our behalf."[486]

As we explore human dilemmas, we come inexorably against major issues at the core of clients with which they are struggling. The most fundamental concerns may not be wedded to developmental stages in early experience but the way we are now and how we respond to matters that threaten us.

At the deepest level of being, a client may be pursued by two ghosts: guilt and shame. These loom large in the psychological lexicography of therapy and will be explored with considerable awareness. They are fundamental to how we are in the world and deal with what has happened to us. Clinicians will attempt to handle guilt and shame from their own therapeutic approach but also with some sense of resonance. In various ways and to differing degrees, we have been there. This is common human experience. A psychodynamic therapist will want to probe the link between feelings of guilt and shame as currently experienced with sources of anxiety arising from the earliest conflicts people have. Clients may well be those who soak up any guilt going spare and be prone to feeling ashamed.

Guilt and shame are aspects of the human situation that most recognize as definitely pathological at one end of the spectrum. Yet this is the stuff of life. Novelists and journalists know about these ghosts. So do priests and practitioners who have laboured for centuries in the fields of complexity. Those who live with a guilty secret or a shame are all around us and indeed take residence within.

This seems to go beyond the Freudian instinct-powered approach to human conflict. The reason why guilt and shame turn up so regularly in the consulting room is that they strike loud notes on the moral register of the human situation as well as our social sensitivity about how we are with others. Guilt and shame may indeed become destructive but fundamentally are not to do with parts of ourselves that become pathogenic so much as related to our very being and how we deal with life.

Redemptive reconstruction can best be brought into the frame by juxtaposing two major themes of pastoral theology—namely acceptance and forgiveness. We can use the analogy of a daguerreotype (the first commercially successful photographic process; each daguerreotype is a unique image on a copper plate). On the daguerreotype of shame we can capture the imprint of acceptance. Our other copper plate captures guilt with which we can group forgiveness in a family of resemblance.

People tend to believe stories that reinforce previous belief—so called "motivated reasoning." But new narratives are possible. Those who feel shamed can learn to tell a different story.[487]

Shame v guilt is played out in the difference between collectivist cultures compared to individualistic ones. Honor and shame cultures rely on external sanctions and pressure to enforce the social rules. Guilt cultures rely on internalized conviction of sin. Shame requires an audience. Guilt does not. It is internal. Guilt is remorse for behaviors, actions, or thoughts and is usually separate from the person's core. Collectivist cultures place a greater salience on shame, emphasizing interdependent relationships and prioritizing of group *goals* over personal ones. Shame taints family name and honor. In collectivist cultures, mental illness is stigmatizing; it reflects poorly on family lineage and can influence beliefs about the suitability of someone to be linked with a family.

Shame is a powerful emotion and a potent social force. It can assert collective values, hold power to account, and uphold the social good. The prime need is to "save face." Saving face brings honor to oneself and one's culture. Hiding true feelings is essential. It will not do to reveal what one is really thinking. Saving face results in the ability to preserve the public appearance of the patient and family for the sake of community.

Consider the issue of furious husbands killing their wives for sleeping around. In many cultures, such a "crime of honor" was not even punished by the courts in the past. The reason the husband behaves this way is not just insane jealousy. He believes his honor has been irretrievably damaged. It is a social question, not just an internal mental event. A sense of sin or personal guilt was not the point.

Many cultures are tight knit communities where everyone knows everyone else and everything about them! In the Middle East and central Asia, a major objective is to accumulate honor and avoid anything that could deplete it. Honor is eroded through shame. Shame brings disgrace down on one's head and dishonors the family. It must be avoided at all costs. To prevent letting the side down, people will preserve appearances. Honor comes from age, from family connections and from hard work and success. In Islamic societies, honor is inseparable from religion. It is not confined to Middle Eastern culture. Entire societies made maintaining honor a vital task, especially to adult males in the community. It is the ultimate humiliation to be seen as weak. Having an addiction goes against Asian social norms for example. Dishonor flows from breaking the honor code and responding with insufficient vigor to an insult or an injury. Sin and guilt and the notion of individual, rather than collective responsibility, were the province of Western societies. This is changing.

Honor and social shame still have salience when it comes to paedophilia and marketing. The former dark practice is called out and its self-justifying advocates treated to public shaming. Their ranks were swollen by "greedy bankers" or offenders in public or private advertising campaigns. Some marketing relies on shame; their campaigns becoming the superegos of late modernity as they challenge bad breath for instance. Large sectors of the economy are built to capitalise on our wishes to live up to certain ideals, targeting those—often the powerless and vulnerable—seen to be falling short. The shame associated with bodies, health, habits, money, and morals is a lucrative industry.

Socially and commercially, shame is manufactured and mined by industries that grow big when we feel small. The weight of shame tends to fall upon those who are marginalized. "Poverty-shaming" or "fat shaming" is thought, wrongly, to imply an easy choice. The burden falls on the least powerful member. On social media, people shame others. Shame is an exercise in profiteering, designed to keep someone in place and silenced. It is so debilitating, keeping you half-way out. The incapacity to feel shame can be a social problem. Yet the word "shameless" is problematic. There is a rule you feel regarding your own notion of community or norms of interpersonal life that have been infringed. People can be ashamed in not feeling rich, strong or powerful; keeping down those parts of ourselves we dislike that feel like "dirty secrets."

We saw in this chapter that shame arises from childhood sexual abuse and has a detrimental effect on esteem. It brings with it "feelings of isolation, alienation, stigmatisation and 'powerlessness.'"[488]

So what is shame and what does it represent in clinical contexts? One perspective is that it is a "response to an encounter we have with someone else."[489] Although the line between shame and guilt is not clear-cut (there can be much false guilt), "objective shame . . . has a . . . source outside the judged individual." Rather than it being a person's own evaluation of self-worth that leads to judgement, "shame is pronounced according to the measure of the . . . group."[490] It comes from external factors. As Izard notes, shame is a social emotion, typically felt after failures, inadequacies, and moral or social transgressions.[491]

The presence of others who scrutinise lies at the heart of shame: "the experience of one's felt sense of self disintegrating in relation to a dysregulating other." Coping strategies cope involve dissociating from the agony of shame, "[disconnecting] from self and from others . . . [holding] identities of unworthiness [and fabricating] a performance of self."[492] Indeed, De Young observes that chronic shame brings back the devastating, hopeless meaning of one's self-image that will "confirm core badness."[493] "I AM a bad person" highlights the shame-filled state the client experiences.

How then does anyone move on from an experience of shame that belongs to our wounded history?

By understanding how shame operates, we can dismantle its toxic effects on us and turn it into the power to fight back.

Psychotherapeutically, shame comes up so very often in client distress and an effective therapist needs to know how to address it. Standing up for oneself without shame is a powerful to be in—for many, tremblingly so. Here is a woman whose partner is having an affair. Note the role of value and worth in what follows. She feels shame in allowing him to stray, as if it is her fault; shame in being a complete failure as a person and as a wife. The antidote was to discover her worth—recover her value and gather more and more of herself as a person in her own right.[494]

You feel guilty about something you did and shame about what you are. There is a grey area between them. Shame reflects on your actual self. It defines you socially. There might be marks on our record that cause us to be denied in an application, for example, for credit, a loan, or housing.

Shame is deeply relational. Therapeutically, it suggests the value of relational attunement; the therapist reaching into the places that have been silenced and drawing them out. For the most part, we hate the parts of ourselves that we see in others and experiences of shame latch on to this.

Sin and Guilt/Right and Wrong

Shamed people shame others. Those prone to guilt place guilt trips on others or, alternatively, can compel us to distance myself from and reject others as a means of punishment.

Life is a struggle. Guilt and suffering: conscience and contingency are not occasional interruptions into the norm. They represent our true situation: they are the norm.[495]

Being in the world creates guilt and shame at an existential level. The realization that we must take responsibility for our own lives and take charge of our identities evokes a pain of existential anxiety, described by Paul Tillich as anxiety of guilt and condemnation. We have not been all we could be.[496] Existential guilt strikes at the conscience. This does not represent specific shortcomings and sins so much as issues that face our very being. Moral self-affirmation is profoundly threatened by guilt and condemnation. Responsibility for our own lives is something we must take with both hands.

Shame tends to be more public; guilt is a largely private affair. Consciousness of personal sin, of rights and wrongs, is a feature of a society where individual responsibility is stressed. It is no doubt related to the impact of Judaeo-Christian civilization.

> The word of the Lord came to me: "What do you mean by using this proverb concerning the land of Israel: The fathers eat sour grapes, and the children's teeth are set on edge?" As I live—this

> is the declaration of the Lord God—"you will no longer use this proverb in Israel. Look, every life belongs to Me. The life of the father is like the life of the son—both belong to Me. The person who sins is the one who will die. . . . "Therefore, house of Israel, I will judge each one of you according to his ways." (Ezek 18:1–4, 30)

This was in contrast to the group responsibility for someone's actions whereby an entire family could fall under collective penalty. Allied with legal theory in the West in which jurisprudence established the "mens rea" of personal culpability, a sense of sin and individual blameworthiness has been a strong social driver. It was not just a case of particular individuals being held to account, a sin-based society was fundamental to a worldview, to a moral framework of accountability. Transgression incurred sanction because that was how things should be.

Punishment to absolve personal guilt for failure or trying to remove the experience of shame are recurrent themes in client history. People embark on a range of endeavours to free themselves from the cage. What is shameful to the self is discomforting and must not be allowed to be the last word.

Shame and weakness were re-cast by psychoanalysis as personality problems, a sickness. Sin and guilt came to be much stronger drivers of life in the West. A sense of sin went hand in glove with a sense of "ought." Moral duty was a strong imperative. It is perhaps one of the strongest markers of societal shift that "duty" has completely gone out of fashion. Almost no-one is buying shares in it anymore. There remains a strong and rising "blame culture." Someone must be called to account!

The presence of guilt in everyday life is pervasive nonetheless, even without recognition of a moral code that brings consciousness of sin. Guilt is both an intrapsychic and an interpersonal emotion. It is therapeutically useful to distinguish two senses of guilt, deontological and altruistic guilt, induced through different experimental paradigms. Deontological guilt comes from having offended moral authority or norms, while altruistic guilt arises from selfish behavior and the reactions of others.[497] There is an existential guilt that arises from not having embraced what one could be and failure in life. Guilt can also take the form of a neuroses; a guilt stemming from the loss of someone and sense. Depression appears as proof of one's worthlessness.[498]

But there is also a very real guilt from transgressing what we know as right and wrong. Humans are not only complicated, we are prone to considerable heights of self-deception and depths of murky motivation.

Blind to our blind spots, we fail to trace the wolf to its lair. A moral code (especially the sense of God's law in Judeao-Christian backgrounds) highlights this but as the New Testament describes, there is a moral law inside (Rom 2:14). Conscience generates regrets.

Somewhere to Go

High amongst the imperatives for meaning-making in the human situation is the need to make sense of our moral experience. Our sense of right and wrong and all too often trail of wreckage has to fit into a coherent perspective.

Theologically, where should we look beyond a postmodern focus to find meaning where we can, albeit nowhere with any authority? Biblical texts shows that "humanity dishonours God . . . we bring shame upon God . . . [regarding] the Creator God as though he has little value . . . [and] exchanged the basis of [our] own glory [and self-worth]" (Rom 1:18–21). "God works to defend and restore his honour [through Jesus' work on the cross]" so that those who "understand their identity in Christ" are enabled to honor God and others.[499]

Through this lens, how does that help us understand the cross? Here are five steps to walk through.

i. Sin violates sacredness; it devalues other people and dishonors God.
ii. Some kind of payment is needed to acknowledge that this matters. Everyday interpersonal tensions demonstrate it. Impaired relationships require reconciliation and compensation.
iii. In solidarity with humanity, Jesus steps in as divinely appointed representative to make a one-off payment for our indebtedness. He identifies as "one of us." Solidarity is the key.
iv. At the cross Jesus absorbs both what people do us and what we do to others. He pays the price.
v. An exchange is made in our state whereby human beings can be reconciled and participate in the standing and Spirit of Christ. This is a complete reversal of our lack of worth.

It is fundamental to Christian belief that there is somewhere to go with the guilt that clings on. There is an equation between the problem and the antidote:

Guilt	—	Forgiveness
Shame	—	Acceptance

When conditions of worth function well, they are life-enhancing. When they take on an absolute form they assume the character and oppressive function of the principalities and powers. People can be treated as guilty without being personally guilty (racism for instance). The unconditional love of God comes into contact with conditions of worth at the cross and invites responses out from illusion to reality.[500] Developing this model, the American pastoral theologian Don Browning sees the cross in terms of God's unconditional acceptance.[501]

Acceptance is powerful. The New Testament speaks of a position before God that brings a reversal of having a deep insecurity about where we stand. Paul's letter to the church in Rome refers to this: "Therefore, since we have been justified through faith, we have peace with God through our Lord Jesus Christ, through whom we have gained access by faith into this grace in which we now stand. And we boast in the hope of the glory of God" (Rom 5:1–2).

This is a profound reality that can be understand both through a theological lens but also a psychological lens. A psychological reading of what it means to be acquitted and declared righteous speaks of divine approval against a backcloth of not being acceptable to oneself, not being okay. Unconditional acceptance is a ticking bomb that detonates shame-filled experiences of dishonor. This has potent implications for those who have had difficult experiences with where they stand with human caregivers. There is a warm embrace and crucially, a new position, a new status. This is the lost son who comes to be reinstated, made a fuss of and given fresh robes to wear. He can hold his head up high again in a state of grace, not disgrace. Instead of faltering self-verification there is a complete reset of humiliating circumstances.

This has enormous potential for building a new self-concept based on the ultimate affirmation, namely, divine approval. Such faith in God permeates the relative with the absolute.[502]

Being accepted and placed in a new position with God means that those who have lived with shame have somewhere to go that can reverse how they feel about themselves and the impact of wounded history. This is an antidote to relational shame as it reflects the ultimate acceptance that trumps what social dishonor is projected.

Jesus takes on himself human shame and guilt. For much of Christian history, the cross has been seen as addressing guilt and effecting forgiveness. Someone is trashed. Their value is walked all over. Some sort of compensation, of recompense is called for by way of response. Opponents of any kind of idea of payment are simply not being true to life. In everyday life, we find that letting someone down or hurting someone matters. "You will pay for this" is an instinctive response either spoken or unspoken. This is not tribal or antiquated but a fact of psychological life. Either we make others pay in some way or we demand payment from ourselves. This is the essence of guilt. We go cool with those who annoy us. We cut people up on the road. The value of persons means that infringement sets up a deficit. Something happens that can only be discounted at the expense of denial of the value that someone has.

When we experience being written off or trashed, something has been breached in our depths. It is core material, primal wounding. It evokes a primal cry of "I'm worth more than that!" Indebtedness arises. Someone must pay. The same desecration that has been inflicted on us must be visited upon others. Recompense will ensure that my depleted bank account of debt is met. This is what makes forgiveness hard work. "Forgive us our debt" is a way of articulating the need to cover the aggrieving by the aggrieved. Atonement theology is usually expressed in terms of the law courts, sacrificial language or that of the slave market and its overtones of redemption. But the demand for compensation is utterly true to life. It pursues us across the years. A judge sentencing an offender will work with a scale of tariffs. We have to pay; we always have to pay. Impaired relationships require reconciliation and compensation, restitution or even prison (depending on the seriousness).

Forgiveness is a complex issue. An internal sense of guilt and being a bad person is antithetical to any notion of being saved and forgiven by God. But human beings are summoned in the gospel of Christ to forgive others in turn: "forgive us our sins as we forgive those who sin against us." It is deeply challenging since it comes up against a real sense of what stands in the way: our worth and value before God or that of others we seek to defend. It feels like betrayal. That must be overcome for there to be progress and the release of bitterness.

In personal or social relationships, if people are devalued, some form of redress or compensation is always sought. They are valuable; that worth deserves to be respected when it is breached. When personal beings are trashed, something needs to be done or said to put it right. It is akin to payment. Sin sets up an obligation that can only be met by means of transfer. It is not a monetary transaction but a symbolic one. Sin needs paying for as persons have immense value.

At the cross, what we owe is "paid in full" (*tetelestai*; John 19:30). An exchange is made in our state whereby human beings can be reconciled and participate in the standing and Spirit of Christ.

Looking at the cross through the lens of Jesus paying the price for our sins is instructive. Second Corinthians 5:21 speaks of an exchange in our state, rooted in impaired relationships and the need for reconciliation. The heart of the atoning sacrifice of Jesus is that when sin occurs, something has happened that needs to be addressed. It cannot be "unhappened" and time doesn't erode it away.

This central part of Christ's identification with us meets our need because it is true to life. When we do wrong something has just taken place which it would be wrong to ignore. Someone must pay. Indebtedness inevitably arises. "Dying in our place" (the just for the unjust) sets up a kind of symbolic exchange, a transfer of value akin to what happens in everyday transactions when we purchase something. Similarly, when Jesus offered to pay for the damage as the human representative it sets up an exchange—the righteous for the unrighteous; his life for ours, his riches for our poverty. He switches states. It enables us to be reconciled to God and enter a new humanity embodied by Jesus. At the heart of the atonement is exchange. It brings together two ideas in fruitful combination:

i. The value and worth of personhood
ii. The identification principle

Identification is at the heart of incarnation. The embrace of the human by the divine is fundamental to the incarnation and represents an affirmation of it. The incarnation does justice to the material side of our existence. It gives value to the material order. In embracing the life that people live, God assigns importance to the human body, the body that was torn apart by violence to pay the price.

The cross is a stunning turning of the tables on the powers of darkness (who thought they had won their greatest victory in killing the God-man). It was an instant turn-around against those believed that they had finished with Jesus and rid themselves of this man who was both the walking embodiment of goodness and a thorough nuisance. The Gospels do not record the personal reactions of Pilate, Herod and Caiphas—three major players who believed they had stopped the dangerous talk of another King and another kingdom. But their work was to be completely undone.

The destruction of a human life that they had envisaged was turned from defeat into sudden victory because the life they thought they had destroyed was more than human. "Having disarmed the powers and authorities, Jesus made a public spectacle of them, triumphing over them by the cross" (Col 2:15). The death of Jesus was the death-knell of the devil and a trumpet sounding the ultimate defeat of darkness. An enormous stone couldn't stop him, the military guard couldn't stop him, death couldn't hold him, and Satan could only watch incredulous.

It is this complete reversal on Easter Sunday morning that provides potent truth to help the sinful and the hurting. Jesus identified with trapped humanity, to fight our battles. Though Jesus went down into defeat, he trusted God for the reversal, as Psalm 16 has it. Good Friday concluded with doom and gloom, the extinguishing of hope and the death of light. Watch for the third day! The stone was broken through. All that sealed Jesus into coldness of death was replaced by the surprising victory of God. Confident that Jesus had defeated the dark powers that bound the human race, the first Christians went everywhere to sound the ultimate defeat of sin, despair, death and the devil. The Adam humanity had just been declared "old" for a new Christ humanity was beginning to be abroad in the earth).

In the countless situations in our world where it seems evil has triumphed, the victory of Christ and the reversal of God proclaims that evil will be defeated. Death does not have the last word. It looked as if the result was certain but there was extra time and a surprise victory. God has the last laugh and those who tune their ears to Calvary can begin to hear it. The victory of God can be proclaimed in the teeth of those same dark powers that appeared to have won. Those bound by sin, despair, death and evil can be free if they believe the announcement and emerge from their prison. "Say to the captives 'Come out' and to those in darkness, 'be free'" (Isa 49:9).

Being included in the new humanity that Jesus now identifies with is dynamic. The best guide to this is Romans with its paeon of praise to the resurrected life. "There is therefore now no condemnation for those who are in Christ Jesus. . . . [Y]ou are not in the flesh but in the Spirit" (Rom 8:1, 9). Paul moves in a series of film strips to outline the dynamic of the new humanity. Through the death and resurrection where incorporation takes place and the great transfer made, believers have a new status, a new relationship, a new freedom and a new power. This is the Pauline philosophy of history for it shows how God intervened in the face of the creeping paralysis in the moral life of humanity. The way we were has dramatically shifted. There is a "no longer" though also a "not yet" in the story of salvation.

The church in Ephesus received less systematic exposition on what participation means but it did learn this upward trajectory: "Because of his great love for us, God, who is rich in mercy, made us alive with Christ even when we were dead in transgressions—it is by grace you have been saved. And God raised us up with Christ and seated us with him in the heavenly realms in Christ Jesus" (Eph 2:4–6).

A joyful awareness of God can replace feelings of an unworthy self.[503] Shame, guilt, and doubt from the past holds many in the grip of fear, so that the search for love and approval is disrupted.

To use metaphors of space and place, the identification principle took Jesus down to being in human form, down into death, and then up, up to resurrection and the highest pinnacle of all (Phil 2:7–11). Those who go beyond merely being part of a common humanity and are actively joined to Christ through his death and resurrection, realize that there is someone in the heavenly realms who resembles us. His humanity and ours has been taken up and adopted by God forever. Such revalidation is the ultimate revaluation!

PART FOUR

Positions and Foundations

Chapter Eighteen

Joining the Conversation

Cure of Souls and the Care of Souls

"The feeling of being valuable—'I am a valuable person'—is essential to mental health and is a cornerstone of self-discipline. It is a direct product of parental love. Such a conviction must be gained in childhood; it is extremely difficult to acquire it during adulthood. Conversely, when children learn through love of their parents to feel valuable, it's almost impossible for vicissitudes of adulthood to destroy their spirit."[504]

Leading Idea: Endeavouring to make therapy and theology compatible has a long history. What principles can guide us?

Counseling psychology and theology can seem incompatible: a world apart. "I am looking for a counseling model that is more biblical," someone might say. Or, "I am open to psychology." Like most knowledge, where you stand depends where you sit and what you see. What does it look like to give counseling theological underpinning and how do we set this up such that a Christian worldview open to dialogue becomes the prism through which everything else stands out?

The approach we take here is that secular psychology has been enormously helpful in showing the complexity of human functioning. "Genetic factors, family dynamics, socioeconomic circumstances, educational background and even chance weave intricate patterns that form each individual personality like a snowflake. Secular psychotherapy has been far more sensitive to the texture of the personality and temperament than has its Christian counterpart."[505]

At the same time, the theologically informed self has much to offer. Distortions of the self abound in contemporary society but it has ever been thus and there are many centuries of psychological reflection often undertaken by theologians such as Augustine "who described the slow and bumbling search for God and self as a single undertaking."[506] Grasping the triunity of God, he contended, was analogous to the faculties of human consciousness and therefore vital for understanding the self.

With its particular focus on stimulus and response, when psychology developed as a discipline in its own right, and not just as a department of pastoral practice, there were numerous projects to integrate the new "science" with theology and faith. Christian practitioners and doctors sought to offer remedial therapies that were sensitive to faith while being grounded in some psychological principles. When it crossed over into the search for meaning, psychotherapy entered the terrain traditionally occupied by theologians of the soul and a Christian understanding of personhood.

There has been a proliferation of books and journals, clinicians and doctors developing and applying college courses. Degree and doctoral programmes have been built on the premise that an approach to psychology and psychotherapy is possible built on a Christian worldview. Some of these drew on a restricted menu of psychological models combined with some theology. This was deemed to be integration. How far should a Christian worldview set the agenda for counseling practice? Some were opposed to this tendency, calling it psycho-heresy and a sell-out. Biblical stances should reject it. A well-known book exemplifying this end of the spectrum was that by the Bobgans who objected strongly to the psychologizing of Christianity that seemed to be in evidence everywhere.[507]

Pastors were motivated by the desire to have an approach to troubled people that would offer real help while being faithful to faith as they saw it. Many did not want to go to secular worldviews or witness them smuggled into pastoral practice. Could there be an approach that combined faith with therapy? It depended what form of faith—and what form of therapy. Where a more relaxed view of the Bible was taken or a liberal stance that saw scripture as not just history but as metaphor rather than authority, it did not matter so much. Combining psychology and traditions of faith can be done with a pick and mix approach. When practitioners sought to ground their work in faith rather than draw out principles, the picture was more complicated—especially when faith was biblically based.

In large measure, the issue of how psychological therapy and faith traditions interfaced became more complicated still with growing professionalization. Expert knowledge became lodged with a growing cadre of medical people, who in time were endowed with professional qualifications. This was a world away from well-meaning Pastors who, compared with doctors and therapists, lacked the training in behavioral sciences to help troubled people. Could specialist study of the human mind be separated from centuries-old knowledge derived from spiritual practice? As in all walks of life, specialisms became sources of power and fortresses that were staunchly defended. One strand in what became a growing movement towards integration as a way of aligning the relationship was no doubt a reaction against this professional knowledge driving a wedge between two forms of help.

It is worth asking whether the difficulties about trying to combine psychology and theology are any greater than might arise from wondering how faith and chemistry, for example, might relate? A chemist is not, however, usually in direct competition with a pastor. The turf they occupy is incommensurable and unrelated although a Christian chemist might well adopt a theistic backcloth that can see his or her work as derived from it ultimately. With psychotherapy it is different. Turf-wars are inevitable—at least conceptually—because both pastor and counsellor or doctor seek to help someone, albeit from a different position and view of personhood. What is at stake is the nature of human beings and whether God is relevant. With professionalization of psychiatry and psychotherapy based on medical models came a retreat by many ministers from healing the hurting. Endeavouring to bridge the gap between the claims of counseling and faith-practitioners has given rise to a whole industry. There have been at least five forms of conceptual architecture.[508]

i. *An integration view* of the relationship between psychology and Christian perspectives.

ii. *A distinct Christian psychology* would seem to offer a way of holding both disciplines.

iii. *Different levels of explanation* account for the way that relationship is conceived.

iv. *A transformational psychology* view could signify a renewed vision of psychology's potential.

v. *Biblical counseling* where the Bible has all that is needed and pastors competent to counsel.

I. *An integration view* of the relationship between psychology and Christian perspectives

The findings of psychology must be respected, despite secular naturalism that shaped so many of its assumptions. Yet in its understanding of human beings, a Christian worldview also has something to contribute to counseling literature and practice. Attempts should be made to relate theology and psychology. This leads to interdisciplinary integration, combining "the special revelation of God's Word with the general revelation offered by the psychological sciences and professions."[509]

II. *A distinct Christian psychology* would seem to offer a way of holding both disciplines

This is the challenge for Christian thinkers to develop theories and stances arising from their faith and theology at the same time as continuing to practice professionally. It is quite acceptable for Christian academics to think out their own distinctive positions.

III. *Different levels of explanation* account for the way that relationship is conceived

There is a sharp distinction between theology and psychology as being two different disciplines and levels of thinking. These are incommensurable and should not be confused. Spiritual and moral issues cannot be put in the same category as, say, the psychology of perception. These different levels of explanation have their own methodology and vocabulary. Theology and psychology have their own perspective ("perspectivalism") and to confuse the two undermines the integrity of each.

iv. *A transformational psychology* view could signify a renewed vision of psychology's potential

Should the focus of integration be conceptual and theoretical or on personal and ethical issues? How Christians live out their faith in the practice of counseling is as important as intellectual understanding of human beings.

v. *Biblical counseling* where the Bible has all that is needed; pastors are competent to counsel

From a seminal 1970 text, *Competent to Counsel*, by Jay Adams, professor of practical theology at Westminster Theological Seminary, the biblical counseling program sought to base all counseling on the Bible. Inspired scripture alone could be authoritative in its insights into human functioning. Dialogue between Adams and evangelical psychotherapists has been fraught at times.

Competent to Counsel became a widely read volume advocating a wholly biblical approach that did not draw on modern psychology and psychiatry. Rejecting both as secular compromises that failed to address the real needs of human beings, Adams offered "nouthetic counseling" (from Col 3:15 and "being able to admonish one another" [*noutheto*]).[510] An authentically Christian counseling could find within the Bible sufficient help and resource for pastors to be counsellors in their community. Dismissing Freudian psychodynamics as archaeology and Carl Roger's person-centered approach as being just playing with mirrors, Adams argued that a call to repentance and change should dominate practice. The therapeutic gospel should be shunned as a new version of the modern self. To his supporters, Adams was a Luther-like figure, calling the church to embrace ideas of biblical counseling and eschew reliance on modern psychology.[511]

In course of time, many who worked with distressed people pushed back against such a strict view. Maybe psychology had more value than its detractors suggested. There were growing concerns about the use of the Bible amongst authoritarian subcultures of the Christian church. Even amongst believers, just taking a spiritual viewpoint did not seem to address people's needs and appeared harsh. To unchurched people, a straightforward biblical counseling approach had nothing to say.

There were many who took a different view. Conferences were held on how faith could relate to contemporary psychology and how a redemptive relationship with God would impact mind, body and soul. Some more appreciative writers began to demonstrate how modern psychotherapy could illuminate God's work in the human heart and mind. Figures such as Clyde Narramore (a practising psychologist complete with a high view of scripture and a radio broadcast) began to be influential. In 1968, Narramore went on to found the Rosemead School of Psychology, offering a doctoral programme and a journal. It joined with Fuller Theological Seminary in providing advanced training in theology and psychology. In that wave, books became common that were written on psychological topics by evangelical Christians such as James Dobson.

Psychology has offered a body of empirical evidence and observations clad in scientific complexity. Our science-oriented culture mandated a version of what it means to be human that can seem to relegate faith traditions to the mantlepiece of history. Biblical revelation no longer possessed writ or authority. Psychotherapists became the new priests. A counter-narrative was here to stay. Issues of faith should not intrude into a domain where study of reality was derived from direct observation.

For many of a more liberal cast of mind, modern psychologists were influential and regularly cited when it came to pastoral psychology. But this was a one-way street. Faith and psychology tended to come together through the latter pulling the former into its orbit.

Amongst churches of a more conservative or fundamentalist persuasion, the new psychology was suspect. Anti-intellectualizm went hand in hand with a proliferation of Bible Colleges whose dominant interest lay elsewhere than the inner working of the soul. Moral issues, doctrine and eschatology were the order of the day. The important task was to hold the line and not let the psychology revolution claim the whole field of battle in the pursuit of the therapeutic.

Clearly, when it comes to theology and counseling, there are different ways of understanding that relationship. How then do we place Christian concerns at the heart of the Counsellor's agenda?

A major and recent (2021) text on the importance of integration is from Hathaway and Vernon who propose a "domain-based approach."[512] This is an organizing paradigm that incorporates the domains of worldview, theory, applied understandings, role integration and personal integration. Role integration involves taking leadership in mental health professions. This is an approach that combines a high view of scripture with a sensitive welcome to the findings of psychology.

Here are some principles that could guide us.

i. It is worth saying that reflection on human psychology is not a recent development. Both Old and New Testaments imply a considerable body of theory about human personality.

ii. The quest has been for a fundamental epistemological foundation for an holistic integration of psychology and spirituality. Integration has become a major concern amongst those who seek a faith-based view of science and scripture that will be sensitive to both. This concern is heightened the higher the view of scriptural authority. Does drawing on secular psychology conflict with the Reformation emphasis that the Bible alone contains all that we need for understanding human existence (sola scriptura)? But stressing that wisdom for living is contained in the scripture surely cannot exclude findings and observation based on listening to clients in the contemporary world, for example arising from trauma. Old Testament wisdom literature such as Proverbs clearly contains reflection on extrabiblical material.

iii. Psychology was concerned with the realities of human existence. But its history contains hidden assumptions about what it means to be human. This might seem to be a far cry from loving communion with God until it is realized that spiritual growth and development is an inherently psychological project. Every aspect of human growth "finds its place in the light of persons-in—relation with God."[513] A growing divide emerged when the new "science" of psychology took to itself empirical observations and research methods endeavouring to probe human development and the realm of lived experience. To theology went abstract ideas such as ontological and epistemological conceptualizations. Spiritual development should be seen as basic to human development. Shrunken anthropology cannot be acceptable to those concerned with faithfulness to faith. The cultural context has opened the human sciences rather more to the importance of slippery spirituality but where this is grounded (be it in a form of natural or revealed religion) is a source of continuing debate.

iv. Existential concerns such as the meaning of hope, freedom, life and death lie at the heart of human distress. Indeed, these issues have formed the agenda of a whole branch of therapy, namely existential counseling.

v. Fundamental to the debate is that different approaches think they know it is to be human, to be a person. All models assume this. Clearly there are numerous types of counseling and indeed of theology. Versions and visions of counseling range over the twentieth century where exponents and theorists sought to correct inadequate views of the self as they saw it.

vi. There is no value-free psychology. Values matter and it is a question of where those values are grounded. The APA's Encyclopaedia of Psychology concluded an earlier history of developmental psychology by observing that "there is increased awareness that values matter in development and that science cannot provide those values."[514]

vii. Our model of human flourishing and if that is vital. Should the theoretical foundations of counseling psychology focus on accumulating knowledge about human beings or aim at restoring and reconstructive work with a view to enabling people to live well and flourish?

viii. Is there a distinctive understanding of human functioning which is uniquely validated by theological and biblical concerns and to which only Christians subscribe? A stance of general revelation would presumably say that there is a much wider understanding of ethics and practice that most therapists would sign up to irrespective of their world view.

ix. Epistemology is vital to the debate—how do we know what we think we know? A naturalistic psychology operates with a limited understanding of what it means to be a human person. Restricted by a hard version of empiricism, restricting knowledge to what the senses provide will only take you so far. The sources of knowledge vis a vis scripture, psychological research, philosophy or lived experience will take people in different directions according to whether a trusting or critical posture is adopted. Social science valorises quantitative, qualitative or critical modes of knowledge rather than ultimate questions. These are distinct bodies of research and reflection using different methodologies.

x. Psychology has little to say about final causes and ultimate ends for which we were made. "Psychology does not have the epistemological

> tools to address issues of teleology."[515] Theology, however, has much to say. Material well-being and satisfying relationships are much discussed as ingredients of human flourishing (what philosopher Charles Taylor calls the goods of "production and reproduction").[516] For Paul and numerous Christian writers, the goal is to become transformed, metamorphosized: a human infused with divinity.

The human person is unavoidably spiritual. We are ensouled but also embodied people (1 Cor 2:14–15). Like the word soul, the "image of God" is a fundamental phrase in a theological anthropology. Through relational ontology of the soul to God we remain porous to divine influence.

The question is whether a commitment to counseling psychology with a secular view of personhood be reconciled with commitment to faith grounded in faith. Theology and counseling are problematic for alignment because of contrasting worldview, vocabulary and remedies appropriate to people in pain. These working assumptions are in contrast to a theological lens that anchors the drama of life within the transcendence of divine personhood. God has given general revelation (through which we can study human functioning in the light of our createdness) and special revelation (though which we are informed about sinfulness and redemption). Projects to integrate psychology and theology need to be attuned to both lenses. Unhealthy relationships, distorted thinking and damaging systemic issues and behavior patterns demonstrate a role of human sinfulness in social behavior.

Is God Lost?

An older view of psychology was that it was about mental life and functioning (cf. William James, *The Principles of Psychology* (1890).[517] In the hands of Freud and subsequent twentieth-century psychotherapists, this changed. Psychology now became the science of behavior and functioning. In what may be termed "secular psychology," invoking a transcendent God had little place in theoretical structures. From a faith-based viewpoint, the lack of orientation towards the transcendent was a serious omission that revealed an ideological agenda. The following sketch gives some headlines with reference to a high view of the value of the human.

1. Freud and the Repudiation of a Christian View of Humankind

Twentieth-century psychology on humanistic assumptions generally saw little place for theology. In Freud's psychoanalysis that was a drum roll for the twentieth century, we are not immortal beings whose true home lies elsewhere. We are of the earth and to the earth we return. Set within nature, our life is marked by an ecology of the emotions and the biology of mind. In the absence of theology, there is no overarching means of integration. People who would take their problems to priests now went to doctors. But there was no attempt at forgiveness; no final salvation. Freud saw his role as a guide.

Freud's *The Interpretation of Dreams* was a drumroll, not just for a method of psychological treatment but a new way of looking at human beings. As his hagiographer Ernest Jones remarks, "starting as a theory of certain illnesses of the mind, it went on to become a radically new and momentous theory of mind itself."[518] Freud saw little inherent value in people. "I have not found much 'good' in the average human being," he wrote to his surprising friend Pastor Pfister. "Most of them are in my experience riff-raff."[519] Psychoanalysis did nothing to value females. Freud indeed famously characterized women as being subject to envy; damaged creatures with a lack instead of whole persons in their own right. Karen Horney disagreed. If some women want to be like men, it is because they perceive men as being freer to act.[520] Early psychoanalysis is riven with envy, jealousy, paranoia and ambition—a hothouse of charismatic egos and odd situation for those who claimed that to experience their therapy was to embrace a more exalted state![521]

Psychodynamic counseling, as a pluralistic, relational and intersubjective form of encounter, can address and work with spirituality. Donald Winnicott is arguably the most influential British analyst of the twentieth century. His ideas were adopted across the psychoanalytic world particularly in the UK, Europe, and Israel. Through extensive clinical experience with mothers and babies he developed a creative form of Object Relations theory that focused on the central ontological question of *being* and how a person forms as an integrated, independent self-capable of intrapersonal, interpersonal, and extrapersonal being. Winnicott was central to post-Freudian rethinking of the psychoanalysis of religion. He developed concepts of particular significance for thinking about spirituality and religion. This includes the notion of transitional phenomena, illusion and the capacity to believe. Transitional phenomena, objects, and space are "a hypothetical area that exists (but cannot exist) between the baby and the object." It allows a baby to separate, to play and to create, psychically and physically, in its inner and outer world. This builds a connection to culture, through experience of transitional phenomena such as music, art, theatre and religion. Although Winnicott never suggested this, it allows for a belief in an internal god/God and an external god/God without a false dichotomy.[522]

The French psychoanalyst Jacques Lacan proposed a rather different formulation of our psychic structure, the *real* (roughly corresponding to Freud's "id"), the *symbolic* (superego) and the *imaginary* (the ego).[523] The "*name of the father*" is an entity that separates a baby from its mother and knots these psychic processes together in a way that achieves the birth of a child's own subjectivity. In the Lacanian orientation, a concept of "*ordinary psychosis*," the kind you can just about live with, is key. Ordinary psychosis is characterized by the absence or erosion of the "name of the father" so there is no separating principle and the membrane between a sense of self and the outside world is very porous. From a Lacanian perspective, Parker describes the revolution in subjectivity to do with the politics of the subject, subverting the link between therapy and capitalism, objecting to "the bio-political management of populations."[524] There is an assumption that the individual counts but there is little scope for the role played by "value" in the dramatis personae of psychic forces.

Adlerian psychology—The approach taken by Freud's one-time associate, Alfred Adler, carves out a little more space for the value of other human beings as well as oneself."[525] It was configured as a problem of inferiority. Adler argued that individuals are motivated to attain equality or superiority over other people to compensate for organ inferiority. The typically masculine need to act and become powerful to compensate for feeling inadequate undergirded Adler's Masculine Protest.[526]

II. Jung's Project

Should we re-theologize counseling psychology or to psychologize such aspects of theological reflection as to render them useful knowledge? There are many psychological projects emphasizing that we must experience the life of the spirit anew for ourselves. It is the only way we can break free from the cycle of biological events. For many Christians, another of Freud's colleagues Carl Gustav Jung is often important. Jungian depth psychology proposed a rather different approach to that of Freud, urging us to get in touch with our unconscious. Religion had an important place when speaking of archaic and primeval terms: violence of the unconscious, strange forces and phantasies surfacing in the minds of his patients, drawn from the world of mysticism. Strangely echoing Calvin, for Jung knowledge of God is the same as self-knowledge. Jung sought to find a way back to religion as a condition of inner integration our psyche is pursuing. Yet Jung never speaks of God in terms other than God-image in the human psyche. An external realm of meaning and value is irrelevant.

Through dreams or intuition, we get in touch with our real needs and listen to what our unconscious is saying to us. Freud's approach was that the human situation can be analyzed in terms of what constrains us, be it class, gender, ethnicity or psychology. Jung went beyond this analysis, seeing human problems as essentially spiritual blockages. Struggles of people over the age of 35 were almost always of this nature.[527] Jung counseled clients to listen to their unconscious and pursue integration. Religious archetypes embedded in the collective unconscious were useful categories in this healing agenda. So was love! Jung said, "where love rules, there is no will to power, and where power predominates, love is lacking. The one is the shadow of the other."[528] Does this imply a valuing of self? Jung's own journey of individuation in search of the structure of human personality depicted how an individual is split between the "I" of conscious existence and the "self"—the total personality including the unconscious.[529] The search for the deep level of the mind common to all humanity—the collective unconscious—looms large in this journey. But a dynamic concept of value does not assume any role amongst components of personality Jung describes.

III. The Imperative of Hope

Personalism points us back to views that seem most compatible with Christianity. By 1938, Victor Frankl spoke of existential analysis which extended psychotherapy beyond earlier categories to include meaningfulness and spiritual dimensions of human experience. It was his three years at Auschwitz and Dachau though that led to *The Unconscious God: Psychotherapy and Theology*.[530] Frankl applied the imperative of hope to the existential morass of post-war society with strong resonance for our own time of not being at home in the world, ill at ease. We are an enigma to ourselves yearning for a more comfortable past. Human self-transcendence should include the spiritual within the unconscious. Existential analysts took issue with the reductionism in much psychotherapy—bringing human functioning down to a few basic drives. Philosophical analysis objected too on grounds of critical realism, arguing that mental processes cannot be caused purely by identifiable factors already present. There must be more to a clinical model of the human person. Existentialists object to scientific positivism inherent in behaviorist models. A deeply personal human experience must include ultimate concerns—death, freedom, isolation, or meaninglessness.[531]

IV. Beyond Ourselves

Concern with the numinous and the other-worldly led to a search for meaning and fulfilment beyond ourselves in some post-Freudians. Maslow is perhaps best known as a humanistic psychologist who went beyond his own "self-actualization" project. "Towards a Psychology of Being" sought to discover something bigger than we are.[532] This is not theism; his "Fourth Psychology" wants to find meaning in the cosmos. Maslow sought to build a comprehensive, systematic and empirically based general psychology and philosophy which includes both the depths and heights of human nature. Mention could be made also of the psychosynthesis of Roberto Assagioli pointing to a higher self[533] or the work of Ken Wilber arguing for an essential unity of all things. Wilber believed that human obsession with boundaries vitiated against a transpersonal psychology.[534] The contemporary interest Wilber notes in things like psychic phenomena, eastern religion, mystical, out-of-body experiences, yoga, misuse of drugs, occultism indicates the need for a spiritual dimension in human make-up. This fits with interest amongst non-materialist neuroscientists in religious experience.[535]

Every counseling psychology has its presuppositions. Contemporary potent therapeutic models have their own understandings of human behavior. Transpersonal theories deal extensively with matters relating to higher human development and spiritual experience. Referencing larger existential themes, reflection on the human situation can draw on an immense body of ancient faith-based tradition. This is pre-eminently a theological project rather than what might seem the more practical task of aligning with Christian faith and pastoral practice by the church. Can that align with any psychological theory? Does theology translate into a discrete therapy and biblical psychology?

A major lack also, distinct from loss of the transcendent God is the absence of a horizon: embedding responses to social context right into our models of human functioning. At the heart of the approach we take is a dynamic impulse towards being of high worth. Valuable personhood is, we contend, at the heart of psychic structure. From that imperative and a struggle in everyday life for its realization comes much else. It is a principle through which alignment with psycho-social scripts becomes possible but also theology. The struggle to realize our value is a common theme in theological understandings of humanity but also features in newer psychologies. We now look at this.

Chapter Nineteen

Epistemology and Integration

A Proposal

Leading Idea: We need to find a place and principle of alignment in bringing together two different disciplines—social science/counseling theories and biblical theology

New Directions in Theological Method?

Conceptual strategies are available to articulate the link between theology and counseling psychology as modes of understanding human behavior. Are they mutually exclusive or complementary in their ontology and epistemology? Should we re-theologize counseling psychology or to psychologize such aspects of theological reflection so as to render them useful knowledge?

Inter-disciplinary enquiry is highly complex because multiple languages are involved. Though all are set on meaning-making in their own way, dynamic encounter between differing bodies of knowledge is immensely challenging. An approach that recognizes critical enquiry pertinent to each is vital.

Our proposition here is that *an applied understanding of the value and worth of people* provides an intersection between theology and human dynamics. Specifically, it is the value of humankind lovingly fashioned by God and made in the divine image (Gen 1:26) that can provide a bridge between what is known as theological anthropology and cultural and systemic dynamics within which human personhood is embedded. The centrality of the struggle to realize this in human experience is derived from client work, from listening to people in pain.

It is as we hear clients talking about negative experiences that have impacted their lives that we can hear how the impetus to maintain their sense of a valuable self is fraught with all that seeks to undermine it. Social experience (sociology) wraps around interpersonal life (psychology) to frame this struggle, that is so characterizes human identity. It goes beyond the knowledge of self, the conscious awareness that we exist in relation to other minds. What we are talking about here is the secret knowledge that we are worth it, that we have a self that deserves respect, a personhood that might not be affronted and a dignity that must not be invaded. This pertains to fundamental drives.

Such knowledge informs the approach we take in this book and is detected most easily when clients refer to distressing circumstances. Here it was a journey of autoethnography that could highlight what seems to be going on but the range of responses to being made invisible, put down or trashed are clearly discerned in the therapeutic room. This stands out most obviously in the contrast pole; in response to negative experiences that arise between people or between people and organizations.

> I was vulnerable, a lost child with low self-esteem. I had to dig deep, deeper than I had ever dug. I had a sense of self. The longer I stayed in care, the harder it was. . . . I have given up on people believing in me. I don't care what their opinions are. When people are ready, they will believe in me.[536]

But it is no less true of dehumanization arising from social experience, for example arising from racial stressors that are common among Black teens. Psychologists who study racial socialization and identity found that Black adolescents experience an average of five discriminatory encounters every day, either online or in person.[537] These encounters take a toll: one meta-analysis, for example, showed that teens of color who report greater perceptions of racial and/or ethnic discrimination have higher rates of depression and distress, and poorer self-esteem. They are also more likely than their counterparts to suffer low educational attainment and to engage in risky behaviors such as substance use. Systemic thinking is a vital concept to grasp, witness the spotlight on race and gender in the "Black Lives Matter" and "Me Too" movements (not the only frontiers of disadvantage).

The struggle for valuable personhood is fundamental now to non-discriminatory practice and ethical frameworks. It is underlined in person-centered approaches with "conditions of worth" and also cognitive behavioral therapies with "worthlessness" as a maladaptive core belief. Approaches such as Gestalt therapy assumes human beings have worth. Here we reframe it as a central driver, the struggle for which provides a strong impetus for love, belonging, significance and hope or purpose.

Is it possible to integrate theology and counseling psychology and what would that look like? "Integration" itself is a big word in psychology and is problematic, implying a smooth finished result: a terminus rather than direction. There should though be a tie up between the two, given that both traditions of reflection lay claim to valid insight into how people function. This can be harder to do where there is a commitment to theological reflection rooted in a high view of scripture.

The theological category that speaks of humanity is that of theological anthropology. This is a branch of enquiry that investigates the origins and destiny of humankind. It deals with the nature and condition of being human before God rather than the comparative study of human society that constitutes anthropology. Thinking out the human story as it is lived out before God encompasses biblical revelation but also general revelation about the knowledge of God and of ourselves (an order that much modern theology has reversed). Knowledge of the self need not be the gateway to knowledge of God as modernity avows, for it to be a basis for discovering evidence from the natural and social sciences that can help us discover many things that are true about us. A theological anthropology rooted in human value can underpin a model of integration between faith and therapy. As referenced in the previous chapter, there are numbers of ways we can go here.

One way of conceptualizing the link between theology and counseling—different strategies is an oppositional stance. The question is how do we reconcile two contrasting traditions of reflection (systems of thought?) that have been antagonistic at times or at least complex and contrasting? The sociological imagination has whittled away theological territory. Social science stresses quantitative, qualitative, or critical modes of knowledge rather than be concerned with ultimate or transcendental questions based on high value. Protestant theology had to suffer the near complete erosion of the scripture principle, notwithstanding the turn to the human subject epitomized by Schleiermacher. Catholic thought was buttressed rather more by an appeal to the magisterium of tradition. But nothing seemed to prevent the marginalization of religion and any sense of the sacred beyond what was relocated in humanity. The context we face is that of reduced circumstances. No longer the Queen of the sciences, theology is embattled in its confrontation with secular social science. It seems as if it is the social theorist, enhanced by differing psychologies, who aims at a comprehensive interpretation of human life-worlds. Psychology is seen as *the* vehicle of enlightenment. As philosophy has moved steadily in empirical directions, the theological residuum has shrunk.

We could note John Milbank's emphasis of Christian linguistic and cultural practice in repudiation of sociology as heretical secular thought.[538] There is no such thing as social *science*—you can describe cultures but that does not mean you can make predictions. This rescues theology as a valid way to explain how and why societies are the way they are—it is because God made them like that.

Yet entrenched oppositional stances are open to serious question. Over the centuries, there have been numerous projects to take a Christian view of the natural sciences and scripture and seek to harmonize them. Do we believe that a theological approach provides a deeper understanding of people's problems, aiding recovery and helping them grow resilience? As we saw in the previous chapter, a mediating position is often taken by some who seek to make use of insights of psychology in their work. We must not allow scope for evangelical theology rooted in the Bible to become simply a question of scriptural justification through such devices as silencing proof texts.

If biblical psychology is valid, there must be an engagement between at least two sets of horizons: divine command and the human. Theology is at its best when contextual as well as systematic, listening to ordinary people as well as itself. For purveyors of strict humanism, there is no external reality, simply a radical individualism in which it is down to you and your feelings. Individualism has marked a time in our culture and political life with its insistence that there is no reality to which we are beholden. It makes everything "all about me." Globally, as religion exploded in the twenty-first century it has become more important about how people see the world.

Methodological Neutrality?

A crucial role when it comes to investigating and testing our understanding of reality is that of the status of knowledge. How do we know what we think we know? This is the issue of epistemology.

The loss of a transcendent perspective for the most part is a serious but also curious absence in models of counseling, given that human beings seem incurably hard-wired to whatever they think is ultimate. Another curious lack is the absence of sociological grounding, given the extent to which socialization through culture conditions the unconscious. This is important as it is commonplace amongst those who give serious thought to social realities to say that where you stand depends on where you sit, or where you are situated.

The liberation theologian Juan Segundo introduced the phrase a "hermeneutic of suspicion" to uproot selectively deployed ideologies that rationalise self-interest.[539] We have a problem with counseling theories. For the most part, they were worked out in a vacuum. Many faith-based approaches to therapy are simplistic; lacking theological depth or sociological input. The approach to therapy developed here takes full account of social context as most would claim to do but it does so by bringing our inner response to external pressures (that are giving rise to distress) into the model. Social imperatives come into the unconscious. It is not only that people are reacting to what is going on, that very reaction is supplying momentum for change. The response to being devalued is to assert our value and worth. Feminist critiques of psychotherapy have long insisted that a person's issues should be looked at within the framework of a person's social context.

There is a presupposition in very many counseling models and approach to therapy. It is that the model of the human person is generic, looking at an individual per se. This individual is colorless and genderless. Devoid of context, the person is both neutered and neutral. The person does not in fact exist. The realities of existence depicted, despite being reiterated as universal truths, are rarely those of men and women of color or align with the female experience. They do not accord with the lives of those who feel the imperatives of disability or of class, for whom the whole psychotherapy project is usually out of reach financially. External worlds do not reach past the front door and into the interior castle. Yet it is just such confluence of external and internal factors that is constitutive.

It is vital for counseling theory to bring in patterns of social relations between individuals and groups that organize and structure the broader society. Most societies attach social meanings, including roles and institutions, to certain groupings or categories—most commonly gender and sexuality, race/ethnicity, and class. Often these meanings derive from a hierarchy that accords some groups more social value and others less.[540] The human quest for validation is distorted by society.

Methodological neutrality with regard to the concrete situations in which human beings find themselves in does not allow for the kind of formulation and diagnosis that takes on board the pressures arising from that social influence. Consequently, it fails to prepare for counsellors to work with real clients—only the cardboard cut-out evoked by a psychotherapeutic model.

Despite feminist scholars insisting that to understand a person's behavior, we must understand not only that individual but also the social system in which that person is embedded,[541] sweeping changes to society at best only have a walk on, walk off part. The social realities they signify are not a part of the way of looking at a particular counseling theory. That might be because counseling theories were developed in the last century by white Western men. Feminist psychology argued that historical psychological research has been done from a male perspective with the view that males are the norm. Psychology was more interested in individual differences than social systems about which there has been a strong neglect. More recently, feminist psychologists have addressed the importance of considering intersections of gender, race/ethnicity, sexuality, and class when seeking to understand and explain problems and patterns of distress. Influential sociologists like Talcott Parsons discussed the importance of individual psychology as both a product and a determinant of social structures.[542] Social class position and race/ethnicity often define relative access to resources, which in turn shape traits reflecting mastery, agency, and dominance[543] Equally, a child's gender influences teachers' and parents' expectations for that child's abilities and future achievements. These expectations in turn shape children's own developing motivations and expectations.[544]

In social science, the idea of situated knowledge has wide currency. The American Psychology Association (APA) defines this as "knowledge that is embedded in, and thus affected by, the concrete historical, cultural, linguistic, and value context of the knowing person. The term is used most frequently in perspectives arising from social constructionism, radical feminism, and postmodernism to emphasize their view that absolute, universal knowledge is impossible."[545] It sometimes carries the implication that social and historical factors constrain the process of constructing our very ways of knowing. To the extent that knowledge is situated, it is hard to avoid epistemological relativism. The systems that shape the social experience of clients quite profoundly also structure our ways of perceiving and gathering knowledge. Knowledge is socially produced. How we know what we think we know (epistemology), is altered radically by our view of the world and our experience of it.

Given that psychology itself has always been divided between scientific status and inductive approach, how we know anything to do with counseling psychology is problematic. The scientific method claims to be the sole apparent means of securing objectivity, replacing speculative accounts of the inner world with rationally tested results. Thinking scientifically was cast as a saviour for a world locked in outmoded beliefs. Psychology replaced moral and religious understandings of human behavior with accounts that stressed scientific standing. Can we ground theologically-based knowledge claims in distillation from observations in the client space? Theology seems to rely on innate fundamental ideas, such as archetypical moral and religious notions. Yet it was growing disputes in the nineteenth century between conceptual v empirical accounts of the mind that led neurologists to try to join medical Faculties. Rebuffed, they formed their own discipline. With their experimental techniques, psychology took up the mantle of behaviorism with a focus on phrenology or neurology. This was in contrast with an outward looking anthropology or social studies that focused on society and culture. Psychology has a strong emphasis on the scientific method—though arguably what it actually brought us was classification. Research in psychology often delivered ideas of mental testing that have since been shown up as power in disguise. Scientific methodology is taken as yielding objective results despite experiments in cognitive or social psychology failing to be reproduced by subsequent experimenters. Over half of such studies fail reproducibility test and should probably be distrusted.[546] Researchers are after all committed to quantification but not to the inner lives of real people.

The Sigh for Endorsement: Client Work

The foundation for our approach to psychotherapy is a quest for endorsement and recognition. The need to be of high worth pertains to psychic structure, not just service delivery. This we will set up in such a way as shapes much else in psychic life and therefore client distress and in the therapy room.

How though do we substantiate this contention? Secular psychology has its own epistemological assumptions. Every discipline has its presuppositions, its vocabulary, and its method. On what basis are we making certain statements and testing claims to saying something truthful about the world?

The key in our method was to build theoretical foundations on the basis of listening to clients. From Freud onwards, psychotherapy and counseling work has advanced in this way rather than the observation and laboratory testing common to placing psychology on a scientific foundation.

She sat the opposite side of the consulting room, her sullen face enlivened periodically with flashes of hot indignation. "I wish he could just tell me what he wanted," she said in exasperation about the way her new partner had dumped her. "He gives me the run-around," she complained, puzzled about the "missing-you" texts that belied the thrust of his conversation. "I'm worth more than that," she said. It became clear how the sense of a valuable self that had been growing in recent months was, as she put it, "something to grab hold of." It is this sense, not just of self but of "value in oneself" that is our focus. Another client is ascending into a new sense of self after years of the "put-downs" and persistent denigration. "I'm beginning to feel valuable," she proclaims. "And I'm enjoying it!"[547]

In a ménage of impressions and memories, a particular client expresses his gut-wrenching experiences when she left him. It was shattering, it was flattening; it was as if she had punched him, kicked him and he lay, winded on the floor in disbelief and fraught astonishment. If only it had been limited to a quick rough and tumble between the sheets. But from the way he had seen them out together, he knew it went far deeper.[548] A piece of commentary is volunteered that deserves pondering. It was his use of what is now a common term, "she disrespected me . . . she dis'd the family." Slowly, there came a reaction that was whispered. In time, the whisper became a shout. "I'm worth more than that!" Notwithstanding Freud's contention that dreams are the royal road to the infernal realms of unconscious life, within this *cri de couer* there lurks something of potential significance about human action. A profound layer of motivation and reaction is evoked.

In our culture of enquiry, extending a sense of value gradually became an important concern to what it meant to operate ethically. Because it seems to say something fundamental about how people function, the pursuit of worth is a lens on how personal problems are configured and analyzed as well as best practice. Even with newer psychotherapies, assumptions about the unique value of individuals have yet to be set against a systematic framework of psychodynamic theory.[549] Arguably, the struggle for human worth is not simply located in a moral practice of relationships or how humans ought to be treated.[550] It has to do with the way we are wired with motivational impulse.

The question that began to arise in client and pastoral work was where this way of framing experiences fits into classic accounts of the inner world? What would it mean to say that the impetus towards high value is fundamental? Should inner worlds be re-configured? Here, personal and social worlds intertwine in lived experience. Post-modern critical thinking looks for the silences in text or discourse rather than what is present, whether post-existentially[551] or de-constructively.[552]

What began a period of sustained reflection in client observation was noticing how, in various domains, issues of worth were being constantly generated when people were facing its erosion. On being repeatedly struck by how many clients spoke of experiences of devaluation and how they languaged their indignation in terms of value—"I'm worth more than that!"—the role that worth and value play in everyday life was listened to with careful attunement. Working with clients began to provoke sustained reflection on usual accounts of the motivational drivers. This was interleaved with client's personal relationship to their organization, interpersonal dynamics and their own responses.

The particular approach used in applying the listening in client work was rooted in *autoethnography*, encapsulated in the following: "beginning in the 1970s, there was a shift in emphasis from participant observation to the observation of participation."[553] Autoethnography is reflection as research where the focus is on how the researcher is engaging with what is being encountered in relation to theory. It is an approach to research and writing that seeks to describe and systematically analyze personal experience to understand wider cultural or psychological experience.[554] The "auto" part of autoethnography refers to the researcher, who uses his or herself as a sample of one, and his or her own experience as a "story" revealing or instancing wider cultural or social issues. The idea is to be as rigorous as possible about this, using research methods but applying them to oneself. A researcher uses tenets of autobiography *and* ethnography that becomes in effect both process and product.[555] There is growing recognition that research cannot be done from a neutral, impersonal, and objective stance; that it is not value-free. Working with stories and everyday lives, the auto-ethnographer is hearing these analytically, deploying a set of theoretical and methodological tools and a research literature.[556] The methods are those of writing accounts based on participant's stories, fieldwork or interactive interviews that provide an "in-depth and intimate understanding of people's experiences with emotionally charged and sensitive topics.[557] Various moves allow a researcher working with this approach to analyze, categorise and draw conclusions.[558]

Voice as the researcher and research lies at the heart of autoethnography.[559] It is an autobiographical genre of writing and research that demonstrates multiple layers of consciousness. Developing an approach using this method involves tentative integration of new with established theory. So where could we locate in the literature the role that issues of value or sense of a valuable self play in the architecture of the mind, within *a* psychic structure of helping us to flourish?

The twentieth century was the psychological century, replete with attempts to change people and bring peace and transformation. Therapy after therapy unfolded in the West offering redemptive messages of great power and persuasiveness in a coercive social order where oppression and repression had become synonymous and where self-repression was self-abuse. Different psychologies offered their own brand of liberation based on a diagnosis of the human condition and a desire to understand how the interior world worked. There are some forms of counseling psychology where linkage can be made with according a key role to the quest for high value and worth as being central to human functioning. Here are some that will offer some common ground.

Gestalt Therapy: Based at Ersalen in California, the Human potential movement connected with the 80s and 90s in a big way. Self-help books became hugely popular. Fritz Perls had been a key figure in the 60s, a pioneer in applying to psychotherapy the approach worked out in psychology at the Berlin Gestalt School by Wertheimer et al. "Each person is a complex arrangement of figure-ground relationships."[560] When our sense of self is subsumed within a relationship of studied predictability, for instance, we lose a sharper identity. It is distinction between emerging figures and receding grounds that brings excitement and growth.[561] Through creative experimentation and "aha" moments, past and future can be brought into the "here and now." There is some explicit sense of human value in this project and the statement by Mackewan about assumptions is instructive:

"A dialogic relationship [the ever-shifting relationship between people, life-spaces, fellow human beings] is one in which the uniqueness of each person is valued."[562] This is a definite marker to Gestalt working with the value of the human. As Hycner and Jacobs argue, "the paradox of the human spirit is that I am not fully myself until I am recognised in my uniqueness by another—and that other person needs my recognition in order to fully become the unique person she or he is. We are inextricably intertwined. Our valuing of another brings value to ourself."[563]

Cognitive Behavior Therapy: Some notion of human value and worth is assumed in CBT, widely practiced today. It is contested territory—some arguing that it does nothing to address the cause of psychological problems and that the evidence for long-term benefit is simply not there. Others argue that it does deal with the effects that negative experiences have on your thinking patterns and it is up to the client to internalize reflection about this into more permanent results—the short term evidence base being more impressive than other therapies. One CBT manual argues that disturbing feelings of depression, anxiety, shame, guilt, anger, envy and jealousy are often rooted in your view of self. Low self-esteem shows your estimate of your value is low. But you have worth because you're human; an individual, too complex to measure, more than the sum of your parts. Learn to change negative thinking, value your uniqueness. Improve attitudes towards yourself![564]

Central to CBT is the idea of core beliefs; enduring understandings that are so fundamental and deep that people find it hard to articulate them, even to themselves.[565] Amongst these are worthlessness—the fixed idea that one is morally bad and unacceptable, even that we don't deserve to live. Correcting that deeply rooted belief relies on the opposite assumption; that one is valuable.

Client-centered therapy: Carl Rogers, the psychotherapist who emphasized person-centered counseling, proclaimed the importance of "unconditional positive regard."[566] This was respect for the client,[567] aiming to maintain a relationship that is as free as possible from value judgements. The client should not be blamed or condemned. While they may not be helping themselves, the strategies they have adopted are an effort to manage their lives and emotions. This does not mean that clients cannot change or that the therapist should collude with self-destructive behavior. Clients should be given respect, their experiences should be given credence and their emotions validated. We should distinguish carefully between the behavior of the clients and clients themselves, who are "valuable because they are human."[568] To be sure, the adequacy of the person-centered model is being questioned. There are many tribes in this particular part of the therapeutic jungle.[569] The overall quality of the relating between therapist and client remains not only fundamental to its core principles but crucial to the healing of the suffering soul.

Arguably, the struggle for human value is not simply located within the moral practice of interpersonal functioning or how humans ought to be treated. It goes deeper: it is based upon the interaction of unconscious drives and forces within the person[570] and between different structures of the personality. In short, an impetus towards a high value belongs to the psychodynamic zone.

Critical Correlation

There are various strategies for integration available. One approach to integration between social science and a theology of culture is David Tracy's revised correlational approach in contextual theology. Tracy drew on Paul Tillich as a conversational partner to advance two principal sources for theology: Christian texts and common human experience and language. The theological task involves a critical correlation of the results of one's investigations of the "Christian texts" and of "common human experience. "Theology is the attempt to establish, in both theory and practice, mutually critical correlations between two sets of interpretation: an interpretation of the Christian tradition and an interpretation of contemporary experience."[571]

It is significant that Tracy aligns "common human experience" with "contemporary experience" and that any idea of "investigation" is replaced by one of "interpretation" (hermeneutics). With this emphasis on interpretation, "contemporary theology shares with the humanities, social sciences, and, more recently, natural sciences, a turn to reflection on the process of interpretation itself."[572]

In this, he followed Paul Tillich's who popularized the method of correlation between message and situation.[573] Both are clear that the Christian self-understanding expresses an understanding of authentic human existence.[574] Niebuhr's model of transformation becomes a means of correlation; building on the integrity of human experience and transforming human reality through dialogical encounter. Dialogue works both ways for it to be authentic. Social science and counseling psychology can talk to theology but this can go the other way. Tracy argues that with transformation in mind, it is the particular needs and questions of concrete human situations that principally determine which way the "correlation" will go. Each becomes a source and target for the other.

This is transdisciplinary. A fruitful model for preparing for dialogue is a perichoretic relationship, defined as oneness without losing the identity of those involved. The Greek term "*Homoousios*" (*homo*: same; *ousios*: being), describes the complete mutual indwelling in each Person of the Trinity. Each person remains in himself as Father, Son, and Spirit but nevertheless, fully in the others, fully in themselves. Theology retains its own identity as does psychology, without either losing itself. A trinitarian perspective in our theological anthropology can not only serve as a model for mutual exchange and dialogue but can ground our humanity in a personhood related to other persons.

Constructive engagement—the basis on which we pursue enquiry—is affected by how far attitudes to textual authority have shifted hugely across the years. The Reformed perspective saw the special revelation of scripture as the sole authority by which claims to knowledge must be tested. By contrast, the modern mind of the Enlightenment made human thinkers supreme on the assumption that we are capable of objective rationality. Perhaps inevitably, this led in turn to the critical gaze being turned on its own principles. The result of this universal solvent was the post-modern mind.

What then is our authority for a theological method? In what used to be dubbed "the post-modern turn," word has it that it was not possible to know the truth about anything. Our take on reality could never be anything more than a local version embedded in cultural and power-laden imperatives.

Christian theology has its own language that differentiates it from other ways of looking at the world. As noted, every discipline has its presuppositions, its vocabulary, and its method. With its centuries of writing and reflection, theology raises its own challenges and questions about what can be said about God in any kind of a coherent way. This is at the heart of theology—the study of God—and everything else lies in often puzzling relation to it. All complexities of human existence are illuminated by and derived from general revelation. A biblically based worldview is a particular kind of speech. Learning the theologian's craft is to learn that language of faith but also to grasp cultures where that language was shaped as a social construct as well as contemporary cultures.

Bearing in mind that the latest generation is not the first to do serious work on the basis of faith, there are, in Christian history, various collections of sources for authority when it comes to faith and reliable knowledge. In, for example, the Lambeth Quadrilateral, four points that are important as markers of Anglican identity are: acceptance of Holy Scripture as the rule of faith; the Apostles' and the Nicene creeds; the sacraments of Baptism and the Lord's Supper; and the historic episcopate as representing that faith and a providing a source of contact. The four-fold chair model has been deployed also in what has been termed "the Wesleyan Quadrilateral," invoking:

- The texts of Scripture that define the faith
- Tradition as the inescapably persistent way of keeping adding to understanding
- Reason that provides some sense of coherence
- Religious experience that highlights how theological knowledge is grounded in human lives

For Karl Barth, the Bible was the sum total of the sources in terms of which Christianity could be defined. Human experience and reflection on that experience became irrelevant to decide what God had revealed in Jesus Christ.[575] Barth spoke of discovering "the strange new world within the Bible."[576] Viewing this though has to be brought into conjunction with a second lens; namely the life and times of the familiar yet constantly changing world of the here and now.

Graham McFarlane articulates a distinctive way of doing evangelical theology rooted in revelation and the relational and five reference points: scripture, tradition, reason, experience and community. This last is often missing as the grounding and language for sources of knowledge but is vital.[577] Theology is only possible in the presence of others with whom we are transformed. It is not solitary.

A discipline must establish its own methodology and assumptions. Re-theologizing counseling psychology can be done in a conviction that evangelical affirmations ought to mean something but also that theology *directly applicable to counseling* needs to offer a vocabulary of hopeful critique. Moreover, that double listening ought to pay attention to sociological dimensions of psychology (the latter being interior logic of the former). Rather than simply reading a counseling psychology off biblical texts, arguing from first principles drawn from traditions of reflection suggests some specific content. The problem of knowledge within the interaction between theology and counseling psychology is in seeking to align two different discourse fields. So what do we bring from theology?

Chapter Twenty

Openness to Humanity

The Theology of Personal Experience

Leading Idea: Every counseling theory has its own assumptions. There are theologically-driven insights on human functioning and which are highly relevant to counseling theory.

We will argue in this chapter for a contextual theology rooted in messy human experience.

Much in the cultural mood music supporting the counseling revolution has been antithetical to a Christian world view. The most articulate prophet of the modern creed was Jean-Jacques Rousseau. When looking for life's rules of conduct, he said, he found them "in the depths of my heart, traced by nature in characters which nothing can efface. I need only consult myself with regard to what I wish to do; what I feel to be good is good, what I feel to be bad is bad."[578] "Carefully examine your feelings!" It is what someone will do these days about embarking on a new relationship or a new job. "Does it feel right? What does your heart say?" After all, humans are the ultimate source of meaning. We do not rely on an external source of authority to tell us what to do, like a parent in the sky. Instead, "listen to yourself, follow your heart." To justify an affair, feelings rather than divine commands are a litmus test. This signified the move from revealed religion to natural religion that usually now goes under the name of spirituality. This contemporary stance could be characterized as an "anti-theology" position.

A common critique of theology has been that it is other-worldly, living in a rarefied atmosphere divorced from human concerns.

That may well be true for many strands of historical theology. Patently though there are myriad versions of theology and as many approaches as there are human beings who reflect on ultimate concerns. The purpose of this chapter is to show that theology in general does indeed have something to say to the human situation and the very real contexts in which humans play out their dramas.

Consider subdivisions of systematic theology, using in this case Wayne Grudem's approach:[579]

i. The Word of God
ii. The being and nature of God
iii. Our study of humankind (anthropology)
iv. Christ and the Holy Spirit
v. The application of redemption (soteriology)
vi. The church
vii. The future

How do these categories support an approach that should be taken where someone being counselled is vaguely aware of deep-seated reasons why they do destructive things or are being rejected by others? What does out theology say to people in pain? The dynamics of the human mind are foreign to the traditional concerns of theology; weightless in respect of the distress that carries much weight for clients. Of the knowledge and cure for our problems, typically that has been left to pastoral care.

The perspective of this counseling approach is that theology does, however, have something to say about the human situation. Biblical tradition and text have sustained a wealth of reflection on human functioning. This applies not only to the big existential themes but practice as counsellors.

Ethical norms may sometimes clash and skilled counsellors may sometimes need to hold them in tension. A hierarchy of norms is precluded by the reality that every situation is different. It is not always possible to set out which principle takes precedence. Within the centuries-old traditions of both the cure and care of souls, however, there are broader

Christian ethical norms such as love, grace, holiness and forgiveness that can help resolve dilemmas.

There are, moreover, different emphases within the various faith-based counseling traditions. Some Christian approaches are more at ease than others in drawing on insights from secular theory and practice. Not all Christian counsellors think the same or counsel in the same way. An explicitly Christian umbrella organization such as the UK Association of Christian Counsellors (ACC) does expect its counsellors to have a specifically Christian worldview.[580]

> 2.1. Basis of Christian Counseling
>
> 2.1.1. It is not our purpose to make These may be implicit or explicit. They should be consistent with:
>
> 2.1.2. What the Scriptures reveal about the nature and activity of God—that He is both the creator and judge of human beings and their redeemer in Christ.
>
> 2.1.3. People being created in the image of God—although, because they are fallen and sinful, they are in need of God's redeeming grace.
>
> 2.1.4. Christ as the one true Saviour and Lord. Through His life, death, resurrection and the gift of the Holy Spirit, God has made available all the resources of His grace torescue people, heal them and bring them to maturity and wholeness.
>
> 2.1.5. God's work of justice and mercy in the world and His love towards all people.
>
> 2.1.6. His work of rescuing people, even though they do not deserve it, and bringing them to faith and maturity in Christ, through the work of the Holy Spirit.
>
> 2.1.7. The reality of a fallen world where suffering, pain, guilt, fear, broken relationships and fragmented communities occur.
>
> 2.1.8. God's desire for His people to work to bring healing and wholeness of spirit, mind and body.
>
> 3. Christian Counseling
> In light of the above, we may define Christian counseling as: "that activity which seeks to help people towards constructive change and growth in any or every aspect of their lives through a caring relationship and within agreed relational boundaries, carried out by a counsellor who has a Christian worldview, values and assumptions.

Though the learning can indeed go in both directions (Christian practitioners have much to gain from social and neurosciences) psychology has largely neglected the theological and religious traditions that have underpinned it. An overtly Christian counsellor works with overall assumptions. There are ultimate themes that can be articulated theologically that play out in the therapeutic space. Within the broader landscape of psychological forces, fundamental to the human situation are the impetus towards at least seven themes that constitute a biblical worldview:

i. Transcendence centered on God as the ultimate reference point and circle
ii. Revelation, both general and special
iii. Spiritual nature of humanity as those who are born to relate upwards and outwards
iv. Connection and belonging, love, valuable personhood and endorsement
v. Desire and destructiveness
vi. Sinfulness, guilt, and shame
vii. Redemption and hope centered on a Redeemer, the Christ, who defeats the dark powers that haunt human existence and who imparts the Holy Spirit

First Theme: Transcendence: Beyond Ourselves

We are oriented to what is beyond. The quest for meaning beyond ourselves and ultimately rooted in God. "Spirituality" is a greatly overused word today. But the importance of a relation with God, the Absolute, The Eternal (however it may be described), is at the core of being human. It is fundamental to what it means to be an individual, what it means to live a fulfilled life. Spirituality is always relational. The question is what the individual is related to, and this absolutely reflects on what sort of a human being a person is. A person who is relational in terms of finite goods, whether these be money, sex, power, reputation, nationality, politics, or wife and family, is barely human. They define themselves in terms of other finite goods. Fewer people look to the heavens for meaning: they search on earth. It is no longer a voice above and beyond that can save us and give our lives structure. The inner voice is what counts. Being true to an external, transcendent voice such as comes from God and divinely inspired scripture has been replaced. But arguably, the idea that there is no meaning out there, no reality—only human life-worlds—sells human beings short. The reality of human experiences, however, is that God is not an agent among others in the world we see. For a model of psychotherapy rooted in biblical theology, the ultimate reference point is to God who is there, who speaks and shows.

Second Theme: Revelation

Biblical theology is rooted in the speech-acts of a God who does not hide. God discloses, God shows. Revealed knowledge is offered to humanity as a way by which we can know the ultimate power behind everything, beyond which there stand no other principle or potentate. Human beings catch more than a glimpse of this God—the only one there is—through what is called *general revelation*. This is the means by which human knowledge is mandated in a cosmos that is knowable, testable and empirically discovered. It is often said that "all truth is God's truth." Science, ranging from the truths of mathematics to the observations of physics, chemistry and biology, bring to the cinema screen of our own mental projections an astounding cosmos and stage scenery for all who live here.

There is much that we discover about human functioning through the sheer fact that the world is discoverable. This allows us to explore the human body and ascertain how humans work physiologically but also psychologically. Advances in neuroscience, for example, have transformed the potential for us to inquire into our own brains and make remarkable discoveries. Approaches to counseling that do not demonstrate any openness to this are denying general revelation.

There is also a *special revelation*. Some proposals to align psychology with theology end up confusing the two if they insist that the only permissible realm for ascertaining valid perspectives on human functioning must be derived from the special revelation of biblical text. The approach we take here is that biblical revelation does indeed give us huge insight into the ultimate truth of the human situation which we ignore at our peril. We take a high view of scripture as being both historical (within its genres) and redemptive. Yet there are countless truthful observations to make from the realm of everyday mental and emotional functioning allowing for enormous expertise in those who study them. Assumptions and presuppositions need establishing as for any enterprise.

Third Theme: Createdness and the Spiritual Nature of Humanity: Theological Anthropology

Theologians who offer the results of their insight to counseling and psychotherapy should be able to speak validly to the psychodramas where the guilty, the confused, the pathological, and the neurotic play out the pathos of their lives. The human situation is manifestly different from the divine reality, in which there is always divine presence and divine grace, but in which our sense of ourselves does not feel much at home. Not only are human beings oriented towards something beyond ourselves, we have a spiritual dimension. "Body, soul, and spirit" is a biblical description of a human constitution. The word "soul" used to approximate to "psyche." We are "ensouled" beings, embodied people with a spiritual nature that can ask questions about purpose, what we are here for, why life hurts, freedom and ultimately death. This existential capacity is deeply rooted in human life. The Roman poet Ovid observed that we were not made like dogs to go on all fours and look down on the ground but to walk on two legs and look up. Routinely touched, it is our createdness that cries out in the night. It is createdness that sighs when confronted by ageing, nostalgia, melancholy or romantic turbulence. It is troublesome feature of how we are made; the human condition that cries out in the night. Often, the dramas of war and turbulence in political and interpersonal spheres are so pressing it feels like the world is an abandoned place. For divine grace to be present and not just rooted in a God who is far away requires a different set of questions to those normally posed in the systematic theology faculties. We go to fiction writers of sharp insight such as Shakespeare or Dostoyevsky who depict our humanity yet the texts of narrative scripture are ruthlessly fierce about the human situation.

Fourth Theme: Connection and Belonging, Love, Valuable Personhood, and Endorsement

Humans are relational and, echoing Levinas, shaped by recognition, not just cognition. What an entity is is inseparable from its relations. Relationality is central for understanding persons rather than human action seen in solitary terms. In face-to-face relations we are obligated to the other. We are formed in relationship with others; significant encounters leave sediments that build up. Community (family, neighborhood, city) represents markers of a relational self. We long to be connected. The cost of commitment is matched by the price people pay when love breaks. A lonely self longs for connection. Love and lonely betrayal are the stuff of life. Though reaching constantly to go beyond ourselves, everyone must live inside themselves. That is our home with all the physicality and social location that anchors us to the ground. In a pandemic, social distance has meant we withdrew from community so as to preserve the body. Often it is easier to communicate through an on-line identity. Being part of a community of some sort is essential to identity formation, to who we are. Yet we are full of contradictions. Fallible as we know ourselves to be, texts of scripture reflect free diversity of human interaction with all its messiness. What makes human life work or not is played out there. The tragedy and comedy of human relations is richly depicted and needs to enter our theology. This is the theology of ordinary people, though no life is ever ordinary.

Fifth Theme: Sin: Desire and Destructiveness

As the psychiatrist Karl Menninger lamented a generation ago, "Whatever became of sin?"[581] By slow but steady rejection, the concept of sin was eroded in Western society. Sin became almost a non-entity. Sin moved from being associated with duty or its deficit to cohabitation being the subject of frown by the 1970s. Then it was ironed out of existence or collapsed into penalties or allowances (it mattered not) in dieting. The shift resulted in a changed understanding of sin through the years, shifting the responsibility of sin from the individual to society. Actions and attitudes that destroy human beings we tend to say it was due to the way perpetrators were raised, their mental illness or previous traumas. Or we say that the global environment—such as destruction of the Arctic—is the planetary sphere of our moral concern rather than interpersonal actions. Sin was seen as a guilt-inducing moralizing attitude emanating from institutions now exposed as fatally flawed. Any concept of wrong focused on harm to others, harm to animals and to the environment. This leaves a gaping hole. How on earth does society cope conceptually with radical evil that seems to be not on earth?

In traditional, biblical forms of theology, the Fall was upheld as the only explanation of man's present discordant state, notwithstanding the reality that little is made of this afterwards explicitly and directly in biblical narratives. Human evil arises out of the very freedom of reason with which humanity is endowed. "Sin is not so much a consequence of natural impulses, which in animal life do not lead to sin, as of the freedom by which man is able to throw the harmonies of nature out of joint."[582] Such disturbance arises when we centre our life round one particular impulse (sex or possessiveness for example) or when we try to make ourselves rather than God the centre of existence. It is not a defect of creation but a defect which arises because we have a freedom not known in the rest of creation. We set up ourselves, individually or collectively, as God: as the providers of final answers; final solutions, that are always in reality utterly destructive of humanity. Our commitment to human freedom and dignity includes freedom to be irrational and ridiculous.

Desire lies at the heart of our pain. Satisfying our needs and desires means the outworking of an emotional forces and motivational impulse. The word "passion" expresses some of this. Yet passion is also closely linked with suffering—witness the suffering and death of Jesus.

Desire itself represents our createdness rather than sinfulness. But it is ever only one step away from going in wrong directions. It is from within from the human heart that misery and malignancy spring. Freud categorized desire in sexual terms. Whether for sex, power or money with which it is associated, desire is a powerful driver that shapes us. The oppression under the sun spoils everything. In chains to *desire* we try to position ourselves better in the win or lose game of life. The thread running through oppressive categories humans experience is that of devaluing each other and dishonoring God. The high value of the human is eroded by our capacity to devalue others. That takes place on a spectrum descending to the heart of darkness through:

i. *Denigration* on an interpersonal level

ii. *Depersonalization* at the level of social prejudice but also machine-economics

iii. *Desecration* through violence which constitutes assault of sacred personhood

iv. *Dehumanization* that many will experience through state-sponsored action

v. *Demonization* where social groups have been reduced to folk devils or animals

The potential for radical evil has been a feature of the twentieth century with special resonance in theology after Auschwitz. As Richard Rubinstein, the first Jewish thinker to name the Holocaust as a crisis for traditional Jewish theology observed, "At the time I wrote 'After Auschwitz', one could search through almost everything written by the contemporary establishment without finding the slightest hint that they were living in the same century as Auschwitz."[583]

Sixth Theme: Guilt and Shame, Justice and Accountability

The fully honest, fully human person does not exist. Self—deceit is too pressing a reality. The quest for just deserts, for justice and resolution (both in right relationship to God and others) is a major theme of life. The vindication of good is not for morality plays only. It is our personal and group story. Our own sense of guilt reflects inner knowledge that someone must pay—often us! Following the philosopher Kant, the invoices are often addressed incorrectly in this life. There is a strong role that guilt plays in the human situation, as illustrated in client work. Interpersonal transactions carry much moral freight. Yet moral suppression carries on regardless. Such are the issues of life.

Exploring psychological aspects of the atonement provides a very relevant lens such as with reference to guilt in everyday life. When conditions of worth function well, they are life-enhancing. When they take on an absolute form they assume the character and oppressive function of the principalities and powers. People can be treated as guilty without being personally guilty (witness racism).

Shame too is a prevalent disposition (emotion?) arising from perception that one is socially outcast or out of favour and not accorded status or approval. Its essence is not so much that "I *have done* morally bad actions" but that "I *am* a bad person." Shame contrasts with honor both in terms of psychological experience but also in the biblical culture of an honor-shame social system that cradled it.

Seventh Theme: Soteriology and Spirit (Redemption and Hope)

We are strongly motivated by hope. It is at the core of being human. Without struggle there is no growth. Clients need to feel that they can get through this. Potential for repair and recovery lead to establishing therapeutic alliances; then keeping going. Meaning in suffering is possible as is capacity to be future orientated. What sustains us are unfulfilled dreams. Dreams are to dream, not to realize. In death, all are the same, no matter what their dreams. Through the cross the liberator Christ is the breaker of chains. By him we have hope and connection with the God who is. Our flight from meaning and reality is addressed for it is the real Jesus (not just a Christ-figure) who gives us hope and redemptive reconstruction.

The true humanity of Christ is important to assert in concrete terms: "The Redeemer appears not as man-in-general, i.e. not simply as a bearer of human nature but as a definite human being in history—Jesus of Nazareth. . . . Jesus, the Son of God who has become man, is a genuine man."[584] As Bonhoeffer points out, this man was no abstract God. The doctrine of the incarnation begins by asking not, "How is it possible to conceive of the incarnation?" but "Who is he?" Jesus is not adopted by God and is not God clothed in human characteristics.[585] The incarnation, for Bonhoeffer, means that Christ shared in an unqualified way human nature as we know it. This meant there was some element of the incognito about the incarnation. It was possible to mistake him for an ordinary man.

This was the first phase in a distinctively Christian scheme of a recovery programme. The incarnation of the Christ revealing God in a new way in an authentically human life leads directly into the events of the last week of Jesus culminating in the death and what Christians believe to be resurrection. The dark powers of alienation, death, sin and despair are overcome by Jesus and decisively routed.

In an unbroken line, this is the same one who brings about the regeneration of a new order of things. Imparting the Holy Spirit is not so much a personal experience to enjoy as emblematic of a new creation. The project is transformational in the direction of the Christ life as revelatory of what that new condition looks like and how it comes about. Resurrection leads inexorably to Pentecost with which it is tightly knit. This presents therapy with enormous resources and power for change. The Spirit is in the room; present to effect growth and freedom for those battered and baffled.

Formidable resources are available in Christian theology for the restoration of troubled people. There is in the New Testament a strong message of what is known as soteriology—human rescue and repair. Much could be said about this that defies any more than a few headlines but essentially:

- There is a common grace and general revelation applicable to humanity, not just the community of the faithful. Theories of human functioning that can be developed from client work or scientific testing are probing the richness of this. Medical doctors and mental health practitioners are drawing on general revelation available in principle to anyone.
- Justification and acceptance by God looms large in the scheme of human salvation. A wholesale change of status is on offer arising from the atonement of Christ which intersects the experience of our standing with God being riddled with sin and guilt. The result is a divinely initiated exchange in which merit and new standing is substituted for demerit.
- Not only guilt and a deep sense of unworthiness but purification is available whereby the stain of defilement is addressed by a powerful washing of the soul that cleanses the past.
- Deep uncertainty about the vagaries of life, our position with God and what is ultimate is replaced by assurance of "salvation" and a confidence in the future that overcomes death.
- The human need to connect with what is ultimate is addressed by relationship with what is at the heart of things; namely a God who is relational and calls humanity into a live link.
- A sense of weakness and impotence to face the challenges of life is addressed by divine empowering that comes from the Holy Spirit. "Strength for today and bright hope for tomorrow" is a classic hymn that depicts some of this.

There is, in addition to these themes of Christian reflection a definite theology of pain that connects with human experience in a major way. The Bible is replete with struggling souls. It rubs our noses in it except that its purpose is relentlessly redemptive. We see people in pain through making choices, being trampled on and trampling over others. We witness the spectre of suffering and the unfairness of life's puzzle as to why some are successful and while for others, bad things happen to good people. We see trauma. We witness Empires and Kings exercising cruelty. "How long, O Lord, who long?" is an oft repeated refrain.

Until then we are faced with those struggling with their inner demons, with anger, alcoholism, addictions of all kinds, unmet needs, wounded history, longings and belongings. Rationalizing and blame-shifting are all too common. What though has theology to say to code-pendency or borderline personality disorders? How are fears and phobias to be addressed?

Development of a systematic theology of counseling represents fresh theological work about human nature and everyday experience. Enough though has been said to indicate that there is a theology for therapy that connects people in pain with ultimate issues as set forth in scripture combined with centuries of insightful reflection. It is a theology that can scrutinise the enlightenment construction of the individualized self growing like a plant and argue instead for a self that is related to others, anchored to traditions of past, present and future and above all, oriented to a transcendent God.

Postscript

Spiritual Transformation and the Answering Echo

WHAT DOES IT MEAN to change?

In many personal biographies lies the statement that they went somewhere and did something and as a result they were a changed person. Very likely it was an experience that acted as catalyst for what lay out of sight previously.

Latent change lies within us all: be for the worst as well as for the better. We cannot consider, even briefly, the direction of change without invoking centuries of ethical reflection about the good life and what that means in practice. Being a better person might not be an obvious reason to want to change but it is an important aspect of the moral and spiritual ends to which transformation ensues.

The Goals of Therapy

To what end do people seek therapy? Reparative work might be sought for example for:

- A better adjustment to life
- Healthier and more satisfying relationships
- Dealing effectively with the many challenges that are weighing heavily on someone
- Anxiety and depression

- Nagging problems inside that just won't go away
- Repeat behavior that results in emotional desolation
- Different parts of ourselves in conflict

It is a real question for evidential assessment to know if short-term or immediate therapeutic gains are genuine and if they will translate into sustainable change long term. Gains or if the gains mean something different for the patient, therapist, and progress of therapy, respectively. A theory of therapeutic change depends on past experiences and the trajectory of a life.

In humanistic counseling, following Abraham Maslow, "self-actualization" is key. The goal is a fully functioning person, open to experience, not defensive, who lives existentially (constantly in process, adaptable and flexible).[586] That is a different focus to faith-based counseling where there is a God-context. Self-determination and fulfilment are vital aspects of humanistic counseling but would not be considered goals of a faith-based approach.

The idea of different personas arises in the work of C. G. Jung who stressed the different parts of the psyche in competition. This was not, as in Freud, driven by past experiences only but also future goals. Growth towards harmony means that different personas come into alignment. Until then, in *The Undiscovered Self*, Jung argued we experience progressive alienation from ourselves.[587]

When most people think of therapeutic change, they probably think of amelioration of symptoms, improved mental models and internal representations of self, other, and relationships. They may also think of healthier and more satisfying interpersonal and relationships, handling their emotions better and the need to facilitate insight and greater self-awareness.

There seems little doubt that self-awareness and knowledge of self can equip one to better deal with the problems of everyday life. Spinoza foreshadowed psychotherapy in his book *Ethics*. "Emotion, which is suffering, ceases to be suffering as soon as we form a clear and precise picture of it."[588]

In considering the goals of therapy, With Aristotle, the focus is on being a good person and the right actions will follow.[589] Eudaemonia—the life well lived or human flourishing—is about proper functioning, following natural law so we do the right thing in the right way. If you are virtuous, you know what to do. Robust character traits will show you what to do. The golden mean results in doing the right thing in the right situation as a mid-point between extremes. Honesty is about being truthful but also realizing what need not be blurted out. Character is developed action by action as someone pushes themselves to be the best person they can be and emulate moral exemplars. Aristotle influenced Aquinas in a natural law theory, that human beings could and should act in a way for which God has fitted them.

Alasdair Macintyre picks up this trajectory. His *After Ethics* sought to chart a way out of the moral bleakness of our times by reintroducing the idea of a *telos* into morality. This is the notion that things have a given end or purpose, and something is "good" if it helps the object or entity attain that end. It represented a move away from situation ethics or straight de-ontological ethics based on absolute notions of right and wrong. Focus instead on narrative, the shape of a life, as if the subject of a novel can be described and it is a good life that ends well. The good life is the life spent in seeking for the good life for human beings. The virtues necessary for the seeking are those which will enable us to understand what more and what else the good life is.[590]

Intrinsic to Aristotle's conception of eudaemonia as summing up the goal of ethics include both ones that contribute to our flourishing as members of a community, and ones that allow us to engage in spiritual contemplation. This brings us to the shape of a life as has been drawn in Christian reflection down the centuries.

Face to Face

Intrinsic to the experience of meeting online in the COVID-19 pandemic that greatly accelerated previous social trends in psychotherapy no less than in personal interaction was a reworking of time and space. Remote working entailed counseling that was face to face yet many felt that this was not the same as being "in-person," even though the face was recognizable.

In social life, recognition—the power of the gaze—is hugely important.

At different points in our learning journey we have encountered the importance of the face.

In experiences that might be shame-inducing, "saving face" results in the ability to find a way out.

A sense of a valuable self is formed in the face of someone who smiled when they saw you. Positive looks from parents are a crucial stimulus to growth of a social brain.[591] Through positive messages written across the face of the significant Other, pleasurable biochemicals help brain development.[592] It is here we build a valuable self.[593] Someone lights up when we are around.

It begins with a gaze. To be seen (noticed) and heard communicates that I am worth listening to. It begins with a gaze. To be seen (noticed) and heard communicates that I am worth listening to.

Consider some biblical texts.

Some very real sense of "seeing the face of God" is the culmination of a good life lived in a way that someone—and those around—will be blessed. "Blessed are the pure in heart, for they will see God" (Matt 5:8). In this well-known statement from the Sermon on the Mount, purity will have its reward; not just as defined by Kierkegaard as to will one thing. The ends for which we live reach their culmination. Destiny and destination reach their finale.

> And we all, who with unveiled faces contemplate the Lord's glory, are being transformed into his image with ever-increasing glory, which comes from the Lord, who is the Spirit. (2 Cor 3:18)

This looks similar to the thought in Psalm 84:7: "They go from strength to strength, until each appears before God in Zion." The difference is the reference to the Spirit.

There is a concept of "thirdness" in psychotherapy, linked to the "relational unconscious." This is defined by Gerson as the fundamental structuring property of each interpersonal relation in modes of engagement specific to that dyad and influences individual subjective experience within the dyad. The way a client pursues enactments and intersubjective resistances are viewed as clinical manifestations of the relational unconscious. Therapy can help alter the structure of the relational unconscious that binds therapist and client.[594] It is the jointly created unconscious life of the analytic pair that constitutes the analytic third.[595]

In Christian theology, the Spirit may be considered to represent thirdness as being essential in the interaction between Father and Son. This is different to the psychotherapeutic idea clearly but the idea of there being "you, me and the space between" is the linkage of interpersonal interaction.

There is a transformation, a direction of travel enabled and empowered by the Spirit that goes beyond human endeavours by signposting beyond them.

In Christian theology, sanctification is a state of separation to God that results in real change. This is not self-directed change but transformation facilitated by the Spirit in a step-by-step process as deep inner states of being are cleansed and re-directed and new neural pathways are forged.

> For whom he did foreknow, he also did predestinate to be conformed to the image of his Son, that he might be the firstborn among many brethren. Moreover whom he did predestinate, them he also called: and whom he called, them he also justified: and whom he justified, them he also glorified. (Rom 8:29–30)

Arguably, such transformation encapsulates what is intrinsic to the ethical direction signposted by Aristotle. The good life is one that represents the goal of human endeavours and how we should live. This is inseparable from the change process as conceived by biblical theology rooted in the God who calls us into being by seeing us and affirming our existence through knowing and self-knowing.

> When I was a child, I talked like a child, I thought like a child, I reasoned like a child. When I became a man, I put the ways of childhood behind me. For now we see only a reflection as in a mirror; then we shall see face to face. Now I know in part; then I shall know fully, even as I am fully known. (1 Cor 13:11–12)

There is a profound question arising from this journey. If our fundamental quest is for endorsement, for someone or something out there that responds to my humanity, what are the horizons of this? Our personhood is in need of validation, of recognition by what is ultimate? This can be put in the form of a question. Is there anything out there that corresponds to what is in here, inside us?

That is a metaphysical question that will have to be pursued into a subsequent book. Does a cosmic order derived from what we see as spiritual but impersonal force? Does it point to a personal God?

Finding the Valuable Person

Working with the Model

WRITING A THERAPEUTIC FRAMEWORK means that we are able to state clearly how we work. Defining our **practice rationale** helps articulate what we aim to do and provides a vocabulary for good practice.

The theoretical allegiances that underpin our work need to be clear. Being theory-led, "doing therapy," should naturally evolve towards being "therapy-informed," 'being a therapist.'[596]

As consistent research demonstrates, there is more value in the process than the content of theory. Yet a body of theory should come to life in the counselling room and should resonate with values.

Pre-suppositions are important to state. The therapy proposed here does not draw on a humanistic view of human nature if by that a purely secular assumption is meant. Neither does it rest on the presuppositions of behavioural science or an existential framework that is in search of meaning.

Core Theory/Philosophy

Spirituality rooted in biblical theology that takes faith seriously to do with a transcendent God.

Linked with that, the value of human beings as a psycho-social fundamental drive.

Relational theory in its different aspects.

The importance of transference and counter-transference as windows on dynamic processes.

The importance of embodied experience, the existential quest for meaning and capacity for agency.

Informed by

Psychodynamic view of unconscious influences to do with client history and which shapes what is being enacted in the therapeutic space.

Person-centred approaches for conditions of worth in a therapeutic relationship to probe "the here and now" of what the client brings.

Cognitive behavioural therapy with the need to work on faulty working models and thought patterns.

Gestalt theory emphasising phenomenological, experiential approach to build awareness supporting client to articulate meaning and find agency in shifting and enduring shapes or patterns in their lives.

Interested in

Biblical theology and the Christian tradition.

Neuroscience.

Cultural factors and the relevance of social experience in shaping a devalued self.

The motivation to pursue a high worth is carried out against the background of everything in inter-personal life and society that generates the devalued self.

1. **Indifference**—does the client feel invisible or silent; being unseen or unheard?
2. **Inferiority**—does the client feel belittled, diminished, put down or made to feel second class?
3. **Indignity**—does the client feel rejected, trashed or have dignity compromised or invaded?

Drivers of Human Functioning and Hungers of the Soul

The impulse in our approach to human functioning is the relational drive to be recognised, endorsed and validated. Soul-hungers through which this quest for validation is expressed are four lenses to help us discern what is going on deep down. These are four domains in which we can work fruitfully.

a. In the way people *relate* to others.

b. In the way people experience themselves incarnationally as *embodied.*

c. In the way people attach *meanings* on situations in their lives and lack of purpose.

d. In the way people exercise responsible *agency* or find exercising their voice challenging.

I BELONG (relational connection and the power of place)

I WANT (pursuit of desire, whether for sex or power that is a deeply embodied experience)

I MATTER (valuable personhood, longing for meaning, worthwhile, significance, and purpose)

I WILL SURVIVE (hope and a positive future, evoking our inner resources as responsible agents)

Applying that to our four REMA domains, a therapist will want to probe some far-reaching questions. These relate to the client but also therapist since the link between them is living and interactive.

When belonging and relational connection is thwarted, the outcome is insecurity and isolation. When the hunger for joyful embodiment is unfulfilled, the frustration will generate disturbance. When meaning and significance is frustrated, the result is a strong feeling you do not count. When impetus towards hope and agency is blocked, this can lead to depression and often despair.

Working relationally with the Rema framework means that the therapist does not just reflect on the client experience, but also and equally importantly on their own experience of the therapeutic relationship. The sections below outline fruitful questions for the therapist to reflect on as they reflect on their work both by themselves and in supervision. These questions apply equally to the client experience and the therapist experience- both offer valuable insight into the therapeutic process. They are grouped in the four domains of the REMA framework and are intended as a starting point, not to be used definitively.

Working in the First Domain—Relational

Relational disruption brings a need for repair and restoration. Created by a relational and trinitarian God, we relate and look for relationship within ourselves, with the divine, with humanity and with the created world in order to nurture a sense of worth. It is connection that imparts a sense of value.

What we are, we are in relationship; a screen on which we project our inner world and act out our psychodramas. What different parts of ourselves are like a cast of characters in the room life now? Object relations illuminate why we may operate from different positions and are not integrated.

What is going on in the way client relate to others currently? What *has been* a pattern of relating?

What is happening in the therapeutic relationship? How do you as therapist feel in this relationship?

What about counter-transference the therapist is experiencing? How is this to be interpreted?

Do clients have difficulty forming relationships or want to sabotage in search of something elusive?

What relationship patterns are emerging? Are they familiar to the client or therapist?

How are the cultures and intersectional identities of client and therapist (both sameness and difference) influencing the therapeutic relationship?

How much do clients feel loneliness or relational connection to somewhere they feel they belong?

This is encapsulated in the transference projected on the therapist. "Who do I remind you of?"

What deeply formative patterns in how they related to parents are influencing clients now?

Working in the Second Domain—Embodiment

Embodied Personhood. Our identity is mediated through embodied experience be it emotionality, physicality, sexuality or disability.

How are clients aware of their bodies? how connected are they to their body? How is this changing?

What about the therapist? What is your bodily awareness? (Remember this can include numbness and desensitisation)

What role does desire have in their bodily experience? Where and when and how do client and therapist experience embodied desire?

How do clients treat their body and look after themselves?

What emotions or sensations are being experienced? where? How? How is client expressing them either physically or verbally?

What signs of trauma are emerging? How is pain being embodied or that might need to come to the surface?

What aspects of embodied spirituality are emerging as being important?

How has social location influenced the client. How is embodied sameness or difference between client and therapist impacting the relationship?

Working in the Third Domain—Meaning-making

In what way are client and therapist grappling with meaning? What gives life meaning?

How is therapist's meaning making impacting the client's meaning making? Are there blind spots?

What is therapist countertransference of trying to make sense of life?

What metaphors, images or repeated body postures or movements are emerging in the work?

What about our sense of significance? What may be lacking or make it complete? How is the search for significance and a sense of worth present in the room (for both therapist and client)?

Is there a void within the "me" at the heart of our experience? What is being avoided or unspoken?

How far do questions of purpose, loss or the reality of death loom in client consciousness?

However languaged, what meaning does God and their spiritual dimension have for the clients? How is this rooted in their identity?

What meanings are coming up in the situations being described?

Why do clients think they are placing such interpretations? What are the underlying core beliefs?

What meaning is emerging from client dreams?

What meanings are being placed on the transferences between therapist and client? How is this impacting the therapeutic relationship?

Is there a sense of meaninglessness, boredom or "stuckness" for client or therapist? How is this embodied? Or evoked?

Working in the Fourth Domain—Agency

More than fulfilling physical urges, we need to know that we matter—that we are *noticed.* We can though move beyond the script handed out to us and take responsibility for our own lives.

What prevents the client from exercising agency and capacity in the situations they face?

How is the client exercising agency in the working alliance? How is this impacting the therapist?

How are clients taking response-ability for their life and direction so as to move forward? How are they being prevented from growing? What defences are emerging in the therapeutic relationship?

Where is their voice in situations that might be crowding in upon clients? What would be ideal? Whose voice is being heard in the therapeutic relationship? How?

What would it mean for clients to hold head up high and ensure dignity?

How much is hope and any sense of a positive future missing in the client's life and situation? Where in the client's life is there hope or despair? Do these figure in the therapeutic relationship?

What is NOT being expressed in the room that seems important to emerge and be voiced?

Endnotes

1. Tauler, J. (1985). *Sermons* (Maria Shrady, Trans.). Paulist.
2. Jones, E. (1964). *The life and work of Sigmund Freud*. Penguin, p. 181.
3. Rogers, C. (2012). *Client centred therapy* (New ed.) Robinson.
4. Rogers, C. (1951). *Client centred therapy*. Constable, p. 437.
5. Gill, M. (1982). *Analysis of transference*. Vol. 2, *Studies of nine audio-recorded psychoanalytic sessions*. International Universities Press.
6. Frances, A. (2014). *Saving normal: An insider's revolt against out-of-control psychiatric diagnosis, DSM-5, big pharma, and the medicalization of ordinary life*. William Morrow & Company.
7. Boyle, M., & Johnstone, L. (2020). *A straight talking introduction to the power threat meaning framework: An alternative to psychiatric diagnosis*. PCCS.
8. Mahrer A. (1989). *The integration of psychotherapies*. Human Sciences.
9. Beck, A., et al. (1979). *A cognitive therapy of depression*. Guilford.
10. Van der Kolk, B. (2014). *The body keeps the score: Mind, brain, and body in the transformation of trauma*. Penguin, p. 246.
11. Rosa, H. (2021). *Resonance: A sociology of our relationship to the world*. Polity.
12. Linden, D. (2006). How psychotherapy changes the brain—the contribution of functional neuroimaging. *Molecular Psychiatry*, *11*, 528–38.
13. Layard, R., & Clark, D. M. (2014). *The power of psychological therapy*. Penguin.
14. Rachman, S. J., & Wilson, G. T. (1980). *The effects of psychological therapy*. Pergamon, p. 665.
15. Brand, R. (2013, March 9). *Russell Brand: My life without drugs*. The Guardian. https://www.theguardian.com/culture/2013/mar/09/russell-brand-life-without-drugs.
16. Van de Castle, R. L. (1971). *The psychology of dreaming*. General Learning.
17. Persinger, M. (2001). The neuropsychiatry of paranormal experiences. *Journal of Neuropsychiatry*, *13*, 515–24.
18. *Study finds that suicides are far more likely to occur after midnight*. (2014, June 1). American Academy of Sleep Medicine. https://aasm.org/study-finds-that-suicides-are-far-more-likely-to-occur-after-midnight/.

19. Loder, J. (1981). *The transforming moment.* Harper and Row.
20. Tillich, P. (1952). *The courage to be.* Yale University Press, p. 66.
21. Schreiner, M. (2014, August 14). *Existential loneliness.* Existential Psychology. https://evolutioncounseling.com/existential-loneliness/.
22. Higham, N. (2018). *Living the life that you are: Finding wholeness when you feel lost, isolated, and afraid.* New Harbinger.
23. Yalom, I. (1980). *Existential psychotherapy.* Basic Books, p. 5.
24. Troyat, H. (1971). *Leo Tolstoy.* Penguin, p. 523.
25. Cate, C. (2003). *Friedrich Nietzsche: a biography.* Pimlico.
26. Kaufmann, W. (1974). *Nietzsche, philosopher, psychology, antichrist* (4th ed). Princeton University Press, p. 97.
27. Troyat, H. (1971). *Leo Tolstoy.* p. 519.
28. Tolstoy, L. (2009). *A confession.* Merchant.
29. Troyat, H. (1971). *Leo Tolstoy.* p. 524.
30. Maunsel, J. B. (2014). *Susan Sontag.* Reaktion, p. 124.
31. Nunez, S. (2011). *Sempre Susan: A memoir of Susan Sontag.* Atlas, pp. 115–16.
32. Nunez, S. (2011). *Sempre Susan: A memoir of Susan Sontag.* Atlas, p. 183.
33. (2004, August 10). Obituary. *The Times.*
34. Levin B. (1978, May 3). An ideal way to clear the mind. *The Times*, p. 16. Republished in Levin, B. (1979). *Taking sides.* Cape, p. 123.
35. Brand, R. (2013, March 9). *Russell Brand: My life without drugs.* The Guardian. https://www.theguardian.com/culture/2013/mar/09/russell-brand-life-without-drugs.
36. Kierkegaard, S. (2004). *The sickness unto death: A Christian psychological exposition of edification and awakening by Anti-Climacus.* Penguin.
37. Cited in Becker, E. (1973). *The denial of death.* Free, p. 70.
38. Wurmser, L. (2003). Abyss calls out to abyss: Oedipal shame, invisibility, and broken identity. *The American Journal of Psychoanalysis, 63*, 299–316.
39. Schopenhauer, A. (1909). *The world as will and idea* (R. B. Haldane & J. Kemp, Trans). Vol. 3. Paul, Trench, Trübner, & Co., p. 573.
40. McCabe, I. (2015). *Carl Jung and alcoholics anonymous: The twelve steps as a spiritual journey of individuation.* Routledge.
41. Grof, S. (1979). *Realms of the human unconscious: Observations from LSD research.* Souvenir.
42. Tarnas, R. (1991). *The passions of the western mind.* Pimlico, p. 426.
43. Dearborn, M. (2018). *Ernest Hemingway: A biography.* Vintage.
44. Clark, T. W. (1995). Death, nothingness, subjectivity. In D. Kolak & R. Martin (Eds.), *The experience of philosophy* (pp. 15–20). Wadsworth.
45. Janov, A. (1988). *Primal scream: Primal therapy, the cure for neurosis.* Abacus.
46. Janov, A. (1991). *The new primal scream: Primal therapy twenty years on.* Abacus.
47. Goldman, A. (1988). *The lives of John Lennon.* Guild.
48. Mithers, C. L. (1994). *Therapy gone mad: The true story of hundreds of patients and a generation betrayed.* Addison-Wesley.
49. Johnson, S. (2018, September 17). *Separation anxiety disorder.* Heathline. https://www.healthline.com/health/anxiety/separation-anxiety.
50. American Psychiatric Association. (2013). *Diagnostic and statistical manual of mental disorders* (5th ed.). APA.
51. Greene, G. (1999). *A sort of life.* Vintage.
52. Bowlby, J. (1975). *Attachment and loss.* Vol. 2. Pelican.
53. Freud, S. (1995). *Introductory lectures on psychoanalysis: Part 3.* Norton.

54. Novak, M. (2017). *The experience of nothingness*. Routledge.
55. Tillich, P. (2014). *The courage to be* (3rd ed.). Yale University Press.
56. Berkouwer, G. C. (1956). *The triumph of grace in the theology of Karl Barth*. Paternoster.
57. Barth, K. (2010). *Church Dogmatics*. Vol 3. Hendrickson, p. 335.
58. This quote is popularly attributed to Charles Cooley.
59. The daughter of the writer William Golding recounting how Golding's children were put in second place to their parent's projects and had to work twice as hard for their parent's attention and approval. Golding, J. (2011). *The children of lovers: The memoir of William Golding by his daughter*. Faber.
60. Berne, E. (1968). *Games people play*. Penguin.
61. Harris, T. (1995). *I'm ok—you're ok*. Arrow. See also Clarkson, P. (1992). *Transactional Aanalysis: An integrated approach*. Routledge.
62. Stewart, I., & Joines, V. (1987). *TA today: A new introduction to transactional analysis*. Lifespace, p. 7.
63. Alexander, J., & Lara, M. P. (1996). The struggle for recognition. *New Left Review*, *220*, 129.
64. Honneth, A. (1995). *The struggle for recognition: The moral grammar of social conflicts* (J. Anderson, Trans.). Polity.
65. Tangney, J. P. (1999). The self-conscious emotions: Shame, guilt, embarrassment, and pride." In T. Dalgleish & M. J. Power (Eds.) *Handbook of cognition and emotion* (pp. 541–68). Wiley & Sons.
66. Tajfel, H., & Turner, J. C. (1979). An integrative theory of intergroup conflict. In W. G. Austin & S. Worchel (Eds.), *The social psychology of intergroup relations* (pp. 33–47). Brooks.
67. Frankl, V. (2004). *Man's search for meaning*. Rider, p. 62.
68. Frankl, V. (1973). *The doctor and the soul*. Penguin, p. 27.
69. Frankl, V. (2004). *Man's search for meaning*. Rider, p. 60.
70. Miller, A. (2000). *Death of a salesman*. Penguin.
71. Author's client notes. Name withheld and used with permission.
72. Rawlings, B. (2010, October 29). *A life without work*. BBC2 documentary.
73. Author's client notes. Name withheld and used with permission.
74. Maslow, A. (1977). A theory of metamotivation: The biological rooting of the value life. In H-M Chiang & A. Maslow (Eds.), *The healthy personality* (p. 28). Van Nostrund.
75. Culliford, L. (2011). *The psychology of spirituality*. Kingsley, p. 16.
76. Royal College of Psychiatrists. (2021). *Spirituality and mental health*. www.rcpsych.ac.uk/mentalhealthinformation/therapies/spiritualityandmentalhealth.aspx.
77. Hindmarsh, B. (2019). End of faith as its beginning. In T. M. Crisp, S. L. Porter, & G. A. T. Elshof (Eds.) *Psychology and spiritual formation in dialogue*. IVP Academic.
78. Ovid. *Fasti*, I.211–12 ('petulant' for 'volunt').
79. Tolstoy, S. (2009). *The diaries of Sofia Tolstoy* (C. Porter, Trans.). Alma.
80. Gay, P. (2006). *Freud: A life for our time*. Max, p. 390.
81. Freud, S. (1922). *Beyond the pleasure principle*. Hogarth.
82. Freud, S. (1927). *The ego and the id*. Hogarth.
83. Gay, P. (2006). *Freud: A life for our time*. Max, p, 390.
84. Freud, S. (1922). *Beyond the pleasure principle*. Hogarth.

85. Freud, S. (1927). *The ego and the id*. Hogarth.
86. Gay, P. (1988). *Freud: A life for our time*. Papermac, p. 147.
87. Lacan, J. (1977). *Écrits: A selection*. (A. Sheridan, Trans.). Tavistock. See also http://lacan.com/
88. Klein, M. (1957). *Envy and gratitude*. Tavistock.
89. LaCugna, C. M. (1991). *God for us: The trinity and Christian life*. HarperSanFrancisco, p. 314.
90. Augustine. (1991). *The trinity* (E. Hill, Trans.). New City, p. 379.
91. Whitton, E. (2003). *Humanistic approach to psychotherapy*. Whurr, p. 39. See also Thorne, B. (2001). *Therapeutic and spiritual dimensions*. Whurr.
92. Yalom, I. (1980). *Existential Psychotherapy* New York: Basic Books.
93. Frankl, V. (2004). *Man's search for meaning*. Rider, p. 75.
94. Neil, S. (1959). *A genuinely human existence: Towards a Christian psychology*. Doubleday, p. 190.
95. Ellis-Jones, R. (2022). *What is identity? https://ellisjones.com.au/the-importance-of-identity/*.
96. Anderson, D. L. (2008). *What is a person?* The Mind Project. https://mind.ilstu.edu/curriculum/what_is_a_person/what_is_a_person.html.
97. Torchia, J. O. P. (2007). *Exploring personhood: An introduction to the philosophy of human nature*. Rowman & Littlefield.
98. Pecere, P. (2020). *Soul, mind, and brain from Descartes to cognitive science: A critical history*. Springer.
99. Nimbalkar, N. (2011). John Locke on personal identity. *Mens Sana Monogr*, *9*, 268–75.
100. Taylor, C. (1992). *Multiculturalism and the politics of recognition*. Princeton University Press, p. 38.
101. Fukuyama, F. (2018). *Identity: The demand for dignity and the politics of resentment*. Farrar, Straus & Giroux.
102. Mead, G. H. (1934). *Mind, self, and society*. University of Chicago Press.
103. De Waal, F. (2021). *Different: Gender through the eyes of a primatologist*. Norton.
104. Cooke, L. (2021). *Bitch: A revolutionary guide to sex, evolution, and the female animal*. Basic.
105. Santoro, H. (2022). *Advocating for transgender and non-binary youths*. American Psychological Association. https://www.apa.org/monitor/2022/07/advocating-transgender-nonbinary-youths.
106. Heinrich, J., Heine, S. J., & Norenzayan, A. (2010). The weirdest people in the world? *Behavioural and Brain Sciences*, *33*(2–3), 61–83. See also Arnett, J. (2008). The neglected 95%: Why American psychology needs to become less American. *American Psychologist*, *63*, 602–14.
107. Andoh, E. (2021). Psychology's urgent need to dismantle racism. *American Psychological Association*. https://www.apa.org/monitor/2021/04/cover-dismantle-racism.
108. Marmot, M. (Ed.). (2005). *Social determinants of health*. Oxford University Press.
109. Minns, D. (2010). *Irenaeus: An introduction*. Continuum International.
110. See Irenaeus, *Adversus haereses (Against Heresies)*.
111. Scott, M. S. M. (2010). Suffering and soul-making: Rethinking John Hick's theodicy. *The Journal of Religion*, *90*, 313–34.
112. Wexler, B. E. (2008). *Brain and culture: Neurobiology, ideology, and social change*. MIT Press.

113. Culley, S. (1991). *Integrative counselling skills in action.* Sage, p. 12.
114. House, R. (2010). *In, against, and beyond therapy: Critical essays towards a post-professional era.* PCCS.
115. Tyler, L. E. (1969). *Work of the counsellor.* Appleton Century Crofts. Gilmore, S. K. (1973). *Counsellor in training.* Prentice Hall.
116. Rogers, C. (2004). *On becoming a person: A therapist's view of psychotherapy.* Constable.
117. Egan, G. (1986). *Skilled helpers: A systemic approach to effective helping* (3rd ed). Brooks & Cole.
118. Culley, S. (1991). *Integrative counselling skills in action.* Sage, p. 13.
119. Rogers, C. (1951). *Client-centred therapy: Its current practice, implications, & theory.* Houghton Mifflin.
120. Adapted from Lapworth, P., & Sills, C. (2009). *Integration in counselling & psychotherapy: Developing a personal approach.* SAGE.
121. Freud, S. (1915). *Instincts and their vicissitudes.* Vol. 14. Hogarth, pp. 117–40.
122. Fromm, E. (1956). *The art of loving.* Harper.
123. Freud, S. (1991). Formulations on the two principles of mental functioning (J. Strachey, Trans.). In A. Richards (Ed.), *On meta-psychology: The theory of psychoanalysis.* Penguin, pp. 29–44.
124. Laing, R. D. (2010). *The divided self: An existential study in sanity and madness.* Penguin.
125. Freud, S. (1911). *Formulations on the two principles of mental functioning.* Vol. 12. pp. 218–86.
126. Jacobi, J. (1973). *The psychology of C. G. Jung.* Yale University Press, pp. 126–27.
127. Stein, M. (1988). *Jung's map of the soul.* Open Court.
128. Jung, C. G. *1973 Letters.* Vol. 1. Princeton University Press.
129. Snowden, R. (2019). *Jung: The key ideas.* John Murray Learning, p. 64.
130. Klein, M. (1921). Development of conscience in the child. *Love, Guilt, and Reparation.* Vintage Classics, p. 252.
131. Mate, G. (2018). *In the realm of hungry ghosts: Close encounters with addiction.* Ebury.
132. Freud, S. (1915). *The unconscious* (Standard ed. 14). Hogarth, pp. 159–204.
133. Tulving, E. (1972). Episodic and semantic memory. In E. Tulving & W. Donaldson (Eds.), *Organization of memory,* (pp. 381–403). Academic.
134. Bargh, J. A., & Chartrand, T. L. (1999). The unbearable automaticity of being. *American psychologist, 54,* 462.
135. Greenwald, A. G., & Banaji, M. R. (1995). Implicit social cognition: attitudes, self-esteem, and stereotypes. *Psychological review, 102,* 4.
136. See, for example, Damasio, A. (1999). *The feeling of what happens.* Harcourt Brace.
137. Freud, S. (1974). *Introductory lectures on psychoanalysis.* Pelican, p. 278.
138. Fairbairn, R. (1952). *An object relations theory of the personality.* Basic.
139. Funder, D.C. (1997). *The personality puzzle.* Norton, p. 257.
140. Wilson, T. D. (2004). *Strangers to ourselves.* Harvard University Press.
141. Chomsky, N. (1972). *Language and mind.* Harcourt Brace Jovanovich.
142. Kandel, E. (1999). Biology and the future of psychoanalysis: A new intellectual framework for psychiatry revisited. *Am. J. Psychiatry* 156, 505–24.
143. James, W. (1982). *The Varieties of Religious Experience: a study in human nature* London: Penguin p. 2.

144. Sperry, L., & Shafrankske, E. P. (2005). *Spiritually oriented psychotherapy*. American Psychological Association, p. 19.
145. Olthuis, J. H. (2001). *Beautiful risk: A new psychology of loving and being loved.* Zondervan, p. 12.
146. Freud, S. (1923). *Das ich und das es.* Norton.
147. Strayer, R. (2022). Teaching religion in world history. *World History Bulletin, 38,* p. 67.
148. Jung, C. J. (1933). *Modern man in search of a soul.* Routledge and Paul.
149. Calvin, J. (1960). *Institutes of the Christian religion* (J. T. McNeil, Ed.) (F. L. Battles, Trans).Westminster.
150. Dubay, T. (1989). *Fire within: St. Teresa of Avila, St. John of the cross, and the gospel—On prayer.* Ignatius.
151. James, W. (1982). *The varieties of religious experience: A study in human nature.* Penguin, p. 2.
152. Newberg, A., & Waldeman, M. R. (2020). *How God changes your brain: Breakthrough findings from a leading neuroscientist.* Ballantine.
153. Alper, M. (2009). *The "God" part of the brain: A scientific interpretation of human spirituality and God.* Sourcebooks.
154. Schermer, V. (2002). *Spirit and psyche: A new paradigm for psychology, psychoanalysis, and psychotherapy.* Kingsley.
155. Culliford, L. (2011). *The psychology of spirituality.* Kingsley.
156. Beauregard, M., and O'Leary, D. (2009). *The spiritual brain: A neuroscientist's case for the existence of the soul.* HarperOne.
157. Epstein, R. (2021, August 21). *Your brain is not a computer. It is a transducer.* Discover Magazine. https://www.discovermagazine.com/mind/your-brain-is-not-a-computer-it-is-a-transducer.
158. Churchill, H. (2021). The Churchill framework. *Accord*, pp. 21–27.
159. Rowe, D. (1993). *The successful self.* HarperCollins, p. 192.
160. Bowlby, J. (1975). *Separation, anxiety, and anger.* Pelican, p. 2.
161. Bowlby, J. (1953). *Child care and the growth of love.* Penguin, p. 13.
162. Bowlby, J (1999). *Forty-four juvenile thieves: Their lives and home-life.* Routledge.
163. Rutter, M. (1985). Family and school influences on behavioural development. In P. Barnes (Ed.), *Personal, social, and emotional development of children* (pp. 55–79). Open University.
164. Moulin, S., Waldfogel, J., & Washbrook, E. (2014). *Baby bonds: Parenting, attachment, and a secure base for children.* Sutton Trust.
165. Moulin, S., Waldfogel, J., & Washbrook, E. (2014). *Baby bonds: Parenting, attachment, and a secure base for children.* Sutton Trust.
166. Shaver, P. R., & Clark, C. L. (1994). The psychodynamics of adult romantic attachment. In J. M. Masling & R. F. Bornstein (Eds.), *Empirical perspectives on object relations theory* (pp. 105–56). American Psychological Association.
167. Main, M. (1990). The effect of experience on signals of security with respect to attachment. In K. E. Barnard & T. B. Brazelton (Eds.), *Touch: The foundation of experience* (pp. 461–95). International Universities Press.
168. Shaver, P. R., & Clark, C. L. (1994). The psychodynamics of adult romantic attachment. In J. M. Masling & R. F. Bornstein (Eds.), *Empirical perspectives on object relations theory* (pp. 105–56). American Psychological Association.
169. Main, M., & Hesse, E. (1990). Parents' unresolved traumatic experiences related to infant disorganised attachment status. In M. Greenberg, D. Cicchetti, & E.

Cummings (Eds.), *Attachment in the pre-school years* (pp. 161–82). University of Chicago Press.

170. Main, M. (1999). Introduction to the special section on attachment and psychopathology. In D. Howe, *Attachment theory: Child maltreatment and family support* (p. 37). Macmillan.
171. Konner, M. (2010). *The evolution of childhood: Reason, emotion, mind.* Harvard University Press.
172. Schore, A. N. (2003). *Affect regulation and the origin of the self.* Norton; Schore, A. N. (2003). *Affect dysregulation and disorders of the self.* Norton; Siegal, D. J. (2001). *The developing mind.* Norton.
173. Chugani, H. T., Behen, M. E., Muzik, O., Juhász, C., Nagy, F., & Chugani, D. C. (2001). Local brain functional activity following early deprivation: a study of institutionalised Romanian orphans. *Neuroimage, 14,* 1290–301.
174. Trevarthen, C. (1993). The self born in inter-subjectivity: The psychology of infant communicating. In U. Neisser (Ed.), *The perceived self: Ecological and interpersonal sources of self-knowledge* (pp. 121–73). Cambridge University Press.
175. Schore, A. (1994). *Affect regulation and the origin of the self.* Erlsbaum.
176. Gerhardt, S. (2004). *Why love matters: How affection shapes a baby's brain.* Routledge.
177. Howe, D., Brandon, M., Hinings, D., & Schofield, G. (1999). *Attachment theory, child maltreatment, and family support.* MacMillan.
178. Saarni, C. (1990). *The development of emotional competence.* Guilford.
179. Hoffman, M. (1984). Empathy: Its limitations and role in a comprehensive moral theory. In W. Kurtines & J. Gerwitz (Eds.), *Morality, moral behaviour, and moral development* (pp. 283–302). Wiley.
180. Larson, R. W. (1990). Emotions and the creative process: Anxiety, boredom, and enjoyment as predictors of creative writing. *Imagination, Cognition, and Personality, 9,* 275–92.
181. Sroufe, L. A. (1990). *Emotional development: The organisation of emotional life in the early years.* Cambridge University Press.
182. Collins, W. A., Harris, M. L. & Susman, A. (1995). Parenting during middle childhood. In M. H. Bornstein (Ed.), *Handbook of parenting.* Vol. 1, *Children and parenting* (pp. 65–89). Erlbaum.
183. Tolan, P. A. & Loeber, R. (1993). Antisocial behaviour. In P. H. Tolan and B. Cohler (Eds.), *Handbook of clinical research and practice with adolescents* (pp. 307–31). Wiley.
184. Gilbert, P. (2009). *The compassionate mind.* Constable.
185. Lieberman, A. (1992). Infant-parent psychotherapy with toddlers. *Development and Psychopathology, 4,* 559–74.
186. Joseph, B. (1982). Addiction to near-death. *International journal of Psychoanalysis, 63,* 449–56.
187. West, M. (2016). *Into the darkest places: Early relational trauma and borderline states of mind.* Karnac.
188. Philipps, A. (2010). *On balance.* Hamish Hamilton.
189. Wellesley, J. (2008). *Wellington: A journey through my family.* Orion.
190. See Alexandra Stryon's memoir of her father in *The New Yorker*, December 2007. Also W. Stryon. (2009). *Letters to my father.* Louisiana State University Press; and Stryon's autobiography, *Darkness Visible.*
191. Serwer, A. (2009, July 6). The best advice I ever got: Gates on gates. *Fortune Magazine.*

192. Stockett, K. (2009). *The help*. Fig Tree.
193. House, R., & Loewenthal, D. (Eds.) (2009). *Childhood, well-being, & therapeutic ethos*. Karnac.
194. Paretsky, S. (2007). *Writing in an age of silence*. Verso.
195. Golding, J. (2011). *The children of lovers: The memoir of William Golding by his daughter*. Faber.
196. UNICEF. (2007). Child poverty in perspective: An overview of child well-being in rich countries. *Innocenti Report Card 7*, p. 1.
197. A popular card used in parenting courses. Source unknown.
198. Author's client notes. Name withheld and used with permission.
199. Author's client notes. Name withheld and used with permission.
200. Graber, K. (1991). *Ghosts in the bedroom: A guide for partners of incest survivors*. Health Communications, p. 34.
201. Celani, D. P. (1999). Applying Fairbairn's object relations theory to the dynamics of battered women. *American Journal of Psychotherapy*, *53*, 62–64.
202. BBC. (2017, October 14). Wales' first black headteacher Betty Campbell dies. *BBC*. https://www.bbc.com/news/uk-wales-south-east-wales-41620491.
203. Freud, S. (1963). *Civilisation and its discontents*. Norton & Company, p. 80.
204. Bocock, R. (1976). *Freud and modern society*. Van Nostrand Reinhold, p. 84.
205. Freud, S. (1950). *Totem and taboo*. Routledge, pp. 64–65.
206. Evaristo, B. (2019). *Girl, woman, other*. Penguin.
207. Thompson, N. (2006). *Anti-discriminatory practice* (4th ed.). Palgrave Macmillan.
208. Andoh, E. (2021). Psychology's urgent need to dismantle racism. *American Psychological Association*. https://www.apa.org/monitor/2021/04/cover-dismantle-racism.
209. Steed, C. D. (2018). *Why inequality matters*. Tauris.
210. Brown, L. S., & Ballou, M. (Eds.). (1992). *Personality and psychopathology: Feminist reappraisals*. Guilford.
211. D., G. G. (2021, June 5). Let's talk about sex. *The Economist*.
212. Hill, F. (2021). *There is nothing for you here*. Mariner.
213. Gilbert, P. (2003). Evolution, social roles, and the differences in shame and guilt. *Social Research*, *70*, pp. 1205–30.
214. Mitchell, S., & Black, M. (2019). *Freud and beyond: A history of modern psychoanalytic thought*. Basic, p. 48.
215. Sanderson, C. (1995). *Counselling adult survivors of child sexual abuse* (2nd ed.). Kingsley, p. 76.
216. Diamond, A. (2007). Interrelated and interdependent. *Developmental Science*, *10* 152–58.
217. Biko, S. (1986). *I write what I like*. Harper & Row.
218. Nanni, V., Uher, R., & Danese, A. (2012). Childhood maltreatment predicts unfavorable course of illness and treatment outcome in depression: A meta-analysis. *Am J Psychiatry*, *169*, 141–51.
219. Reay, B. (2004). *Rural Englands: Labouring lives in the nineteenth century*. Palgrave Macmillan, p. 145.
220. Fischer, L. (1997). *The life of Mahatma Gandhi*. HarperCollins, p. 163.
Orbis.
221. As reported in the *London Daily Mail*, August 25, 2007.
222. Case, A., & Deaton, A. (2020). *Deaths of despair and the future of capitalism*. Princeton University Press.

223. Shenon, P. (2013). *A cruel and shocking act: The secret history of the Kennedy assassination*. Holt and Company.
224. Freud, S. (2001). *The complete psychological works of Sigmund Freud*. Vol. 6, *The psychopathology of everyday life*. Vintage Classics.
225. Spoken by a rape victim. www.bbc.co.uk/radio4 Today March 15th 2010.
226. Das, V., & Kleinman, A. (Eds.). (2000). *Violence and subjectivity*. University of California Press.
227. Eshelby, K. (2008, August 15). If a woman says no, we use force. *Church Times*.
228. Gilligan, J. (2001). *Preventing violence*. Thames & Hudson, ch. 2. See also Blau, P. M. (1964). *Exchange and power in social life*. Wiley.
229. Author client notes. Used with permission.
230. Kjærvik, S. L., & Bushman, B. J. (2021). The link between narcissism and aggression: A meta-analytic review. *Psychological Bulletin*, *147*, 477–503.
231. Volkan, V. (1988). *The need to have enemies and allies: From clinical practice to international relationships*. Aronson.
232. May, R. (1976). *Power and innocence: A search for the sources of violence*. Fontana, p. 44.
233. Author's client notes. Name withheld and used with permission.
234. Beitchman J. H., Zucker, K. J., Hood, J. E., daCosta, G. A., Akman, D., & Cassavia, E. (1992). A review of the long-term effects of child sexual abuse. *Child Abuse Negl.*, *16*, 101–18.
235. The phrase is taken from an unpublished PhD thesis: Madden, A. (2021). The defiled self: Towards a theological response to the experimental phenomenon of defilement amongst adult survivors of childhood sexual abuse. Middlesex University.
236. Fossum, M. A., & Mason, M. J. (1986). *Facing shame: Families in recovery*. Norton, p. 5.
237. Unpublished PhD thesis: Madden, A. (2021). The defiled self: Towards a theological response to the experimental phenomenon of defilement amongst adult survivors of childhood sexual abuse. Middlesex University, p. 34.
238. Wurmser, L. (1981). *The mask of shame*. John Hopkins University Press, p. 43.
239. Kaufman, G. (1985). *Shame: The power of caring* (2nd ed.). Schenkman, pp. 66–69.
240. Powell, P. A., Overton, P. G., & Simpson, J. (Eds.). (2015). *The revolting self: Perspectives on the psychological, social, and clinical implications of self-directed disgust*. Karnac, pp. 4–5.
241. Rozin, P., & Fallon, A. E. (1987). *A perspective on disgust. Psychological Review 94*, 23–41.
242. Powell, P. A., Overton, P. G., & Simpson, J. (Eds.). (2015). *The revolting self: Perspectives on the psychological, social, and clinical implications of self-directed disgust*. Karnac, pp. 16–17.
243. BBC Sounds. (2022, March 20). *Desert island discs with Alan Cummings*. https://www.bbc.co.uk/sounds/play/m0015ksq.
244. Freud, S. (1915). *The Unconscious* (Standard ed. 14). Hogarth, p. 194.
245. McGilchrist, I. (2015). Divine understanding and the divided brain. In J. Clausen & N. Levy (Eds.), *Handbook of neuroethics* (pp. 1583–1601). Springer Science.
246. Cozolino, L., Samuelson, C., & Drulis, C. (2021). The interpersonal neurobiology of executive functioning. In D. Siegel, A. Shore, & L. Cozolino, (Eds.). *Interpersonal neurobiology and clinical practice* (pp. 59–72). Norton.

247. Houston, G. (2003). *Brief gestalt therapy*. Sage, p. 3.
248. Beck, A. (1979). *Cognitive therapy of depression*. Guilford.
249. Ellis, A. (1988). *Rational emotive behaviour therapy*. Alleyn & Bacon.
250. Johnsen, T. J., & Friborg, O. (2015). The effects of cognitive behavioural therapy as an anti-depressive treatment is falling: A meta-analysis. *Psychol Bull., 141*, 747–68.
251. Fonagy, P., Rost, F., Carlyle, J. A., McPherson, S., Thomas, R., Pasco Fearon, R. M., Goldberg, D., & Taylor, D. (2015). Pragmatic randomized controlled trial of long-term psychoanalytic psychotherapy for treatment-resistant depression: The Tavistock Adult Depression Study (TADS). *World Psychiatry, 14*, 312–21.
252. DeYoung, P. A. (2022*). Understanding and treating chronic shame: Healing right brain relational trauma* (2nd ed.). Routledge, p. 47.
253. Padesky, C. A., & Greenberger, D. (1995). *Clinician's guide to "Mind Over Mood."* Guilford.
254. Rosen, H., & Kuehlwein, K. (1996). *Meaning making perspectives for psychotherapists*. Bass.
255. Tschacher, W., & Meier, D. (2019). Physiological synchrony in psychotherapy sessions. *Psychotherapy Research, 30*, 558–73.
256. Schore, A. (2019). *The development of the unconscious mind*. Norton.
257. McGilchrist, I. (2019). *The master and his emissary: The divided brain and the making of the western world* (2nd ed.). Yale University Press.
258. Nielsen, J. A., Zielinski, B. A., Ferguson, M. A., Lainhart, J. E., Anderson, J. S. (2013). An evaluation of the left-brain vs. right-brain hypothesis with Resting State Functional Connectivity Magnetic Resonance Imaging. *PLoS ONE, 8*, e71275.
259. MacLean, P. D. (1990). *The triune brain in evolution: Role in paleo cerebral functions*. Plenum.
260. Burkeman, O. (2016, January 7). Therapy wars: The revenge of Freud. *The Guardian*.
261. LeDoux, J. (2003). The emotional brain, fear, and the amygdala. *Cell Mol Neurobiology, 23*(4–5), 727–38.
262. Blakeslee, S. (1996, November 5). Dr. Joseph Ledoux: Using rats to trace routes of fear. *New York Times*.
263. Ramachandran,V. S. (1995). Anosognosia in parietal lobe syndrome. *Conscious Cognition, 4*, 22–51.
264. Blair, R. J. R. (2004). The roles of orbital frontal cortex in the modulation of antisocial behaviour. *Brain and Cognition, 55*, 198–208.
265. Dougherty, D. D., Shin L. M., Alpert, N. M., Pitman, R. K., Orr, S. P., Lasko, M., Macklin, M. L., Fischman, A. J., & Rauch, S. L. (1999). Anger in healthy men: A PET study using script-driven imagery. *Biological Psychiatry, 46*, 466–72.
266. Shore, A. (1994). *Affect regulation and the origin of the self: The neurobiology of emotional development*. Erlbaum.
267. Schore, A. (1999). *Affect regulation and the origin of the self: The neurobiology of emotional development*. Routledge.
268. Mackes, N. K., Golm, D., Sarker, S., Kumsta, R., Rutter, M., Fairchild, G., Mehta, M. A., & Sonuga-Barke, E. J. S. (2020). Early childhood deprivation is associated with alterations in adult brain structure despite subsequent environmental enrichment. *Proceedings of National Academy of Sciences, 117*, 641–49.
269. Schwartz, J., & Begley, S. (2002). The mind and the brain: Neuroplasticity and the power of mental force. HarperCollins.

270. Marrone, M. (2014). *Attachment and interaction: From Bowlby to current clinical theory and practice.* Kingsley.
271. Wexler, B. (2007). *Brain and culture: Neurology, ideology, and social change.* MIT Press.
272. Tallis, R. (2011). *Aping mankind: Neuromania, darwinits, and the misrepresentation of humanity.* Acumen.
273. O'Craven, K. M., & Kanwisher, N. (2000). Mental imagery of faces and places activates corresponding stimulus-specific brain regions. *Journal of Cognitive Neuroscience, 12,* 1013–23. See also Greene, J. D., Sommerville, R. B., Nystrom, L. E., Darley, J. M., & Cohen, J. D. (2001). An fMRI investigation of emotional entanglement in moral judgment. *Science, 293,* 2105–8.
274. Goff, P. (2019). *Galileo's error: Foundations for a new science of consciousness.* Rider.
275. Beauregard, M. (2007). Mind does really matter: Evidence from neuroimaging studies of emotion self-regulation, psychotherapy, and placebo effect. *Progress in Neurobiology, 81,* 218–36.
276. Freud, S. (1952). *An autobiographical study.* Norton, p. 27.
277. Herman, H. J. M., & Dimaggio, G. (Eds.) (2004). *The dialogical self in psychotherapy.* Brunner-Routledge.
278. Bowlby, J. (1988). *A secure base: Clinical applications of attachment theory.* Routledge, p. 158.
279. Kahn, M. (1997). *Between therapist and client.* St. Martin's, p. 107–9.
280. Mitchell, S. A. (1997). *Influence and autonomy in psychoanalysis.* Analytic.
281. Rogers, C. (1951). *Client centred therapy.* Constable, p. 437.
282. Mitchell, S. A. (1993). *Hope and dread in psychoanalysis.* Basic.
283. Greenberg, J., & Mitchell, S. A. (1983). *Object relations in psychoanalytic theory.* Harvard University Press.
284. Mitchell, S. A., & Aron, L. (1999). *Relational psychoanalysis: The emergence of a tradition.* Analytic.
285. Aron, L. (1996). *A meeting of minds.* Analytic.
286. Mitchell, S. A. (1988). *Relational concepts in psychoanalysis: An integration.* Harvard University Press.
287. Mitchell, S. A. (2000). *Relationality: From attachment to intersubjectivity.* Analytic.
288. Kohut, H. (1971). *The analysis of the self: A systematic approach to the psychoanalytic treatment of narcissistic personality disorders.* University of Chicago Press.
289. Kohut, H. (1979). *The search for the self: Selected essays of Heinz Kohut.* University of Chicago Press.
290. Kohut, H. (1978). *Restoration of the self.* University of Chicago Press.
291. Horner, A. J. (1991). *Psychoanalytic object relations therapy.* Rowman & Littlefield.
292. Scharff, J. S., & Scharff, D. E. (2005). *The primer of object relations* (2nd ed.). Rowman & Littlefield.
293. Lothane, Z. (2003). What did Freud say about persons and relations? *Psychoanalytic Psychology, 20,* 609–17; Curtis, R. C., & Hirsch, I. (2003). Relational approaches to psychoanalytic psychotherapy. In A. G. Gurman & S. B. Messer (Eds.), *Essential Psychotherapies* (pp. 69–106). Guilford.
294. Freud, S. (1952). *An autobiographical study.* Norton, p. 30.
295. Freud, S. (1937). *Analysis, terminable and interminable* (Standard ed. 23). Hogarth, p. 235.

296. Slochower, J. (2013). Relational holding: Using Winnicott today. *Revue Roumaine de Psychanalyse, 6*, p. 29.

297. Winnicot, D. W. (1965). *The maturational process and facilitating environment.* Hogarth.

298. Kohut, H. (1984). *How does analysis cure?* (A. Goldsberg & P. Stepansky, Eds. London.

299. Alvarez, L. (1992). *Live company*. Routledge.

300. Freud, A. (1936). *The ego and the mechanisms of defence*. Hogarth.

301. Klein, M. (1946). Notes on some schizoid states. In M. Klein et al. (Eds.), *Developments in Psychoanalysis* (pp. 344–69). Hogarth.

302. Rosenfeld, H. (1971). A clinical approach to the psychoanalytic theory of the life and death instincts: An investigation into the aggressive aspects of narcissism. *International Journal of Psychoanalysis, 52*, 162–78.

303. Bion, W. (1961). A theory of thinking. *International Journal of Psychoanalysis, 43*, 306–10.

304. Freud, S. (1952). *An autobiographical study*. Norton, p. 32.

305. Freud, S. (1905). *Fragment of an analysis of a case of hysteria* (Standard ed. 7). Hogarth.

306. Symington, N. (1986). *The analytical experience*. Free Association, p. 107.

307. Gammelgaard, J. (2011). Love, drive, and desire in the works of Freud, Lacan, and Proust. *The International Journal of Psychoanalysis, 92*, 963–83.

308. Casement, P. (2014). *Further learning from the patient: The analytic space and process*. Routledge, p. 14.

309. Cozolino, L. (2004). *The making of a therapist* (1st ed.). Norton.

310. Stevens, R. (1996). *Understanding the self*. SAGE.

311. Mearns, D., & Cooper, M. (2017). *Working at relational depth in counselling & psychotherapy* (2nd ed.). Sage.

312. Schore, A. (2021). Interpersonal neuro-biology of therapeutic Mutual Regressions in re-enactments of early attachment trauma. In Siegel, D., Shore, A., & Cozolino, L. (Eds.), *Interpersonal neurobiology and clinical practice*. Norton, p. 30.

313. Cozolino, L. J. (2010). *The neuroscience of psychotherapy: Healing the social brain*. Norton.

314. Siegel, D. J. (2010). *The mindful therapist: A clinician's guide to mindsight and neural integration*. Norton. Kindle.

315. Clinton, T., & Sibcy, G. (2012). Christian counselling, interpersonal neurobiology, and the future. *Journal of Psychology and Theology, 40*, 141–45.

316. Orlinksy, D. E., & Howard, K. I. (1987). A generic model of psychotherapy. *Journal of Integrative and Eclectic Psychotherapy, 6*, 6–27.

317. Thorne, B. (1999). *Person-centred counselling*. Sage.

318. Bowlby, J. (1988). *A secure base: Clinical applications of attachment theory*. Routledge, p. 159.

319. Hayton. A. (2011). *Womb twin survivors: The lost twin in the dream of the womb*. Wren. See also Cohen, T. (2017). Considering gestational life. *International Journal of Relational Perspectives, 27*, 557–73.

320. Weissman, M. M., Markowitz, J. C., & Klerman, G. L. (2017). *The guide to interpersonal psychotherapy*. Oxford University Press.

321. Hayes, N., O'Toole, L., & Halpenny, A. M. (2017). *Introducing Bronfenbrenner: A guide for practitioners and students in early years education*. Taylor & Francis. See

also Bronfenbrenner, U., & Evans, G. W. (2000). Developmental science in the 21st century: Emerging questions, theoretical models, research designs and empirical findings. *Social development*, 9, 115–25.
322. Bee, H. L. (1992). *The developing child.* HarperCollins.
323. Piaget, J. (1957). *Construction of reality in the child.* Routledge & Paul.
324. Piaget, J. (1959). *The language and thought of the child.* Vol. 5. Psychology Press.
325. Erikson E. H. (1982). *The life cycle completed.* Norton.
326. Erikson, E. H. (1963). *Youth: Change and challenge.* Basic.
327. Skinner, B. F. (1973). *Beyond freedom and dignity.* Penguin.
328. Vygotsky, L. S. (1978). *Mind in society: The development of higher psychological processes.* Harvard University Press.
329. Vygotsky, L. S. (1962). *Thought and language.* MIT Press.
330. Freud, S. (1905). *Three essays on the theory of sexuality* (Standard ed. 7). Hogarth, pp. 123–246.
331. Winnicott, D. W. (1958). *Through paediatrics to Psychoanalysis.* Tavistock.
332. Freud, S. (2014). *On narcissism.* White.
333. Fonagy, E. P. (1991). *Freud's 'On Narcissism.'* Routledge.
334. Leach, P. (1974). *Babyhood.* Penguin.
335. Kagan, J. (1989). *The second year: The emergence of self-awareness.* Harvard University Press.
336. Freud. A. (1928). *Introduction to the technique of child analysis.* NMD.
337. Rayner, E. (1986). *Human development.* Routledge, p. 113.
338. Heidegger, M. (1962). *Being and time* (J. Macquarrie & E. Robinson, Trans.). Harper & Row.
339. Grenz, S. J. (2001). *The social god and the relational self: A trinitarian theology of the imago dei.* Westminster John Knox, p. 6.
340. Karkkainen, V-M. *The trinity: Global perspectives.* Westminster John Knox.
341. Hall, D. J. (2003). *Imaging god: Dominion as stewardship.* Wipf & Stock.
342. Barth, K. (2004). *Church Dogmatics 3/1* (G. W. Bromiley & T. F. Torrance, Eds.) (J. W. Edwards et al., Trans.). T & T Clark, p. 182.
343. Barth, K. (2004). *Church Dogmatics 3/1* (G. W. Bromiley & T. F. Torrance, Eds.) (J. W. Edwards et al., Trans.). T & T Clark, pp. 184–86.
344. Grenz, S. J. (2001). *The social god and the relational self: A trinitarian theology of the imago dei.* Westminster John Knox, pp. 269–303.
345. Emibayer, M. (1997). Manifesto for a relational sociology. *American Journal of Sociology, 103*, 281–317.
346. Heidegger, M. (1960). *Being and time.* Harper.
347. Hegel, G. W. F. (1999). *Science of logic* (H. D. Lewis Amherst, Ed.) (A. V. Miller, Trans.). Humanity.
348. Hycner, R., & Jacobs, L. (1995). *The healing relationship in gestalt therapy: A dialogic/self psychology approach.* Gestalt Journal.
349. Benjamin, L. S. (1995). *Interpersonal diagnosis and the treatment of personality disorders.* Guilford.
350. Cozolino, L. (2014). *The neuroscience of human relationships: Attachment and the developing social brain.* Norton.
351. Siegal, D. J. (2012). *The developing mind.* Guilford.
352. Gerson, S. (2004). The relational unconscious: A core element of intersubjectivity, thirdness, and clinical process. *Psychoanal Q.*, *73*, 63–98.

353. Greenberg, J., & Mitchell, S. A. (1983). *Object relations in psychoanalytic theory.* Harvard University Press.

354. *Oedipus complex.* Melanie Klein Trust. https://melanie-klein-trust.org.uk/theory/oedipus-complex/.

355. See *Melanie Klein's publications.* Melanie Klein Trust. https://melanie-klein-trust.org.uk/resource_cat/melanie-klein-publications/: Vol. 1, *Love, guilt, and reparation and other works, 1921–45*; Vol. 2, *The psycho-analysis of children*; Vol. 3, *Envy and gratitude and other works, 1946–63*; Vol. 4, *Narrative of a child analysis.*

356. Spillius, E. B., Milton, J., Garvey, P., Couve, C., & Steiner, D. (2011). *The new dictionary of Kleinian thought.* Routledge.

357. Sutherland, J. (1989(. *Fairbairn's journey into the interior.* Free Association.

358. Birtles, E. F., & Scharff, D. (Eds.) (1988, 1994). *From instinct to self: Selected papers of W. R. D. Fairbairn.* 2 vols. Aronson.

359. Pereira, F., & Scharff, D. (Eds.) (2002). *Fairbairn and relational theory.* Karnac.

360. Skolnick, N. & Scharff, D. (Eds.) (1998). *Fairbairn then and now.* Analytic.

361. Grotstein, J. & Rinsley, D. (Eds.) (1994). *Fairbairn and the origins of object relations.* Free Association.

362. Winnicott, D. (1953). Transitional objects and transitional phenomena. *International Journal of Psychoanalysis, 34*, 89–97.

363. Cozolino, L. (2016). *Why therapy works: Using our minds to change our brains* (1st ed.). Norton.

364. Siegel, D. J. (2021). Interpersonal neuro-biology from the inside out. In D. Siegel, A. Shore, & L. Cozolino (Eds.), *Interpersonal neurobiology and clinical practice.* Norton, p. 7.

365. Shilling, C. (1993). *The body and social theory.* Sage.

366. Author's notes, used with permission.

367. Stern, D. (1985). *The interpersonal world of the infant.* Basic.

368. Elias, N. (1991). *The society of individuals.* Blackwell.

369. Schilling, C. (2008). *Changing bodies: Habits, crisis, and creativity.* Sage, pp. 125–43.

370. Damasio, A. (2010). *Self comes to mind.* Pantheon, p. 20.

371. Simmel, G. (1990). *The philosophy of money.* Routledge.

372. Damasio, A. (1994). *Descartes' error: Emotion, reason, and the human brain.* Avon.

373. Damasio, A. (1994). *Descartes' error: Emotion, reason, and the human brain.* Avon, pp. 249–50.

374. Damasio, A. (1994). *Descartes' error: Emotion, reason, and the human brain.* Avon, p.xv.

375. Heelas, P. (1986). Emotion talk across cultures. In R. Harré (Ed.), *The social construction of emotions* (pp. 234–66). Blackwell.

376. Lindquist, K., Wager, T., Bliss-Moreau, E., Kober, H., & Barrett, L. (2012). What are emotions and how are they created in the brain? *Behavioural and Brain Sciences, 35*, 172–202.

377. Ferrari, P. F., & Coudé, G. (2018). Mirror neurons, embodied emotions, and empathy. In K. Z. Meyza & E. Knapska (Eds.), *Neuronal correlates of empathy: From rodent to human* (pp. 67–77). Elsevier Academic.

378. Saarni, C. (1990). *The development of emotional competence.* Guilford.

379. Hoffman, M. (1984). Empathy: Its limitations and role in a comprehensive moral theory. In W. Kurtines & J. Gerwitz (Eds.), *Morality, moral behaviour, and moral development* (pp. 283–302). Wiley.

380. Larson, R. W. (1990). Emotions and the creative process: Anxiety, boredom, and enjoyment as predictors of creative writing. *Imagination, Cognition, and Personality*, 9, 275–92.
381. Yong, A. (2007). *Theology and down syndrome: Reimagining disability in late modernity*. Baylor University Press, p. 13.
382. Cooper, B. (2006). The disabled God. *Theology Today*, 49, 173.
383. Sontag, S. (1978). *Illness as metaphor*. Penguin.
384. Shakespeare, T. (2018). *Disability: The basics*. Routledge.
385. Department for Work and Pensions (2021). *Family resources survey: Financial year 2019 to 2020*. https://www.gov.uk/government/statistics/family-resources-survey-financial-year-2019-to-2020.
386. *Labour force survey October to December 2020*. https://www.ons.gov.uk/employmentandlabourmarket/peopleinwork/employmentandemployeetypes/methodologies/labourforcesurveyperformanceandqualitymonitoringreports/labourforcesurveyperformanceandqualitymonitoringreportoctobertodecember2020.
387. Scope. (2019). *Disability price tag*. https://www.scope.org.uk/campaigns/extra-costs/disability-price-tag/.
388. Barnes, C., Oliver, M., & Barton, L. (2002). *Disability studies today*. Polity.
389. Shakespeare, T. (1998). *The disability reader: Social science perspectives*. Continuum.
390. White, A. (2011). There by the grace of . . . *Therapy Today*, 22, 10–14.
391. Nathanson, D. (1992). *Shame and pride: Affect, sex, and the birth of the self*. Norton.
392. Union of the Physically Impaired against Segregation. (1976). *Fundamental principles of disability*. UPIAS, p. 3.
393. Halacre, B. (2020). *Good practice across the counselling professions*. BACP House. https://www.bacp.co.uk/media/10780/bacp-working-with-disability-gpacp007-feb-21.pdf.
394. Reeve, D. (2014). Counselling and disabled people: Help or hindrance? In J. Swain, S. French, C. Barnes, & C. Thomas (Eds.), *Disabling barriers, enabling environments* (3rd ed.) (pp. 255–61). Sage.
395. Emmy van Deurzen (2020). Surviving and thriving in a global existential crisis. *Therapy Today*. https://www.bacp.co.uk/bacp-journals/therapy-today/2020/june-2020/articles/surviving-and-thriving-in-a-global-existential-crisis/.
396. Olkin, R. (2017). *Disability-affirmative therapy: A case formulation template for clients with disabilities*. Oxford University Press.
397. World Health Organization. (2022, December 2). *Disability*. www.who.int/en/news-room/fact-sheets/detail/disability-and-health.
398. Barnes, C., & Mercer, G. (2010). *Exploring disability*. Polity, p. 11.
399. Watermeyer, B., & Swartz, L. (2016). Disablism, identity, and self: Discrimination as a traumatic assault on subjectivity. *Journal of Community and Applied Social Psychology*, 26, 268–76.
400. Cited in Watermeyer, B. (2013). *Towards a contextual psychology of disablism*. Routledge.
401. Swinton, J. (2010). Disability theology. In I. McFarland, D. Fergusson, K. Kilby, & I. Torrance (Eds.), *Cambridge dictionary of Christian theology* (pp. 140–41). Cambridge University Press.

402. Eiesland, N. (1994). *The disabled god: Toward a liberatory theology of disability*. Abingdon.
403. Monteith, G. (2005). *Deconstructing miracles: From thoughtless indifference to honouring disabled people*. Covenanters.
404. Reynolds, T. E. (2008). *Vulnerable communion: A theology of disability and hospitality*. Brazos, p. 14.
405. Reinders, R. (2001). *The future of the disabled in liberal society: An ethical analysis*. University of Notre Dame Press.
406. Young, A. (1998). *The harmony of illusions: Inventing post-traumatic stress disorders*. Princeton University Press.
407. Stewart, W., & Sutton, J. (2017). *Learning to counsel: How to develop the skills, insight, and knowledge to counsel others* (4th ed.). Robinson, p. 13.
408. Wilson, A., & Fromm, E. (1982). Aftermath of the concentration camp: The second generation. *Journal of the American Academy of Psychoanalysis, 10*, 289–313.
409. Rakoff, V. (1966). A long-term effect of the concentration camp experience. *Viewpoints, 1*, 17–20.
410. Sigal, J. J., Dinicola V. F., & Buonvino M. (1988). Grandchildren of survivors: Can negative effects of prolonged exposure to excessive stress be observed two generations later? *The Canadian Journal of Psychiatry, 33*, 207–12.
411. Krystal, H. (Ed.). (1968). *Massive psychic trauma*. International Universities Press.
412. Antonovsky, A. (1979). *Health, stress, and coping*. Jossey-Bass.
413. Aleksandrowicz, D. R. (1973). Children of concentration camp survivors. In E. J. Anthony & C. Koupernik (Eds.), *The child in his family*. Vol. 2, *The impact of disease and death* (pp. 385–92). Wiley.
414. American Psychiatric Association. (2013). *Diagnostic and statistical manual of mental disorders* (5th ed.). APA.
415. Pai, A., Suris, A. M., & North, C. S. (2017). Posttraumatic stress disorder in the *DSM-5*: Controversy, change, and conceptual considerations. *Behav Sci, 7*, 7.
416. Summerfield, D. (2001). The invention of post-traumatic stress disorder and the social usefulness of a psychiatric category. *BMJ, 322*, 95–98.
417. Scaer, R. (2014). *The body bears the burden*. Routledge, p. 6.
418. Pearce, J. (1989). Whiplash injury: A reappraisal. *Journal of Neurology and Neurosurgery, 52*, 1329–31.
419. Mason, J. (1975). Confusion and controversy in the stress field. *Journal of Human Stress, 1*, 6–35.
420. Shapiro, F. (2002). *EMDR as an integrative psychotherapy approach: Experts of diverse orientations explore the paradigm prism*. APA.
421. WebMD Editorial Contributors. (2021, November 6). *EMDR: Eye movement desensitization and reprocessing*. https://www.webmd.com/mental-health/emdr-what-is-it.
422. Hobb, N. (1962). Sources of gain in psychotherapy. *American Psychologist, 17*, 742–48.
423. Munslow, A., & Harlan, D. (Eds.) (2006). *Re-thinking history*. Routledge.
424. Spinelli, E. (2005). *The interpreted world* (2nd ed.). Sage, pp. 59–60.
425. Carlsen, M. B. (1988). *Meaning-making: Therapeutic processes in adult development*. Norton.
426. Steed, C. D. (2018). *We count, we matter: Voice, choice, and the death of distance*. Routledge.

427. Chapman, G. (2015). *The 5 love languages: The secret to love that lasts.* Moody. See also, Chapman, G. (2016). *5 love languages of children: The secret to loving children effectively.* Northfield; Chapman, G., & White, P. (2007). *The 5 languages of appreciation in the workplace: Empowering organizations by encouraging people.* Northfield.
428. Binswanger, L. Existential Analysis and Psychotherapy. In Fromm-Reichman, F., & Moreno, J. (1956). *Progress in psychotherapy.* Grune & Stratton, p. 196.
429. Brooks. A. C. (2022). *From strength to strength: Finding success, happiness, and deep purpose in the second half of life.* Green Tree.
430. Yalom, I. D. (1980). *Existential psychotherapy.* Basic, p. 29.
431. Breen, L. J., Sherman, A. L., & Neimeyer, R. (2021). Psychological risk factors of functional impairment after COVID-19 deaths. *Journal of Pain and Symptom Management, 61*, e1–e4.
432. Ledger-Thomas, M. (2021). *Queen Victoria: This thorny crown.* Oxford University Press.
433. Choron, J. (1964). *Modern man and mortality.* Macmillan, p. 44.
434. Troyat, H. (1971). *Leo Tolstoy.* Penguin, p. 640.
435. Yalom, I. (1980). *Existential psychotherapy.* Basic, p. 27.
436. Yalom, I. (1980). *Existential psychotherapy.* Basic, p. 29.
437. Cicero, cited in M. Montaigne (1965), *The complete essays of Montaigne* (D. Frame, Trans.). Stanford University Press, p. 56.
438. Heidegger, M. (1962). *Being and time.* Harper, pp. 210–24.
439. Augustine, cited in M. Montaigne (1965), *The complete essays of Montaigne* (D. Frame, Trans.). Stanford University Press, p. 63.
440. Kierkegaard, S. (1957). *The concept of dread.* Princeton University Press, p. 55.
441. Sartre, J. P. (1958). *Being and nothingness.* Methuen.
442. Eagelton, T. (1990). *The ideology of the aesthetic.* Blackwell, p. 155.
443. Fowler, J. (1995). *Stages of faith: The psychology of human development and the quest for meaning.* HarperOne.
444. Yalom, I. (1980). *Existential psychotherapy.* Basic, p. 459.
445. Clare, H. (2021). *Heavy light: A journey through madness, mania, and healing.* Chatto and Windus, p. 21.
446. Jung, C. J. (1966). *Collected works.* Vol. 16, *The practice of psychotherapy.* Princeton University Press, p. 83.
447. Wheelis, A. (1950). The place of action in personality change. *Psychiatry, 13*, 135–48.
448. Worsley, R., & Joseph, S. (2015). *Person-centred practice: Case studies in positive psychology.* PCCS, p. 59.
449. Seligman, M. (1975). *Helplessness: On depression, development, and death.* Freeman.
450. Luther. M. (1990). *The bondage of the will.* Baker.
451. Freud, S. (1961). *The ego and the id.* Hogarth, p. 50.
452. Cited in Russel, J. (1978), Sartre, therapy, and expanding the concept of responsibility. *American Journal of Psychoanalysis, 38*, 258–69.
453. Sartre, J. P. (1956). *Being and nothingness* (H. Barnes, Trans.). Philosophical Library, p. 633.
454. Knox, J. (2011). *Self-agency in psychotherapy* (1st ed.). Norton, p. 111.
455. Vaillant. G. (2009). *Harvard study of adult development.* Little, Brown Spark.

456. Bond, M., & Vaillant, G. (1992). *Ego mechanisms of defence: A guide for clinicians and researchers*. APA.
457. Author's client notes. Name withheld and used with permission.
458. O'Neill, C. (2022). *The shame machine: Who profits in the new age of humiliation*. Penguin.
459. Cabaniss, D., et al. (2013). *Psychodynamic formulation*. Wiley-Blackwell.
460. Sanderson, C. (2013). *Counselling skills for working with trauma: Healing from child sexual abuse, sexual violence, and domestic abuse*. Kingsley.
461. Slochower, J. (2013). Relational holding: Using Winnicott today. *Revue Roumaine de Psychanalyse, 6B*, 15–40.
462. Llinas, R., & Churchland, P. (1997). *The mind-brain continuum*. Carfax.
463. Rosen, C. (2002). *Piano notes: The hidden world of the pianist*. Penguin, p. 151–53.
464. Spillius, E., & O'Shaughessy, E. (Eds.) (2011). *Projective identification: The fate of a concept*. Routledge.
465. Hentschel, U., Kiessling, M., & Rudolf, G. (1997). Therapeutic alliance and transference: An exploratory study of their empirical relationship. *J Nerv Ment Dis., 185*, 254–56.
466. Hauerwas, S. (1996). Suffering the retarded: Should we prevent retardation? In *Suffering presence: Theological reflections on medicine, the mentally handicapped, and the church*. University of Notre Dame Press, p. 104.
467. Heraclitus (1962). *Ancilla to the pre-Socratic philosophers* (K. Freeman, Trans.). Oxford: Basil Blackwell, p. 25.
468. Menninger, K. (1988). *Whatever became of sin?* Bantam.
469. DeYoung, P. A. (2022). *Understanding and treating chronic shame: Healing right brain relational trauma* (2nd ed.). Routledge, p. 47.
470. Eisland, N. (1994). *The disabled god: Toward a liberatory theology of disability*. Abingdon.
471. Schuman, M. (2017). *Mindfulness-informed relational psychotherapy and psychoanalytic: Inquiring deeply*. Routledge.
472. Hildebbrand, D. V. *Transformation in Christ: Recollection and contemplation*. https://www.ewtn.com/catholicism/library/transformation-in-christ-recollection-and-contemplation-9858.
473. Laing, R. D. (2010). *The divided self*. Penguin Classics.
474. Schwartz, R. (1997). *Internal family systems therapy*. Guilford.
475. Freud, S. (1959). Freud's psycho-analytic procedure. In J. Strachey (Ed. & Trans.), *The standard edition of the complete psychological works of Sigmund Freud*. Vol. 7. Hogarth, pp. 261–62.
476. Author's client notes. Name withheld and used with permission.
477. Trinh, M. (1992). *The framer framed*. Routledge.
478. Roberst, W., & Srayer, J. (1996). Empathy, emotional experiences, and prosocial behaviour. *Child Development, 67*, 449–70.
479. Cooper, T. (2009). *Sin, pride, & self-acceptance: The problem of identity in theology & psychology*. InterVarsity.
480. Oden, T. (1966). *Kerygma and counselling: Toward a covenant ontology for secular psychotherapy*. Westminster.
481. Thorne, B. (2002). *The mystical power of person-centred therapy*. Wiley.
482. Brown, B. (2010). *The power of vulnerability*. https://brenebrown.com/videos/ted-talk-the-power-of-vulnerability/.

483. Wimarick, D. J. (2020, June 26). *Towards a psychodynamic-relational theory of psychotherapy: Factors effecting therapeutic change*. Psychology Today. https://www.psychologytoday.com/us/blog/personality-quotient/202006/towards-psychodynamic-relational-theory-psychotherapy.
484. Cabaniss, D., et al. (2013). *Psychodynamic formulation*. Wiley-Blackwell.
485. O'Connor, A. (2021). Moral injury. *Therapy today*, *32*, 35.
486. Wright, T. (2003). *Paul for everyone: 2 Corinthians*. SPCK, p. 66.
487. Thompson, C. (2015). *The soul of shame: Retelling the stories we believe about ourselves* (1st ed.). InterVarsity.
488. Sanderson, C. (1995). *Counselling adult survivors of child sexual abuse* (2nd ed.). Kingsley, pp. 67, 93.
489. Thompson, C. (2015). *The soul of shame: Retelling the stories we believe about ourselves*. InterVarsity, pp. 68, 69.
490. Wu, J. (2018). Have theologians no sense of shame? How the Bible reconciles objective and subjective shame. *Themelios*, *43*, 205–19.
491. Izard, C. E. (1977). *Human emotions*. Plenum.
492. DeYoung, P. A. (2022). *Understanding and treating chronic shame: Healing right brain relational trauma* (2nd ed.). Routledge, p. 22.
493. DeYoung, P. A. (2022). *Understanding and treating chronic shame: Healing right brain relational trauma* (2nd ed.). Routledge, p. 47.
494. Author client notes. Used with permission.
495. Jaspers, K. (1951). *The way to wisdom* (R. Manheim, Trans.). Yale University Press.
496. Tillich, P. (1952). *The courage to be*. Yale University Press.
497. Basile, B., & Mancini, F. (2011). Francesco Mancini eliciting guilty feelings: A preliminary study differentiating deontological and altruistic guilt. *Psychology*, 2, 98–102.
498. Boss, M. (1962). Anxiety, guilt, and psychotherapeutic liberation. In *Review of Existential Psychology and Psychiatry*, *11*, 173–95.
499. Wu, J. (2018). Have theologians no sense of shame? How the Bible reconciles objective and subjective shame. *Themelios*, *43*, 217.
500. Oliver, G. (1995). Illusions of guilt and innocence. In J. Goldinghay (Ed.), *Atonement today*. SPCK, p. 247.
501. Browning, D. S. (1964). *Atonement and psychotherapy*. Westminster.
502. Wagner, M. E. (1975). *The sensation of being somebody: Building an adequate self-concept*. Zondervan.
503. Rizzuto, A. (1981). *The birth of the living god*. University of Chicago Press.
504. Peck, M. S. (1990). *The road less travelled*. Arrow, p. 23.
505. Charry, E. T. (2001). Theology after psychology. In M. R. Mcminn & T. R. Phillips (Eds.), *Care for the Soul*. InterVarsity, p. 133.
506. Charry, E. T. (2001). Theology after psychology. In M. R. Mcminn & T. R. Phillips (Eds.), *Care for the Soul*. InterVarsity, p. 127.
507. Bobgan, M., & Bobgan, D. (1989). *Prophets of psychoheresy*. Eastgate.
508. Johnson, E. L. (Ed.). (2010). *Psychology and christianity: Five views*. IVP Academic.
509. Narramore, B. (1973). Perspectives on the integration of psychology and theology. *Journal of Psychology and Theology*, *1*, 17.
510. Adams, J. (1986). *Competent to counsel*. Zondervan.
511. Powlinson, D. (2010). *The biblical counselling movement: History and context*. New Growth.

512. Hathaway, W. L., & Yarhouse, M. L. (2021). *The integration of psychology and Christianity: A domain-based approach.* InterVarsity.
513. Crisp, T. M., Porter, S. L., & Ten Elshof, G. A. (2019). *Psychology and spiritual formation in dialogue.* IVP Academic, p. 6.
514. Hogan, J. D. (2000). Developmental psychology: History of the field. In Alan E. Kazdin (Ed.), *Encyclopaedia of Psychology* (Vol. 3). APA, p. 9.
515. Balswick, J. O., King, P. E., & Reimer, K. (2005). *The reciprocating self: Human development in theological perspective.* InterVarsity, p. 28.
516. Taylor, C. (1989). *Sources of the self.* Cambridge University Press, p. 211.
517. James, W. (2000). *The principles of psychology: Volume 1.* Dover.
518. Jones, E. (1964). *The life and work of Sigmund Freud.* Penguin, p. 11.
519. Jones, E. (1957). *The life and work of Sigmund Freud.* Vol. 2. Hogarth, pp. 439–40, 457–58.
520. Horney, K. (1950). *Neurosis and human growth.* Norton.
521. Makari. G. (2008). *Revolution in mind: The creation of psychoanalysis.* Duckworth.
522. Winnicott, D. W. (1971). *Playing and reality.* Tavistock.
523. Lacan, J. (1988). *The ego in Freud's theory and the techniques of psychoanalysis* (J-A. Miller, Ed.). Norton.
524. Parker, I. (2010). *Lacanian psychoanalysis: Revolutions in subjectivity.* Routledge, p. 82.
525. Prochaska, J. O., & Norcross, J. C. (1994). *Systems of psychotherapy: A transtheoretical perspective.* Brooks, p. 81.
526. Adler, A. (1939). *Social interest.* Putnam.
527. Storr, A. (1973). *Jung.* Collins.
528. Jung, C. J. (1961). *Modern man in search of a soul.* RKP.
529. Jung, C. J. (2009). *The red book.* Norton.
530. Frankl, V. (1977). *The unconscious god: Psychotherapy and theology.* Hodder & Stoughton.
531. Yalom, I. (1980) *Existential psychotherapy.* Basic, p. 25.
532. Maslow, A. (2015). *Towards a psychology of being.* Sublime.
533. Assagioli, R. (1975). *Psychosynthesis: A manual of principles and techniques.* Turnstone.
534. Wilber, K. (1981). *No boundary: Eastern and western approaches to personal growth.* Shambhala.
535. Beauregard, M., & O'Leary, D. (2008). *The spiritual brain.* HarperCollins.
536. Radio4. (2022, June 14). *Lives in care.* BBC Radio. https://www.bbc.co.uk/programmes/m00187qx.
537. English, D., Lambert, S. F., Tynes, B. M., Bowleg, L., Zea, M. C., & Howard L. C. (2020). Daily multidimensional racial discrimination among black U.S. American adolescents. *J Appl Dev Psychol, 66*, 101068.
538. Milbank, J. (2006). *Theology and social theory: Beyond secular reason.* Wiley.
539. Segundo, J. L. (1976). *The liberation of theology.* Orbis, p. 100.
540. Cortina, L. M., Curtin, N., & Stewart, A. J. (2012). Where is social structure in personality research? A feminist analysis of publication trends. *Psychology of Women Quarterly, 36*, 259.
541. Hyde, J. S. (2007). *Half the human experience: The psychology of women.* Houghton Mifflin.
542. Parsons, T. (1964). *Social structure and personality.* Free.
543. Twenge, J. M., & Campbell, W. K. (2002). Self-esteem and socioeconomic status: A meta-analytic review. *Personality and Social Psychology Review, 6*, 59–71.

544. Eccles, J., Jacobs, J. E., & Harold, R. D. (1990). Gender role stereotypes, expectancy effects, and parents' socialization of gender differences. *Journal of Social Issues*, *46*, 183–201.
545. American Psychological Association. (n.d.). Situated knowledge. In *APA dictionary of psychology*. https://dictionary.apa.org/situated-knowledge.
546. According to the replicators' qualitative assessments, 39 of the 100 replication attempts were successful. Baker, M. (2015, August 27). Over half of psychology studies fail reproducibility test. *Science*. https://www.nature.com/articles/nature.2015.18248.
547. Author's client notes. Name withheld and used with permission.
548. Author's client notes. Name withheld and used with permission.
549. Horowitz, M. J. (1988). *Introduction to psychodynamics: A new synthesis*. Basic.
550. Horowitz, M. J. (2001). *Cognitive psychodynamics: From conflict to character*. Wiley.
551. Loewenthal, D., Cayne, J., Greenwood, D., Thomas, R., Cotton, T., Larsson, P., & Snell, R. (2011). *Post-existentialism and the psychological therapies: Towards a therapy without foundations*. Karnac.
552. Parker, I. (Ed.). (1999). *Deconstructing psychotherapy*. Sage.
553. Tedlock, B. (1991). From participant observation to the observation of participation: The emergence of narrative ethnography. *Journal of Anthropological Research*, *47*, 69.
554. Ellis, C., Adams, T. E., & Bochner, A. P. (2011). Autoethnogoraphy: An overview. *Qualitative Social Research*, *12*.
555. Ellis, C. (2004). *The ethnographic I: A methodological novel about auto-ethnography*. AltaMira.
556. Jones, S. H. (2005). Autoethnography: Making the personal political. In N. K. Denzin & Y. S. Lincoln (Eds.), *Handbook of qualitative research* (pp. 763–91). Sage.
557. Ellis, C., Kiesinger, C. E., & Tillmann-Healy, L. M. (1997). Interactive interviewing: Talking about emotional experience. In Rosanna Hertz (Ed.), *Reflexivity and voice* (pp. 119–49). Sage).
558. Fine, G. A. (2003). Towards a people ethnography: Developing a theory from group life. *Ethnography*, *4*, 41–60.
559. Jones, S. H., Adams, T. E., & Ellis, C. (2016). *Handbook of autoethnography*. Routledge.
560. Van De Riet, V., Korb, M. P., & Gorrell, J. J. (1980). *Gestalt therapy: An introduction*. Pergamon, p. 6.
561. Perls, F., Hefferline, R., & Goodman, P. (1972). *Gestalt therapy: Excitement and growth in the human personality*. Souvenir, p. 25.
562. Mackewan, J. (1997). *Developing gestalt counselling*. Sage, pp. 43–47.
563. Hycner, R., & Jacobs, L. (1995). *The healing relationship in gestalt therapy: A dialogic/self psychology approach*. Gestalt Journal.
564. Wilson, R., & Branch, R. (2006). *Cognitive behavioural therapy*. Wiley, p. 166.
565. Beck, J. (2021). *Cognitive behavioural therapy: Basics and beyond*. Guilford, p. 30–32.
566. Rogers, C. (2004). *On becoming a person: A therapist's view of psychotherapy*. Constable.
567. Egan, G. (1986). *Skilled helpers: A systemic approach to effective helping* (3rd ed.). Brooks & Cole.
568. Culley, S. (1991). *Integrative counselling skills in action*. Sage, p. 13.

569. Sanders, P. (2004). *The tribes of the person-centred nation: An introduction to the schools of therapy related to the person-centred approach.* PCCS.
570. Horowitz, M. J. (2001). *Cognitive psychodynamics: From conflict to character.* Wiley.
571. Tracy, D. (1987). *Plurality and ambiguity: Hermeneutics, religion, and hope.* Harper & Row, p. 142.
572. Tracy, D. (1981). *The analogical imagination: Christian theology and the culture of pluralism.* Crossroad, p. 364.
573. Tillich, P. (1951). *Systematic theology: Volume 1.* University of Chicago Press, p. 64.
574. Tillich, P. (1959). *Theology of culture.* Oxford University Press.
575. Kent, J. H. S. (1982). *The end of the line? The development of Christian theology in the last two centuries.* SCM.
576. Barth, K. (1935). *The word of God and the word of man.* Hodder and Stoughton, p. 28.
577. McFarlane, G. (2020). *A model for evangelical theology.* Baker Academic.
578. Rousseau, Jean-Jacques (1979). *Emilie or On Education.* Basic, p. 348.
579. Grudem, W. (1994). *Systematic theology: An introduction to biblical doctrine.* InterVarsity.
580. Association of Christian Churches. (n.d.). *Ethics and practice.* https://www.acc-uk.org/public/docs/page-pdfs/EandPractice.pdf.
581. Menninger, K. (1988). *Whatever became of sin?* Bantam.
582. Niebuhr, R. (1979). *On myth and its place in the Christian religion.* In E. J. Tinsley (Ed.), *Modern theology.* Epworth, p. 255.
583. R. Rubinstein, quoted in R. R. Ruether. (1999). *The twentieth century: A theological overview* (G. Baum, Ed.). Orbis, p. 77.
584. Bultmann, R. (1979). Theology of the new testament. In E. J. Tinsley (Ed.), *Modern theology.* Epworth, pp. 122–23.
585. Bonhoeffer, D. (1979). Christology. In E. J. Tinsley (Ed.), *Modern theology.* Epworth, p. 310.
586. Patterson, C. H. (2000). *Understanding psychotherapy: Fifty years of client-centred practice.* PCSS.
587. Jung, C. J. (2013). *The undiscovered self.* Routledge.
588. Spinoza, B. (1996). *Ethics.* Penguin Classics.
589. Aristotle. (2009). *The nicomachean ethics* (D. Ross, Trans.). Oxford University Press.
590. MacIntyre, A. (2007). *After virtue: A study in moral theory.* University of Notre Dame Press.
591. Trevarthen, C. (1993). The self born in inter-subjectivity: The psychology of infant communicating. In U. Neisser (Ed.), *The perceived self: Ecological and interpersonal sources of self-knowledge.* Cambridge University Press, pp. 121–73.
592. Schore, A. (1994). *Affect regulation and the origin of the self.* Erlsbaum.
593. Gerhardt. S. (2004). *Why love matters: How affection shapes a baby's brain.* Routledge.
594. Gerson, S. (2004). The relational unconscious: A core element of intersubjectivity, thirdness, and clinical process. *Psychoanal Q, 73*, 63–98.
595. Ogden, T. (2004). The analytic third: Implications for psychoanalytic theory and technique. *Psychoanal Q, 73*, 167–95.
596. Charlesworth, B. (2022). "Developing a Practice Rationale." *Therapy Today*, June 2022

Index

abuse, 104, 114
ACC, 262
acceptance, 216
Adams, Jay, 235
Adler, Alfred, 241
agency, xiv, 5, 6, 8, 55, 60, 189, 282
alignment of psychology and faith, 233–34, 247
amygdala, 82,
APA, 238, 250
Aquinas, Thomas, 59, 274
Aristotle, 155, 273
Assaglioli, Robert, 243
atonement, 224, 267
attachments, xv, 88
Augustine, 51, 59, 104, 232
Auschwitz, 268
auto enography, 246, 253

Barth, Karl, 154, 213, 258
Beauregard, Mario, 86
Beck, Aarron, 117
behavioural approach, 18
Berger, Peter, 126
Berne, Eric, 42
Bible, 232, 270
biblical counselling, 235
Bobgans, Martin & Deidre, 234
Bonhoeffer, Dietrich, 269
Bowlby, John, 39, 88, 92, 127
Brand, Russell, 25, 31
Breuer, Josef, 1, 140
Brief Therapy, 21, 117
British Association of Counselling and Psychotherapy, xiii
Bronfenbrunner, Urie, 147
Brooks, Arthur, 182
Brown, Brené, 214
Buber, Martin, 134, 152, 155

Calvin, John, 83, 110, 242
Campbell, Betty, 98
Chapman, Gary, 181
Chapman, Mark, 113
Churchill Framework, 87
Churchill, Winston, 42
client-centred therapy, 133, 189, 255, 278
Cognitive Behavioural Therapy, 2, 14, 18, 71, 117, 214, 255, 278
cognitive processes, 10, 13, 20
connection and belonging, 265
Conzolino, Louis ,162
Cooley, Charles, 41
createdness, 265
critical correlation, 254
critical race theory, 102–3
Culliford, Larry, 85

Damasio, Antonio, 117, 164, 166
defence mechanism, 138
dehumanisation, 267
demonisation, 267
denigration, 267
depersonalisation, 267
depression, 26
Descartes, 59, 199, 153, 166
describe, review, link, 200, 215
desecration, 267
desire and destructiveness, 266
diagnosis, 17
Diagnostic and Statistical Mechanism (DSM), xv, 17, 155, 174
dialogic change, 9, 131, 156
dignity, 192
disability, 62, 101, 168, 169–71
domain-based approach, 236
Dostoyevsky, Fyodor, 65
dualism, 128
Durkheim, Emil, 191

Eiesland, Nancy, 171
Ellis, Albert, 117
embodiment, xiv, 5, 8, 52, 59, 60, 163, 281
EMDR, 176
emotional cognition, 10
emotions, 92, 167
empowerment, 192
endorsement, 4, 41, 107, 252
epistemology, 192 237, 238, 245, 249
Erikson, 148
ethical framework, 261–62
existential concerns, 237–38, 242–43
existentialism, 185

face, importance of, 274
Fairbairn, Ronald, 154, 160
feminist critiques, 249
forgiveness, 216
Fowler, James (Stages of Faith), 185–86
Frankl, Victor, 44, 56, 242
Freud, Anna, 152
Freud, Sigmund, xvi, 1, 3, 33, 36, 47, 47, 50, 52, 53, 81, 99, 107, 111, 116, 119, 123, 137, 148, 150, 177, 182, 190, 239–40, 252, 273
Freudian theory, 2, 6, 9, 148, 217
Fromm, Eric, 70
frustration, 57

Gandhi, 106
Gates, Bill, 95
gaze, the social, 275
Gestalt, 19, 117, 155, 191, 247, 254–55, 278
Gilligan, James, 112
girl, woman, other, 100
goals of therapy, 272
Goethe, Johann Wolfgang von, 45
Goff, Philip, 129
Golding, William, 95
Groff, Stanislav, 36
Gruden, Wayne, 261
guilt, 35, 261, 268

Hauerwas, Stanley, 206
Hegel, G. W. F., 43, 153, 155, 182
Heidegger, Martin, 153, 155, 183
Hemingway, Ernest, 37
Heraclitus, 71, 206
Hill, Fiona, 104
Hobbs, Nicholas, 177
Holistic approach, 4, 10
Honneth, Axel, 43
humanistic approach to psychotherapy, 4, 10
Humanity of Christ, 269

identification, 204–5, 226
identity, 59, 61, 62
incarnation, 269
indifference, 45, 278
indignity, 45, 278
inferiority, 45, 278
integrative therapy, xiii, 2, 7, 8, 10, 14, 69
interpersonal neurobiology, 141, 157
interpersonal psychotherapy, 145
intersectionality, 102

James, William, 51, 80, 84, 239
Janov, Arthur, 37
Jung, Carl Gustav, 34, 36, 73–74, 81, 145, 180, 182, 241–42, 273

Kahn, Michael, 133
Kant, Immanuel, 35, 268
Kierkegaard, Soren, 31, 184
King, Martin Luther, 106
Klein, Melanie, 53, 54, 75, 139, 159
Kohut, Heinz,
Kraepelin, Emil, xvi

Lacon Jacque, 53, 241
Laing, R. D., 72, 211
Lambeth Quadrilateral, 258
languages of love, 181
Lennon, John, 113
Levin, Bernard, 31
Levinas, Emmanuel, 154, 265
Levine, Peter, 176
libido, 51, 52
limbic system, 81, 122
Locke, John, 59
loneliness, 28
Lothane, Henry, 136
Luther, Martin, 190

MacIntyre, Alasdair, 274
MacLean, Paul, 122
Main and Goldwyn attachment pattern, 91
Mahrer, Alvin, 19
Marx, Karl, 248
Maslow, Abraham, xvii, 47, 71, 96, 243, 273
May, Rollo, xvii, 113
Mead, George Herbert, 62
meaning making, xiv, 5, 8, 54, 60, 177, 281–82
medical model, xvi
Menninger, Karl, 266
mindfulness, 210
Moulin, Sophie, 90

narcissism, 52, 113, 150–51
Narramore, Clyde, 236
Neil, Stephen, 57
neuroscience, 79, 86, 116, 120, 127, 278
Newberg, Andrew, 84
Nietzsche, Friedrich, 29, 72
Novak, Michael, 39

Object Relations, 136, 138–39, 152, 157–58, 240
Oswald, Lee Harvey, 109

Parsons, Talcott, xvi
Pentecost, 269
personhood, 58
Philips, Adam, 94
Piaget, Jean, 148
Plato, 59, 123, 128
postmodern mind, 257
Power, Threat, Meaning Framework (PTMF), 18, 194
practice rationale, 277
protest, the, 192–93
psychoananalysis, 52, 70, 73, 79, 97, 134, 152, 240
psychodynamic therapy, x, 18, 20, 27, 78.152, 278

recollecting, 7, 201, 212
redemptive repair, 199, 213
Reformed perspective, 257,
relational neurobiology, 126
relational turn, 153
relational, xiii, 3–4, 5, 8, 51, 59, 130, 145, 280
REMA approach to counselling, ix, 58176, 200, 215, 279
remembering, 7, 201, 207
repentance, 7, 201, 206
resignation, 106
resistance, 212
resonance, 6, 20–21, 201, 202
resurrection, 269
revaluing, 7, 212
revelation, 257
Rogers, Carl, xviii, 67, 71, 133, 213, 255
Romanian orphans, 92, 126
Rousseau, Jean-Jacques, 147, 260

Sartre, Jean-Paul, 191
Scaer, Robert, 175
Schermer, Victor, 84
Schopenhaur, Arthur, 33, 185
Schore, Allan, 121, 126
Segundo, Johan, 249
Seligman, Martin, 190

Seneca, 183
separation anxiety, 38
sin, 220, 223, 266–67
sociological attunement, 3, 10, 16, 64, 99–100, 246, 250, 278
Sontag, Susan, 30–31, 169
soteriology, 269
soul hungers, 5, 50, 279
soul repair, 197
Spinoza, 273
spirituality, 9, 47, 80–81
Stryon, William, 94
suicide, 26
Sutton Trust, 90
systematic theology, 271
systems thinking, 10, 14

Tajfel, Henry (social identity theory), 44
Tavistock Clinic, 118
Taylor, Charles, 61, 239
theological anthropology, 247, 265
theological assumptions, 251
theology-Christian theological tradition, 2, 8, 147, 153, 262
theology of personal experience, 260
Theresa of Avila, 83
thirdness, 275
Tillich, Paul, 27, 40, 256–57
Tolstoy, Leo, 30, 183
Tolstoy, Sonia, 47
top-layer working, 12–13, 21
Tracey, David, 256–57
transactional analysis (TA), 42
transcendence, 263
transference, 16, 20, 136
transformative change, 276
trauma, 172–73

unconscious processes, 20, 36, 55, 71, 72, 75, 86, 123, 130, 148, 152, 177, 207

validation of the self, 43
valuable personhood, xiv, 5, 130, 244, 252, 266
value, human value, 3, 42, 66, 77, 152, 245
violence, 111
void, 25
Vygotsky, Lev, 149

Wellington, Duke of, 94
Wilbur, Ken, 243

Yalom, Irvin, 29, 56, 182, 186

www.ingramcontent.com/pod-product-compliance
Lightning Source LLC
LaVergne TN
LVHW051051220926
848485LV00001BA/67